★ POLL DANCING

The Story of the 2007 Election

Mungo MacCallum

Black Inc.

❧ *This one is for the grandchildren, Amelia and Finn.*

Published by Black Inc., an imprint of
Schwartz Publishing Pty Ltd
Level 5, 289 Flinders Lane
Melbourne Victoria 3000 Australia
email: enquiries@blackincbooks.com
http://www.blackincbooks.com

The National Library of Australia Cataloguing-in-Publication entry:

MacCallum, Mungo, 1941- .
Poll dancing : the story of the 2007 election.

1st ed.
Includes index.
ISBN 9781863954204 (pbk.).

1. Australia. Parliament - Elections, 2007. 2. Elections - Australia. 3. Political campaigns - Australia. 4. Australia - Politics and government - 1990- . I. Title.

324.99407

Book design by Thomas Deverall
Printed in Australia by Griffin Press

“*All the ills of mankind, all the tragic misfortunes that fill the history books, all the political blunders, all the failures of the great leaders, have arisen merely from a lack of skill at dancing.*

—MOLIÈRE

★ *Foreword*

As will quickly become obvious to the reader, this book was written over the course of 2007 as a sort of election diary. The campaign, which effectively began on the day Kevin Rudd was elected leader of the ALP, ran continuously for nearly a year, and covering it became as much a matter of keeping up as of serious and sober analysis. Thus the account contains predictions and judgements made on the run, not all of which proved in hindsight to be correct. However, I have left them unchanged to try and preserve the ambience of the time. *Poll Dancing* was always intended as a personal memoir rather than as a definitive history, and while I have tried to be as accurate as possible on the facts, the opinions should be treated as strictly impressionistic.

From time to time some readers may experience a sense of déjà vu, for which there is no need to seek medical help: as I was writing the book I was also trying to earn a living by contributing articles to (among others) the *Bulletin*, the *Monthly*, the *Byron Shire Echo*, *Crikey.com* and the community-radio network. Inevitably there was some overlap, for which I apologise to diligent followers of my work, if indeed any such exist. Think of it as positive reinforcement.

I should also take the opportunity to thank my publisher, Chris Feik, my editor, David Winter, Morry Schwartz, who bought me food and drink, John and Romey Stubbs, for help and encouragement, and my partner, Jenny, who put up with the whole fraught process. And as Billy Snedden was wont to say when tired and emotional after a hard day's electioneering, there are probably others I've forgotten, but who gives a fuck.

Cheers.

Mungo MacCallum

> *On with the dance! Let joy be unconfined!*
> —Lord Byron

★ 1.

One morning in his tenth year as prime minister, John Winston Howard awoke in the master bedroom of Kirribilli House to realise that he had become not only omnipotent but invincible.

His demolition of Labor's young pretender, Mark Latham, had probably put the next election beyond the reach of any opponent, let alone one as accommodating as his serial victim, Kim Beazley. The result had also made his leadership virtually unchallengeable. Peter Costello's occasional forays could and would be dismissed as mere showmanship, in keeping with his dilettante approach to politics. Tony Abbott had long ceased to be a threat, and Brendan Nelson was clearly destined for the role of bridesmaid, if that. The only one who went close to matching him in megalomania, Malcolm Turnbull, was a full political generation away.

Howard's courtiers in the parliament and in the media were now assuring him that he could, and should, go on for years – even for another decade, which would put him in reach of the hitherto unattainable record of Sir Robert Menzies, once the immortal nonpareil but now perhaps no more than a John the Baptist heralding the coming of the Messiah. It was no longer a question of the Howard Years; we were now talking about the Howard Age, the Howard Epoch. Future historians would see 1996 as the new Year Zero, the time when it truly all began.

Okay, perhaps the hubris didn't extend quite that far, but there can be little doubt that as the election year of 2007 approached, our Dear Leader felt a bit like his idols in the Australian cricket team: to win, all he had to do was turn up. Of course, he observed the rituals: he was still prime minister only with the approval of his party and the electorate; he was always aware that this approval could be withdrawn at any time; there was absolutely no room for smugness and he was 'umble, very 'umble, kind sir or madam as the case may be. But given his track record as an election winner, 2007 should be a stroll in the park.

True, Iraq was not exactly looking a picture, but the cut-and-run option was still unpopular and could be used to beat Labor about the head if the war loomed as a major issue with voters, which seemed unlikely. The terrorism threat had gone off the boil a bit, but there were plenty of willing bigots among his posse of tame media commentators who could be relied on to ramp it up if the occasion demanded. The great wheat-for-weapons scandal, accurately described as the worst corruption case in Australian history, had been put to bed through a combination of skilled political management, denial and obfuscation; in spite of commendable efforts by the Opposition and the media to explain to the public that the government had, at the very least, been appallingly negligent and incompetent, the punters just weren't interested.

WorkChoices was a bit of a worry, with an increasing number of families being directly affected by its more draconian aspects and so many people knowing someone who claimed to have been treated unfairly; a few of the more excitable commentators were predicting that the angst would still be a major factor by election time. But then, they had said that about the GST, which directly affected absolutely everybody, and that had settled into place very nicely, thank you. There were a couple of other issues exciting the chattering classes, but no cause for alarm: the drought was a nuisance, but surely no one could blame him for that, and the wider question of climate change remained a cloud no bigger than a man's hand on the distant horizon. The Americans still hadn't tried bloody David Hicks, but Australians had put up with his arbitrary imprisonment and probable torture for nearly five years with commendable equanimity; there was no reason to believe that this was about to change.

The only real problem was interest rates – which perversely kept going up, despite his constant appearances during the last campaign behind a banner that said he was keeping them down. Still, look at the fine print: they were an awful lot lower than the 17 per cent under the arch demon Paul Keating (let alone the 21 per cent under the beneficent treasurer John Howard, but we won't go into that). The Big Lie that interest rates would always be higher under Labor had worked well enough last time, and with a bit of a tweak could be adapted to fit the line that in troubled times, you need the steady hand of Honest John to keep things under control. After all, he has guided you through an unprecedented period of prosperity, even if most of it is actually debt – but hey, it's better than paying rent. Most importantly, you still trust him; after all, he got away with the last ten years, proving that even on his worst day he can still fool most of the people for enough of the time.

On 1 December 2006, the first day of summer, the sky was blue, the grass was green, the birds were on the wing and the snails were on the thorn, the Howards were in Kirribilli House and all was right with the world.

★

That, in any case, was the gloomy picture from what is euphemistically described as the beer garden of the Billinudgel Hotel, where I sat brooding over the fact that next year was looking particularly bleak, because I wouldn't even have Arthur Sinodinis to kick around. Sinodinis, for many years Howard's chief enforcer, was moving on; from my point of view, he would be missed chiefly as an almost-inexhaustible subject of limericks. I penned a farewell missive:

Oh Arthur! My lost Sinodinis!
A cloud has descended between us.
If you must quit the game
At least leave me your name
To rhyme with George Megalogenis.

Not even one of my best. But then, right on cue, the cavalry arrived: a message from a usually reliable source assured me that Kevin Rudd, so long as he was supported by Julia Gillard as deputy, had the numbers to knock off Kim Beazley.

I had always been somewhat ambivalent about Rudd – as, it seemed, had the bulk of the population. While polls showed that only 10 per cent actively disliked him (an all-time low, his supporters shrilled gleefully), 49 per cent had no opinion of any kind. In other words, the man was virtually unknown less than a year before he would ask the people to elect him as their head of government. This was not a good start.

Nor was what was known of him particularly encouraging. A former Queensland government apparatchik, he was one of

Kim Beazley's backing chorus of roosters, as Mark Latham called them. Indeed, Latham had been particularly harsh on Rudd in his notorious diary, describing him as personally untrustworthy and an American lackey. Latham believed that Heavy Kevvie, as he had derisively christened his foreign-affairs spokesman, was barely fit to oversee Labor's Pacific Islands policy, let alone to take on the top job. This view was widely shared by the anti-Beazley forces, led by Simon Crean and Julia Gillard – now, incredibly, in harness with Rudd, a man she would previously have moved suburbs to avoid. It was true that through 2006 Rudd had progressively distanced himself from the other roosters (Stephen Smith, Wayne Swan and Steve Conroy) and marked out a more independent path, in preparation, it now appeared, for his tilt at the leadership. But for many, this only made his coup against Beazley more distasteful, particularly as it took an alliance with his former enemies to bring it off.

On the policy side, no one denied Rudd's competence in his own field; in fact, he was almost too good at it. The fact that he had been a professional diplomat – speaking Mandarin Chinese, among other languages – suggested interests far more esoteric than those of the ordinary voter. Then there was his Christianity. Like Howard, he was nominally a middle-of-the-road Anglican, although he had descended to that position from the heights of Roman Catholicism, while Howard had risen to it from the depths of Methodism. But unlike Howard, Rudd paraded his beliefs more openly than some of his colleagues felt was decent. The parallel was less with the prime minister than with his flaky health minister, Tony Abbott, known variously as the Mad Monk and Captain Catholic. In blunt terms, Rudd was not what would conventionally be seen as leadership material, at least in the Australian tradition. The view in the Billinudgel was that he was a wussy, smart-arse God-botherer, and Howard would eat him alive. One of my lefty friends had sworn he could never vote for a Labor Party led by Rudd: it would make him feel smarmy.

And yet, and yet. No one could deny that the prospect of a Labor government under Beazley had become hopeless. The always-likeable Bomber had lost whatever electoral appeal he once possessed, and the more he tried to play the tough guy, the more his support drifted away. Moreover, his political judgements had become increasingly eccentric. His decision to support an appeal against a native-title win by Aboriginals in Western Australia outraged many of the faithful, who saw it as yet another populist betrayal of principle. His proposal that a test on Australian values apply to tourists as well as to new settlers was not only opportunistic but downright silly. And then, perhaps most damagingly of all, he confused the Australian comic Rove McManus with the American ideologue Karl Rove.

In the circumstances, it was probably fortunate that the voters were no longer listening to what he was saying; they had made their judgement, and it was that if the Bomber had ever had it, he had now lost it. Beazley was in the same position as Simon Crean had been three years earlier, a political has-been, a body swinging in the breeze waiting to be cut down. His remaining backers pointed to polls which showed that Labor was still comfortably in front on the two-party–preferred vote. But it was obvious that the primary vote, usually hovering under 40 per cent, was far from solid, and no one really thought Beazley could win against Howard. While at times as many as 54 per cent of those polled said that they planned to give their effective vote to Labor, a large majority – up to 65 per cent – expected the Coalition to win. In other words, a sizeable chunk of potential Labor voters were already resigned to defeat, and that being the case, it would not be hard for Howard to lure them over to what they perceived as the winning side. No matter how you spun it, the situation was dire.

As had been the case with Latham three years earlier, there was really only one alternative. Rudd had come to an accommodation with Gillard and her colleagues on the Left, who realised that they would never have the numbers alone and that this was a golden opportunity to get their star player into the number-two job – and who knew where that might lead in time? He had also cultivated the powerbrokers of the Right, particularly in New South Wales. While they were not entirely convinced of Rudd's merits, they noted that he was from Queensland, a state in which the party desperately needed to win seats, and the hometown boy might have an advantage. And in any case, their own internal polling had made them despair of Beazley. So the trigger was pulled, and on 4 December the Rudd–Gillard ticket (the Dream Team, as they were rather ominously known; please don't mention the last political Dream Team, led by Alexander Downer) comfortably defeated Kim Beazley.

There was genuine regret at his passing. Beazley will go down as one of the great Labor might-have-beens, along with the young Doc Evatt, Arthur Calwell and Bill Hayden. He would, I think, have made a good prime minister, as he made a good defence minister and a good communications minister; but leader of the Opposition is a different task, needing more passion, more mongrel, more grunt. Some years ago Gough Whitlam said to me that Beazley's problem was that he had never had to fight for the position, that he had always had it handed to him on a plate. He could be right. The only three leadership elections Beazley fought – his mid-term challenge to Crean, his contest with Latham and his defence against Rudd

– he lost. On the two occasions he took the leadership, the factions gave it to him without a caucus vote. Compare and contrast, as Whitlam would say, his own strife-torn path to the top. When he finally made it, bloodied but triumphant, the early battles had given him the steel for the real fight that lay ahead. Perhaps if Beazley had faced the same obstacles and overcome them, he would have been better prepared to take on Howard. Or perhaps he was always just too nice a bloke ever to beat the wiliest and most ruthless politician of his generation.

One thing is certain: when Howard saw Beazley as his opponent for 2007, he would have felt utterly, seamlessly confident. From his perspective any change, no matter how bizarre, was a change for the worse. The Rudd–Gillard combination would, at the very least, necessitate a change of tactics.

★

From the Labor side the switch was seen as inevitable; there was no doubt that Beazley was a loser, so anyone was preferable. However, there was a remarkable lack of enthusiasm in the ranks for actually doing the deed. It was, after all, only three years before that the party had found itself in an identical situation and had risked everything on a new and inexperienced leader, and look where that had left them. The Latham experiment, which had started so promisingly, had ended in disaster: while none of the party hard-heads believed that Beazley would have won the 2004 election, few thought that he would have lost it as badly. Moreover, the aftermath had ripped the party down the middle: even by the end of 2006 the feud between the Latham–Crean mob and the Beazley boys continued to smoulder. There were plenty of reasons to doubt that another plunge into the unknown would solve the real problem: providing an alternative government that the punters would find preferable.

And in 2007 the stakes were higher than ever, because of WorkChoices. For the labour movement as a whole and for the trade unions in particular, WorkChoices represented Armageddon. It was never meant to happen; only after Labor strategists' extraordinary incompetence in drawing up their Senate preference lists, delivering control of the upper house to an incredulous but delighted prime minister, did it become a possibility. As a result, the Howard government put the legislation together in a rush, to bed it down well before the next election. It was an untidy package, bristling with unsorted detail and unintended consequences. While it had not produced the industrial devastation that critics had predicted (and hoped for), it still had the feel of a work in progress. If Labor could win in 2007, it would be possible to undo most of it without a great deal of political or social trauma. But if Labor lost, WorkChoices would become entrenched and industrial relations would be changed forever. The heavies were prepared to take any risk to avoid that happening, even one as bizarre as the odd couple they had just installed.

The optimists in the party said that the differences between Rudd and Gillard were not a hindrance, but a virtue: each would appeal to a particular set of voters. Rudd would draw the conservatives, Gillard the radicals; Rudd's appeal to middle-class males would be complemented by Gillard's attraction for working-class females. (Taken to its logical extreme, the argument suggested that Rudd would win over the myopic and Gillard the redheads.) Seductive as it was, it ignored the obvious corollary: for many swinging voters, a liking for one of the pair might be more than offset by a loathing of the other.

In any case, the partnership, while celebrated like a Packer-family wedding, could well turn out to be just as unstable. While the first few days saw the happy couple practically hand in hand, the harsh reality of politics decrees that there can only ever be one leader: election campaigns are not made for double acts. Gillard seemed to understand this, at least early on; she spoke only when spoken to and generally played the role of dutiful helpmeet to perfection. But none of those who knew her well, or even casually, imagined that she could keep it up for the best part of a year. All the tacticians could sensibly hope for was that when she did assert herself, it would be in reasonable harmony with her leader – which, given her record, was far from certain.

But the biggest gamble was Rudd himself. From the start, there was a contradiction: although he had spent his parliamentary career thrusting himself forward with a total lack of modesty, very few people thought that they really knew him. Behind the aggressive self-promotion there was something not only calculating but hidden, an aspect he was reluctant to reveal to the public. It made a lot of people uneasy about him. For a long time I was one of them; like my fellow drinkers in the Billinudgel, I tended to see him as a pious, too-clever-by-half nerd whom I would rather avoid. Yet friends who had dealt with Rudd in Queensland during his time as El Supremo in the Goss government assured me that I was selling him short: beneath the admittedly unappealing facade, they insisted, was a resolute and dedicated Labor man waiting to emerge. I continued to have my doubts.

My epiphany came when I read two essays Rudd wrote in the *Monthly* magazine (to which I also contribute). In one he wrote of the way his Christianity informed his politics, through his admiration for the life and work of Pastor Dietrich Bonhoeffer, the anti-Nazi priest. It was a well-written piece which demonstrated that Rudd not only had an intellectual commitment to the Left but the fire in the belly to go with it. The second essay put the argument that Christianity should not be considered a wholly owned subsidiary of the Liberal Party, as the religious Right in Australia, following its American counterpart, was claiming; the Gospels, if interpreted in a straightforward way, had a great deal in common with the Labor Party's philosophy and platform. This was hardly a new idea, but to put it forward in the current climate required a certain cheek, and also demonstrated that Rudd (like, dare one mention the name, Latham) had the ability to think outside conventional political guidelines. I found myself warming to the man.

Admittedly, there was an element of making a virtue out of necessity in my conversion; Rudd was, after all, the only alternative to the unspeakable, unflushable Howard. But the more I looked for the passion and substance needed in an Opposition leader, the more I found them. Perhaps, just perhaps, Kevin Michael Rudd was the man for the job, if he could make the same sort of breakthrough to the electorate at large. Encouragingly, he had already recognised the need to throw, as Paul Keating memorably put it, the switch to vaudeville every so often. For some time he had been making weekly appearances on Channel 7's popular *Sunrise* program, in company with one of the Coalition's less-horrible ministers, Joe Hockey. These amiable tete-a-tetes with Mel and Kochie, as the hosts like to be known, at least went some way to implanting the idea that Rudd was a regular sort of a bloke, not nearly as far up himself as he appeared on the news; they had the added benefit of ensuring that he would at least know who Rove McManus was, should the occasion arise. Much more was needed, but it was good to see that Rudd recognised the need to balance his evidently superior intellect with a certain amount of earthiness.

Howard and his attack dogs, having spent a decade persuading the voters that any kind of cleverness (Elitism! Latte

Sipping! Chardonnay Drinking! Out of Touch with Ordinary Australians!) was at best suspect and at worst treasonable, took this as their first line of attack. Tony Abbott, almost fainting in horror, said that Rudd talked like a professor – clearly the filthiest insult he could dream up. The commentators, having spent the first fortnight of the new regime being bitchy about Julia Gillard's hair and dress sense (even *Zoo* magazine got in on the act, Photoshopping a picture of her in bra and panties) now turned to the matter of Rudd's lack of familiarity; he would, they announced solemnly, find it a hard job to match Howard in the time available. Well, duh.

But at least he hit the ground running, unhesitatingly attacking Howard on the turf that the prime minister had tried to make his own sacred site. The big problem with WorkChoices, Rudd asserted, was not just that it was unfair, grossly biased toward the bosses and a deliberate attempt to destroy the right of workers to organise, but that it was disruptive to family life. It was all very well for Howard to throw pre-election handouts at working families every three years, but what was the point if those same families couldn't arrange to take holidays together, go to sporting events together, even have meals together? Howard, the great family man, was a double-dyed hypocrite. Howard was a home wrecker.

It caught the government off guard, and the prime minister's response was unconvincing. This probably didn't matter all that much, because the attack took place in the last week of parliament and the silly season was already under way; all would be forgotten by the time the new political year started, at the end of January. But it demonstrated once more that Rudd was capable of what used to be called lateral thinking: taking a new line on an old issue. It was also greatly reassuring to the caucus members who had been worried that Rudd would have trouble breaking through; after all, he had spent months working indefatigably on the wheat-for-weapons affair and had never really looked like cracking the government's stone wall. Perhaps the leadership would be the making of him.

Certainly he wasted no time in asserting his new authority within the party itself. While Liberal leaders can choose their own frontbench, Labor leaders have to take whatever caucus gives them; their only entitlement is to allocate portfolios. In the past few years the real selection has been made by the factional bosses, who work out the numbers between them and then present their lists to the leader. The leader can and does make certain requests, which may or may not be granted, depending on the circumstances, but he seldom gets exactly what he wants. The frontbench Rudd inherited from Beazley was one of the messier compromises. In fact, it wasn't even Beazley's; when he took over from Latham in 2005 he kept Latham's unsuccessful team largely intact, in the name of party unity. All attempts in the next two years to persuade him to call a spill or even reshuffle portfolios failed, leading to well-merited accusations of weakness; the Bomber was notoriously reluctant to take on the party's machine men. At the end of 2006 Labor's shadow ministry was well past its use-by date.

Rudd did not wait for faction leaders to provide him with lists; he told them what he wanted. Room was to be found for Peter Garrett, Craig Emerson, Lindsay Tanner and Bob McMullan, no matter what. And it was, although the process involved administering a direct snub to two of the biggest and nastiest union warlords, Bill Ludwig of the AWU and Joe de Bruyn of the Shoppies. To make it clear that he was no longer bound by the factional system, Rudd announced that he would cease to attend meetings of his own Right faction and Gillard would cease to attend meetings of the Left. Gillard acquiesced, as she did when Rudd refused to make her shadow treasurer; he wanted to leave the hardworking Wayne Swan in the job, in an attempt to mend fences. Instead, she was given Employment and Industrial Relations, set to be the centrepiece of the election campaign. This left another rooster, Stephen Smith, free to take over Education, previously held by Beazley's nearly invisible deputy, Jenny Macklin. Garrett got Climate Change and Environment, although Anthony Albanese retained Infrastructure and Water. Emerson got Small Business and the Service Economy, areas where Labor desperately needed a foothold. McMullan was given charge of Commonwealth–State Relations, which Rudd intended to exploit. Tanner was allotted Finance, as well as overarching responsibility for strategy, his real passion.

The most impressive thing about the choice of line-up was that Rudd did not use it to reward supporters or punish adversaries. Again, he raised hopes: finally the faction system, which had started as a good idea to eliminate intra-party brawling but which had evolved into a totalitarian monster, might be breaking down. Finally the cliques and cabals which had bedevilled caucus for so much of the time in Opposition might be merging into a greater whole. The Labor Party was not quite overwhelmed by the spirit of Christmas, but at least the exchanges of good will at the break-up parties did not sound quite as forced as usual.

On the other side of the house things weren't quite as jolly. In spite of repeated claims by Coalition members to the more gullible members of the press gallery that Beazley was the one they really feared and that Labor had made a terrible mistake, a lot of them were looking rather thoughtful, and it wasn't just because of Howard's by-now-meaningless warnings against complacency. Their initial hope had been that Rudd would prove to be another Latham, an enthusiastic amateur who would eventually succumb to the pressure Howard was so good at exerting. But it was already obvious that there was a professional quality about Rudd which Latham had lacked, together with the steel and determination that Beazley had never acquired. Howard warned his colleagues against dismissing Rudd as just another nerd. After all, he pointed out, he himself had once been put down with the same insult, and look at him now. Perhaps, he mused, the next election was shaping up as the Battle of the Nerds.

The media needed more time to catch on. Initially the cartoonists depicted Rudd as mild-mannered, wide-eyed, a political innocent. The *Australian*'s Bill Leak turned him into the comic-book character Tintin, the boy detective. But the more perceptive noted that Tintin always wins in the end, no matter how big and mean his opponents might be. The *Age* discovered, with a sense of overwhelming relief, that Rudd was not actually a socialist, which was hardly a surprise given that the last Labor leader who had even the vaguest commitment to the socialisation of industry, production, distribution and exchange was Arthur Calwell, who had left office some four decades earlier. But, crowed a fossicker in the *Australian*, Rudd had once described himself as a Christian Socialist: pretty suss. Another banner in the same paper gasped, 'Rudd is a Closet Leftie' – a description which would have come as a shock to his caucus colleagues. Clearly a little more investigative journalism was required. Eagle-eyed reporters may have found a clue in Rudd's choice of holiday reading: *The Search for Stability*, by the former Reserve Bank governor Ian Macfarlane. By contrast, Howard announced that if he could spare time from the cricket he would be dipping into Andrew Roberts' *A History of the English-Speaking Peoples Since 1900*, a tome reviewed under the ironic headline 'Thank God for the White Man.'

A bit of lighter reading would do them both good; at the very least it might freshen up Rudd's sloganeering. Mark Latham had his Ladder of Opportunity, a cumbersome piece of equipment that had us all reaching for our chainsaws after the first month. Then he developed Ease the Squeeze, a mildly offensive image with vaguely scatological overtones. But Rudd is even more banal: we have, he insists, Come to a Fork in the Road. If we don't Take the Right Path, John Howard will make us Cross a Bridge Too Far. Fortunately Rudd's friends (and probably his enemies, too) soon persuaded him to give them a rest.

I was probably the only one disappointed by this; I was about to christen him Mr 2776, the postcode of Faulconbridge. Fork 'n' Bridge, get it? Oh, ho ho. By the end of the year we all needed a break.

> “ *Two things are always the same: the dance and war.* —GERTRUDE STEIN

★ 2.

EVEN BEFORE CHRISTMAS the more excitable Murdoch commentators (those whom Mark Latham called ‘the dancing bears’) had been jumping up and down like a drunken audience at a strip club, chanting at Kevin Rudd, *Show us your policies! Show us your policies!*

This was something seldom demanded of John Howard, and certainly not when he was in a similar position in 1996, a newly elected leader lining up to oppose a long-serving government. But Howard has used his lengthy incumbency to implant a series of myths, among them the ones about never knowing what Labor stands for and how the ALP has become a policy-free area. Neither line stands up to even superficial enquiry, but since most of the press gallery long ago added infallibility to the list of Howard’s political talents – even his lies going unquestioned – they were now treated as received truths.

So Rudd was expected to produce a stack of detailed policies within moments of his ascension. Actually this would not have been as hard as it sounds, because his immediate predecessors – Beazley, Crean and Latham – had put together quite a collection over the years and even if some of them were eminently discardable, there was still a solid foundation on which to draw. But Rudd, sensibly, wanted to start from scratch, to place his own imprimatur on a program he could take to the people, rather than serving up a rehash of rejects.

He had already scored a modest success with his lateral approach to WorkChoices, and now tried a similarly unexpected tactic with education: this was not to be considered in traditional terms, as a social issue, but rather as a core economic one. Education was not just a tool for individual self-advancement, important though that might be. It was a key instrument of national productivity, which was suffering as a result of years of neglect by the Howard government. The way to lasting prosperity, he said, was through an Education Revolution. It was a good line and, like the attack on WorkChoices, it left the government looking flat-footed. The response that (a) the government had not really neglected education, an assertion comprehensively disproved by any number of statistics, including truly damning international comparisons, and (b) if Rudd was really serious about productivity he'd support WorkChoices, did not, as they say, resonate.

Interestingly, when Rudd fell back on existing policy he was less successful. When Howard's hand-picked panel of pro-nuke experts reported that nuclear power should figure in long-term plans for Australia's energy needs, Rudd simply repeated the Beazley formula: nuclear energy was too expensive, too dangerous, and would take too long to implement to be useful in attacking the climate change crisis. The critics pounced. *Cop out*, they screamed: *Prisoner of the Left, bound to the anti-science superstitions of the past.* Howard said that not to plan for nukes in the future would be 'crazy in the extreme' and that he wanted a 'serious, considered, political debate'. The key word, of course, was 'political'. If nuclear power could be proclaimed clean and green – and Howard so proclaimed it – it would be a great wedge to drive into the Left. To cap it off, Howard shamelessly accused the Green and Labor politicians who asked where he planned to locate reactors of playing 'the politics of fear'. If the dinosaurs had possessed hides as thick as John Howard's, they never would have died out. He even announced that he would be happy to live next door to a reactor. Janette, regrettably, was not asked for her own assessment of what it would do to the neighbourhood.

The Howard-huggers in the media rejoiced: the *Australian*'s Steve Lewis handed down his considered judgement that by adopting this lazy, populist stance Rudd had failed the first test of his leadership. (Murdoch journalists love setting Labor politicians tests; it enables them to pretend that they themselves have standards.) But as time went on, it appeared that Rudd might have pulled the right rein. Few seemed to share Howard's desire to have a nuke for a neighbour, and their lack of enthusiasm communicated itself to more cautious politicians. Not only the Labor premiers but also their conservative opposites rejected the Howard plan.

The crunch probably came when the Australia Institute helpfully released a list of twenty suitable sites for the reactors. Rudd would have been delighted to find quite a few of them were in marginal Coalition seats, which he no doubt pencilled in for a visit. And the fact that Howard's experts had suggested a total of 25 power plants were needed left a nice margin for speculation by nervous voters in other winnable electorates. All of a sudden Howard and his ministers were talking a lot more about clean coal and a lot less about uranium.

Exciting as these issues were, the central one was always going to be The Economy, Stupid, and Rudd knew it; he and his brains trust, and especially his chief policy co-ordinator, Lindsay Tanner, believed that the most damaging mistake made by all Rudd's predecessors had been to desert the field, leaving Howard to propagate the lie that Labor could not be trusted to manage the economy – that interest rates would be higher, unemployment worse and the entire country would sink into a slough of despond. It wasn't true, of course, and a cursory glance at the Hawke–Keating years would prove it wasn't true; but Beazley, the only one who had been leader for long enough to get the real story across, had never really tried.

Rudd was determined to use what time he had to give it a shot. Typically, he came at it from an unexpected angle. Perhaps influenced by George Megalogenis's thoughtful book *The Longest Decade*, Rudd began by praising Howard with faint damns: the current government had generally not done a bad job in following up the great economic reforms of the Labor governments from 1983 to 1996. Obviously Howard lacked the daring and imagination of Bob Hawke and Paul Keating, and some of his ideas had been a bit off the track, but by and large he deserved at least a pass mark for effort. Until, that is, his current term, when with WorkChoices he had (wait for it) Gone a Bridge Too Far. From being a modest but well-intentioned reformer, Howard had become an economic fundamentalist, a nutter who treated human beings as commodities and was interested only in the bottom line.

Once again the prime minister was forced to defend himself. To call him a fundamentalist, he said, borrowing a word from his former staffer Gerard Henderson, was hyperbole. Look at his record: a slather of handouts directed at any group that might conceivably vote for him. There was no ideology there. His supporters enthusiastically agreed: far from being a fundamentalist, their man was the ultimate political opportunist, totally devoid of economic principle or indeed of any other kind of principle. And in any case, they added, turning defence into attack, who was Kevin Rudd to talk about economics? We know what he's against, but what is he for? Show us your policies!

The opportunity was just too tempting for the folks over at the *Australian* to ignore. They set Rudd a test – and not just any kind of test, a big test: 'Rudd's Challenge: Big Questions for Rudd.' The chief examiner was the paper's quaintly titled Editor at Large (presumably he's the only one they let out of a cage), Paul Kelly, christened by his colleagues the Professor. The nickname has less to do with erudition than with pomposity, a sanctimonious self-importance that has been nurtured by decades of duchessing by the rich and powerful.

What, demanded Rupert's alpha grizzly, was 'the economic task of the next federal ALP government'?

> ... to cut the fat from government spending, expand competition policy [except, we can safely assume, in the media], de-regulate the universities, introduce more market signals into health, education, transport and energy, eliminate red tape from business, simplify the tax and industrial systems, cut marginal tax rates, encourage the welfare to work transition, invest more in education and training, encourage entrepreneurs in the market place and aspire for a more competitive economy ... Rudd's choice is clear. He can either present as a serious economic policy-maker or engage in the populist positioning that has damaged Labor for too long.

There was just one teensy-weensy problem here: this was not Labor's version of the market economy; it was Murdoch's. Labor's version, as outlined by Rudd (details to be filled in

ASAP) was rather less bleak. Rudd started from the premise that Howard's so-called economic reform had already gone too far, that it had abandoned fairness and decency. Like every Labor leader in the past 40 years, Rudd rejected the idea of economic socialism. But just because he had no plans to nationalise the banks did not mean that he was prepared to embrace laissez-faire capitalism in all its ferocity.

Specifically, he did not believe in the deregulation of just about everything in the name of supposedly greater efficiency, which seemed to be the Murdoch–Kelly agenda. Indeed, perhaps the only point on Kelly's list with which Rudd would unreservedly agree was the one about investment in education and training. The rest, whether or not they were economically desirable, all had social consequences which required rather more consideration. And some, like the total deregulation of universities and further 'simplification' of the industrial system, were quite simply not on. However, it was useful to have the Master's ambit claim on the table; it was going to be interesting (but, I fear, predictable) to see how he dealt with its rejection.

What the *Australian*'s test showed was that Kevin Rudd was still the centre of political attention – which, John Howard had warned his followers, would inevitably be the case for his first few weeks as Opposition leader. This was no doubt the reason for Howard's own behaviour during the silly season being rather more indulgent than usual. Apart from innumerable appearances at the cricket, he turned up unexpectedly on the program of the ultra-right-wing shock-jock Stan Zemanek sounding tired and emotional. He had heard Stan was crook, he gargled, and he wanted his old mate to know that 'we're rooting for you'. Presumably he was using the word in its American sense, but it is still probable that Janette sent him to sleep in the spare room that night.

He sobered up in time to deliver a New Year's message to the nation, a function usually reserved for our Acting Head of State, Major-General Governor-General Thingo. There had been reports that the viceroy was getting a little pissed off about being constantly upstaged, and even more so that no one seemed to be taking his efforts on behalf of the nation as seriously as they should. In an effort to cheer him up, I submitted a Gilbertian ditty:

I made my reputation in the field of bellicosity
But now I serve the nation with impeccable pomposity
And all those years of practice as the army's top banana
    will
Be helpful to my calling as a modern governor-general.
My charismatic bypass makes me almost undetectable
I'm something of a tight-arse but I'm totally respectable
My heritage and ancestry and family and kin are all
Important in the making of a modern governor-general.
I revel in the protocol, embracing it most eagerly
I never miss a photo-call and pose for them vice-regally
I'll boil a boy scout's billy and I'll host a formal dinner – all
The skills that are essential in a modern governor-general.
And when my role's blind-sided by our media-mad prime
    minister
I promise not to find it either seedy, sad or sinister
I won't be controversial or ambitious or original
That's not what is expected of a modern governor-general.
I'm just a public sedative called Whatsisname or Whosis
And if I were competitive I'd be among the losers
At least I can look forward to a lavish public funeral
A fitting culmination for a modern governor-general.

Unaccountably, I still didn't feature in the Australia Day honours list. Ah, well. Perhaps 2007 just wasn't my year. And perhaps, just perhaps, it wasn't going to be John Howard's, either.

Physically he was just dandy, according to his annual personal interview with acolyte Piers Akerman. While this year's effort was not quite so homoerotic as usual, Akerman still found his man 'bursting with enthusiasm and energy', even if his messages for the New Year were a bit of an anti-climax: feminism is dead, and drink tap water. And there was some encouragement for the government: the psephologist Malcolm Mackerras's first prediction was for a Labor win, making such an outcome most unlikely. But no longer completely out of the question, for a quick appraisal of the year ahead revealed that it was not only the Opposition that had changed. The whole playing field seemed to have shifted.

★

Even before Christmas John Howard had been forced to concede that the war in Iraq was going badly. This was hardly the greatest discovery since the Hills Hoist, and Howard's mentor, George W. Bush, had already made the same admission; but hearing it fall from the prime minister's own quivering lips suggested that he was breaking the habit of a lifetime and actually giving ground to his critics. It was not, he hastened to add, an argument for cutting and running; oh, heavens to Betsy no, and Labor policy was still to grant the terrorists a great victory, etc. etc. But it did mean that there might be cause for a minor change of tactics, a nip here and a tuck there.

Howard himself, of course, would not be doing any nipping or tucking; in fact, he wouldn't be doing anything at all. Our troops would remain where they were until Washington said we could bring them home. We must finish the job. But obviously the job had changed; the job now was not the establishment of a model Western-style democracy in the Middle East, but to bog the place up so that it would hold together until we could, in Henry Kissinger's deeply cynical phrase, declare victory and leave. It was hardly an inspirational call to arms.

The prime minister insisted that the basic strategy would not change; if his great and powerful friend George was having a bit of a re-think about tactics, well, that was only to be expected: from time to time Julius Caesar, Napoleon and Jubilation T. Cornpone had taken the same approach to their campaigns. But Bush himself, in a much stickier political mire than Howard, realised the new approach had to be sold as something more profound: a change of strategy; at the very least, a new and positive direction. Hence the deployment of another 20,000 units of cannon fodder was not a temporary reinforcement but a 'troop surge', as irresistible as a tsunami. (In-SAN-ity, noun: 1. Inability to come to terms with reality; a constant state of derangement. 2. The belief that repeating the same action will eventually lead to a different result.)

Almost no professional believed the new strategy was anything more than a face-saving device, designed to provide a buffer period during which Bush could blame Iraqis for the manifest failure of his grand project. Bush himself admitted that it would cost some American lives, and the lives of who knows how many more Iraqis, but he was still unable to offer a coherent justification for the huge and growing sacrifice, for his apparent demand for yet more victims to join the multitudes already dead. There was by now both a popular and a political majority of Americans opposed to any escalation of the war; even in his own country Bush was a clear loser, and international opinion was overwhelmingly in favour of withdrawal.

So where did our own Dear Leader stand? Well, he said, emerging briefly from a pressing round of photo opportunities at sporting events, it's got to be worth a try; anything's better than a perceived American defeat. Back to the cricket, or tennis, or whatever it was. For once it was hard to disagree with the dreaded Sheik Al-Hilaly: our prime minister was indeed Mr Me Too.

As always, Alexander Downer was frothier: the Labor Party, he bubbled, wanted to leave Iraq in the hands of thugs and terrorists. Well, so, apparently, did the American Democrats, large sections of the Pentagon and nearly two out of three American voters. And in any case, who did he think was running the place now? The YWCA? As usual Lord Downer seemed stranded in Fantasy Land, the happiest kingdom of them all. If he really believed that the extra troops would somehow bring to Baghdad (let alone the rest of the country) sufficient stability to enable the Iraqi forces to look after their own security for more than a week, then he was the only one in the world who did. But even Downer isn't that silly; at least he was sharp enough to have refused any request for additional Australian troops even before the request was made. He, like Howard, was simply being polite to his great and powerful friend, in the manner of Evelyn Waugh's editor who used the formula 'Absolutely, Lord Copper' when his boss was right and 'Up to a point, Lord Copper' when the boss was wrong. Reading between the lines, Canberra's response to the Bush initiative was the latter: 'Up to a point, Mr President.' And incidentally, from now on you're on your own.

Bush's response to all this negativism was a defiant 'Well, what would you do?' Which actually wasn't such a bad question. While there was now almost universal acceptance that the invasion of Iraq had been a disaster, there was still a marked reluctance to cut and run; and Howard was right when he said that to do so would not only humiliate America in the propaganda war against terrorism but also hamstring any effort to involve Washington in more productive intervention in the future – we could forget about sending peace-keepers to Africa, for instance. But the problem was that, short of a miracle, this was going to happen anyway.

The troop increases were spun as one last chance for the Iraqis; if, by the end of 2007, they were still not capable of looking after their own security, then no one could say Bush didn't try. This just might play within the US (which is all that really matters to Bush) but in the wider world it wouldn't fool anyone. By now it was obvious to all but the most purblind (Alexander Downer) that Australia's interests were not served by propping up a political campaign designed purely for American consumption. Yet this remained Howard's position: he would leave our existing forces there, do his best to ensure that they were not put in any serious danger, and withdraw them as soon as Washington agreed, all the while loyally pretending that the troop surge was something more than his mate's desperate attempt to salvage his reputation, to be paid for in blood. Mr Me Too indeed, still happy to go on pushing against doors clearly marked 'pull', so long as his big buddy told him it was a good idea.

★

George W. Bush's announcement of his mighty troop surge came on the fifth anniversary of another event which was starting to look a bit tacky around the edges: the opening of the prison camp at Guantanamo Bay. As the stories of prisoners being mistreated and abused and consequently deteriorating to the point of madness continued, efforts had been made to brighten up the camp's image. Bright-eyed visitors on a tight leash were shown licks of fresh paint here and there, a television set, even a games room. Conditions, they were assured, were really much better than those in most prisons in the US itself, with air-conditioning in the main block and each cell having its own toilet, sink and mirror.

Unfortunately none of this was of any comfort to the Australian David Hicks, who, it was revealed, had spent the last ten months in solitary confinement, shackled to the floor for up to 22 hours a day, just in case the walls fell over in an earthquake and he was tempted to make a run for it and impale himself on the razor wire before being shot by the guards. This penalty, he told his lawyers, was in retaliation for a complaint he made about his maltreatment to the Australian consul during a brief visit; unsurprisingly, he was unwilling to risk further contact and further punishment.

These reports and others like them did not stop John Howard, Alexander Downer and Phillip Ruddock declaring that Hicks was absolutely fine, in tip-top physical and mental condition, and the worst that could be said of the treatment he was receiving was that it was firm but fair. This must be the case, because the Americans said it was. When sceptics suggested that this was just a touch naive, Downer replied huffily that he had it on first-hand authority that just a week before, Hicks had been absolutely, demonstrably sane. It turned out that Downer's source was the public-relations officer from the American Embassy in Canberra who, during his leave, had called in at Gitmo and asked to see Hicks. The prisoner had been paraded before him for just three minutes, during which time they had not exchanged a single word. Hicks was then returned to his chains and the PR man departed to work on his expert psychiatric diagnosis.

This piece of Downer smart-arsery provoked an outcry, and if the foreign minister had had any credibility left, it would have destroyed it. As it was, it just confirmed what most people by now suspected: the government couldn't care less about Hicks or what the Americans did to him – unless it became a political embarrassment. In the meantime, the Pentagon could have carte blanche.

This, of course, was the whole point of locating Camp X-Ray outside American borders: to put it beyond the reach of American law. The US Supreme Court had decided that the tactic was at least partly spurious; the original conditions for the trial of the prisoners by military commission were scrapped, because they did not accord with American – or for that matter international – legal requirements. The new conditions under which Hicks was to be charged might or might not do so; on the face of it they seemed very little different from those already rejected. But whatever the outcome, the intention of Guantanamo and the even more inhumane practice of 'rendition' – sending prisoners to secret camps in countries where no limit is placed on interrogation techniques – was clear: to allow the American military to do abroad what it is specifically forbidden from doing at home.

Bush began saying that even Guantanamo has its limits: prisoners may not be tortured. So the spin doctors invented a new syllogism, which goes like this: *Americans do not torture. Therefore what happens at Guantanamo is not torture; let's call it something else, like coercion. Simply because it happens, coercion must be legal, so evidence obtained by coercion must be admissible, in military commissions at least. Therefore all our prisoners will get an absolutely fair trial before being convicted by evidence obtained under coercion, QED.* Well, Howard, Downer and Ruddock believed it, anyway. Asked if he thought prolonged sleep deprivation added up to some form of mistreatment (perhaps, just perhaps, a form of torture) the first law officer of the commonwealth made a joke of it: why, he knew all about sleep deprivation, he often had to take long aeroplane flights, ho ho ho. Ruddock might have added that the undead have no need for sleep anyway.

But in 2007 the issue could no longer be brushed aside. After five years of complacency, the electorate – or enough of it to make a difference – had finally decided that enough was just about enough. Some credit for this must go to the efforts of Hicks's indefatigable US military lawyer, Major Michael Mori, whose tireless integrity had gone some way to redeeming the reputation of both his country and his calling. More belongs to the internet-based GetUp organisation, which turned public unease into a formal campaign. By the middle of January the message coming to the government was clear: it was time to piss or get off the pot. If Hicks was guilty of whatever it was the Americans and their Australian mouthpieces insisted he was guilty of, then it was time, long past time, for trial and sentence. And whatever he may have done, surely he had suffered enough, abandoned by his own government to the hell of Camp X-Ray. It was time to bring David Hicks home.

Sensing the change in mood, Howard had already begun a slow but stylish back flip. Yes, he said, he too was unhappy that things had dragged on, although it was partly Hicks's own fault – after all, his lawyers had been part of the challenge to the previous system of military commissions. Well, sure, but they had been found to be illegal. Would Howard, a lawyer himself, have allowed his client to be tried under an illegal system? Okay, moving right along, let's try something even more preposterous: it must be admitted that Hicks is entitled to the presumption of innocence. This from the man who had spent the last five years declaring Hicks guilty of everything from genocide to jay walking.

Ruddock had gone so far as to set a deadline: if Hicks had not been charged by the middle of November, we might actually have to consider bringing him home. The middle of November passed without action by the Americans or comment by our fearless attorney-general. So did all of December. But finally, as the public rumbling increased throughout January, Howard issued what sounded a little like an ultimatum: Hicks was to be charged by the middle of February, or else ... well, or else. Perhaps he was planning to hold his breath until he went blue in the face.

But as the smart money had already assumed, there was no need for either. Howard is not a gambler: the fix was in. In the first week of February, the day after Hicks's Australian lawyers had flown home from Guantanamo, the word was handed down from Washington: the intention was to charge Hicks with attempted murder and providing material support to terrorism, crimes which carry a maximum sentence of life imprisonment. Howard crowed triumphantly that his deadline had been met, but in fact it hadn't; before the charges could actually be laid they had to be approved by some kind of military convention which had not even been constituted, let alone got around to considering them. The best that could be claimed was that there was at last some progress, albeit of a glacial kind.

And the proposed charges raised a whole new set of questions. Giving material aid to terrorism was a new offence; the law had apparently not existed when Hicks was picked up in 2001. Was the government happy to see Hicks tried retrospectively, having repeatedly said they would not allow that to happen in Australia, and that this was why he could not be brought home? Howard blustered; Ruddock trotted out some legal weaselry to the effect that it wasn't actually a new law, more a recodification, a sort of Clayton's retrospectivity.

The Pentagon prosecutor, Colonel Moe Davis, shouted that everything was quite okay. Asked how Hicks could be charged with attempted murder when it was agreed that he had never fired a shot at anyone, Davis bellowed that the Australian had been holding a gun and had intended to use it against American troops; it was just lucky that there were none around at the time. In other words, Hicks was to be tried firstly for something which was legal at the time he did it, and secondly for something he might have done but didn't, a form of thought crime. Then Davis yelled helpfully that he was open to plea-bargaining, a form of legal blackmail by which Hicks was invited to confess to some lesser crime he didn't commit, to avoid the risk of either life imprisonment if found guilty, or indefinite incarceration even if found innocent, a prospect the military had also foreshadowed. Alternatively, he could opt for a trial based on evidence obtained by hearsay and coercion, with the military acting as prosecutor, judge and jury, a travesty deemed by the Americans to be unfit for their own people.

Such was the fate of an Australian citizen in John Howard's Australia, and by the time parliament resumed it was making a lot of backbenchers feel a little queasy. They were hardly reassured when Howard boasted to his party room that he could bring Hicks home anytime he wanted, but he chose not to, so there. Absolutely powerful, and absolutely corrupted.

> *And the dancing has begun now*
> *And the dancers whirl round gaily*
> *In the waltz's giddy mazes*
> *And the ground beneath them trembles.*
> —HEINRICH HEINE

★ 3.

KEVIN RUDD'S DECISION to place education at the centre of his platform was what Sir Humphrey Appleby would have called a courageous one. Just two losing elections ago Kim Beazley (Remember him? Ah, well) had taken the same course, with disastrous consequences. Beazley, musing that he would like to be remembered as the Education Prime Minister, announced in 2001 that if elected he would transform Australia into the Knowledge Nation. Even then it was a risky idea. Education was, of course, a good thing, especially if it followed the Tom Paxton model:

> What did you learn in school today, dear little boy of
> mine?
> I learned that America must be strong
> We're always right and never wrong
> Our leaders are the finest men
> And we elect them again and again
> That's what I learned in school today, that's what I
> learned in school.

But to make some sort of fetish of it was deeply suspect – an indication, perhaps, of unforgivably unAustralian elitism.

Beazley put the loveable but impractical Barry Jones at the head of his taskforce, and Jones duly produced a report on how almost the whole of the country, from outback to opera company, could be drawn in to the idea of an information-based society. To illustrate the concept he provided a simple connectivity diagram of the kind widely used in primary schools. The Forrest Gumps of the government and the media instantly declared it incomprehensible; Peter Costello, showing that he could not be trusted with a set of counting blocks, let alone the economy, called it spaghetti and meatballs, Noodle Nation. And that was the end of that.

In the years that followed, Howard and his attack dogs continued to defame the state-education systems, demanding they be recast in good old-fashioned terms, with an emphasis on the three Rs, the English classics and history taught as a timeline of Great Events. The leader of the pack was someone called Kevin Donnelly, a former staffer of Kevin Andrews who was granted the unusual privilege of apparently unlimited space by the *Australian*. The privilege was more extraordinary in that all his articles were exactly the same: a rant at unnamed lefties for conspiring to destroy children's minds by taking over the schools and universities and filling them with gobbledegook and propaganda. Exactly who these lefties were or why they should aim to destroy children's minds was never explained, but Donnelly's paranoia fitted in nicely with the campaign of the then minister for education, Brendan Nelson, to base secondary education around schoolyard flagpoles and pictures of Simpson's donkey, so it became part of the political mainstream, along with the promotion of the private system at the expense of the public one. Rescuing our children from leftist ideology (which in the

Howard government's case was code for the teachers' unions) became yet another Murdoch–Coalition crusade.

It took a brave man to step into this shitstorm, but Rudd had already demonstrated that beneath his mild-mannered exterior there was a touch of the political daredevil. To drive up economic productivity, he proclaimed, a highly educated workforce was vital. And there was plenty of evidence that Australia was falling behind, particularly when compared to the emerging giants China and India. Tables were produced to prove that Australian spending on education at all levels was now at or near the bottom of the list of our competitors, and heading further south. Labor's comprehensive approach would attack the problems from all angles, starting with basic learning at the kindergarten stage.

Howard was caught unprepared. He had a new education minister, Julie Bishop (Nelson was now floundering in Defence), who had already embarked on a moderately ambitious reform program, but it did not include a lot of extra spending. Rudd was clearly making the running, and a blockbuster response was required.

First, however, let's clear the decks with the long-awaited ministerial reshuffle – although after all the build-up, this became another anti-climax. Rod Kemp, known affectionately to his colleagues as Elmer Fudd, finally retired and the obnoxious Gary Hardgrave got the chop. But the only other victim was Amanda Vanstone, who both as a woman and a moderate had represented a token presence in Howard's macho ministry. Great piles of dead wood remained: Ian Macfarlane, Jim Lloyd, John Cobb, De-Anne Kelly and Fran Bailey, to mention only the silliest. Some Costello supporters were brought into minor positions, among them George Brandis, who had christened Howard the Lying Rodent; clearly the treasurer no longer represented even the mildest of threats. But the big news was the creation of the new superhero, Aquaboy: Malcolm Turnbull had greatness thrust upon him. Just how much greatness was soon to become apparent.

There was another spin-off from the reshuffle: multiculturalism was formally abolished. Howard had always hated it, had spent years denigrating and undermining it, and was now ready to consign it to the dustbin. The old Department of Immigration and Multicultural Affairs (DIMA) became the Department of Immigration and Citizenship (DIC), which confirmed that the new minister, the unlovely Kevin Andrews, was a DIC-head. He was not amused.

The change of name also signalled an even more aggressive outbreak of nationalism from the government, and fortuitously there was an immediate chance to demonstrate it. The previous year's Big Day Out concerts had produced some ugly incidents involving the Australian flag. Groups of thugs ordered anyone of what is known as 'Middle Eastern appearance' to kiss the increasingly grubby piece of cloth, and if they demurred, they were beaten up. Aware of the violence, in 2007 the concert organisers suggested (and it was no more than a suggestion) that participants leave their flags at home.

Howard was outraged: it was stupid, offensive, the organisers were running a political agenda, the flag should never be banned under any circumstances, bluster bluster. To his shame, Rudd joined in the mindless chorus of jingoism. Flags blanketed the concert in the form of capes, hats, beach towels, picnic rugs, underwear and handkerchiefs, among other less-than-reverent uses. The sacred design made a number of appearances on T-shirts accompanied by such patriotic slogans as 'Love It or Fuck Off'. Howard presumably found all this entirely appropriate; at least, he raised no objection.

If the Australian flag ever commanded genuine reverence, those days are long past; like others before it, it has been hijacked by various nasties as a cover for their bad behaviour. Howard should know: he himself is, of course, a constant flag abuser. He seldom goes anywhere without a large Chinese-made replica which he uses as a background for obfuscations, smears and lies. And his brand of nationalism would have been quite at home among the yobbos at a Big Day Out.

'Jelly-bellied flag-flappers', as Rudyard Kipling called them, were brought back to reality by the publication of the latest Newspoll, which confirmed that Rudd was not only enjoying an extended honeymoon with the electorate but breathing down Howard's neck as the preferred prime minister, a more worrying statistic. The poll also made it clear that the electoral tide had well and truly turned over both the Iraq war and David Hicks. To top it off, Rudd went all prime ministerial and announced that he, and of course the Labor state premiers, would convene a summit on water and climate policy. Something had to be done. Howard decided the answer was a super flip of such magnitude that it would shock even the most blasé observers: a really Great Big Splash.

★

To describe John Howard as a climate-change sceptic, as he and his opponents frequently did, was something of an understatement. Howard was not sceptical, or even agnostic; for many years he had been a card-carrying atheist, as his actions made clear. He would not ratify the Kyoto agreement; he would not consider carbon trading, let alone a carbon tax; he would not set serious targets for renewable energy, or even for a reduction in greenhouse-gas emissions. From time to time he would politely suggest that the bigger polluters might like to have a look at ways to cut back; if they did, good, and if they didn't, so it went.

As the number of headlines about global warming increased through 2006, Howard remained unconvinced, but he recognised the political usefulness of the issue. If, he mused, there really was a problem (though the jury was still out), then perhaps we should try for cleaner coal; and, of course, any solution had to include nuclear power, because that would wedge the ALP. And would everyone please remember to turn off unwanted lights and put a brick in the cistern, because although Australia was such a small player in the emission stakes that nothing it did by itself could have the slightest effect, individuals could still make a difference, and what do you mean, 'Humbug'?

None of this amounted to much, so when Malcolm Turnbull, the newly appointed water and environment supremo, was asked whether the government had a policy on climate change, he was in a sense quite right when he replied that the government had had a policy for ten years. What he didn't say was that the policy went like this: *Climate change probably isn't happening. But if it is happening and there is a problem, then the scientists will fix it. And if they can't fix it, then we'll have to adapt. And if we can't adapt, well, tough. But in any case, it probably isn't happening.* This is less a policy than a state of mind, a fatalism of which Mother Teresa might have been proud. It is, however, an unsuitable attitude to take for a government which is meant to prevent rape, rather than invite the prospective victim to lie back and enjoy it.

It was always going to be risky for Howard if the issue suddenly became a significant one, which it duly did at the end of 2006. A wet American political has-been produced a science-fiction movie and a chinless British dilettante came out with a doomsday prophecy, and the bloody mob went mad. Or that's the way it must have looked to Howard: after all, there was nothing really new in either Al Gore's film or Sir Nicholas Stern's report. The scientists had been saying it all for months, if not years, and the lavishly funded critics had successfully held them at bay. Now, suddenly what had been a scary but far-fetched hypothesis was received truth.

The drought probably had something to do with it; even if, as Howard maintained, there was no proven link to climate change, it was a taste of what might be in the not-too-distant future. Even in the Billinudgel Hotel, normally a fairly cynical haven in one of the few places in New South Wales without any kind of water restrictions, the punters were talking seriously about conservation: recycling might mean more than just pissing on the lemon tree.

There were still sceptics around, and they were getting an inordinate amount of media play. Interestingly, many of them were economists: the pseudo-scientists who delighted in their own warnings of doom and gloom were apparently unwilling to accept the same when it came backed up by hard evidence. In the *Sydney Morning Herald* Michael Duffy unearthed a couple of economists who not only rejected climate change but even regarded global warming as spurious: presumably they had been deprived of access to thermometers all their lives. With a little effort he could probably have found a handful of hairdressers, a few fan dancers and even an unemployed lion tamer who held the same views. Indeed, he could have quoted two climatologists, as did many of his colleagues. Always the same two; the other 99.9 per cent are busy doing the real science, which proves conclusively that climate change is happening and proves beyond reasonable doubt that human activity is responsible for it.

Certainly denial was no longer a tenable position for Howard; whatever his own views, the voters demanded action. So they got it – up to a point. They got the Great Big Splash. Announcing it, Howard drew on *Crocodile Dundee*: Rudd called his education policy a revolution, laughed the prime minister. Well, that wasn't a revolution – this was a revolution. And so it was: a proposal to put $10 billion towards fixing the Murray-Darling Basin, if the states would hand over their water powers to the commonwealth – which meant to Aquaboy, Malcolm Turnbull. As policy, it presented problems, not least the almost complete lack of detail. But as politics it was Howard at his best, or so it appeared at the time. The government burst back into the game, grabbing the very territory on which it was thought to be weakest. Howard audaciously challenged the traditional federal structure, which Rudd had marked out for reform. He trumped Rudd's water summit and wedged the Labor premiers: in spite of some huffing and puffing, it was really an offer they could not afford to refuse. And of course, the sheer scale of the announcement drove all the other problems off the front pages.

With splendid serendipity the popular environmentalist Tim Flannery was named Australian of the Year. A week earlier this would have been an embarrassment to Howard: Flannery had been a constant critic of the government for its lack of action on global warming, and indeed warned that he would continue to be so. But in the circumstances, the front-page snaps of Howard and Flannery shaking hands seemed to presage a new dawn of environmental concern. You wanted the big picture? They don't come much bigger than this.

And it worked – for nearly a week. But even before the premiers assembled in Canberra, the Great Big Splash was starting to disappear down the gurgler. The first problem was that not one cent of the bonanza was going to the places where most of the voters lived: the cities. With the exception of Adelaide, which takes what passes for its drinking water largely from the Murray, urban Australia missed out completely. Not that rural Australia did all that well; while the Murray-Darling Basin is undoubtedly the country's most important water system, it isn't the only one. At first there was some thought that there might be a bit of spare cash left over from the $10 billion for other dying rivers, but it turned out that this was just part of the confusion which surrounded the whole operation.

Indeed, Wendy Craik, the impeccably National Party head of the current Murray-Darling Basin Commission (which had not been consulted or even warned before the announcement of its impending termination), complained that $10 billion wasn't enough; Howard was nearly a billion short. After a short session behind closed doors in Howard's soundproof office, she staggered out to admit she may have been mistaken. But given that no one was entirely clear what the $10 billion was meant to cover, she may not.

The figure itself was more than somewhat suspect; it turned out that neither the Treasury nor the Department of Finance had been involved in its preparation. Indeed, neither had done any significant work at all on the problems associated with global warming and the consequent water shortages. The head of Finance confessed that his involvement with the Great Big Splash had been limited to a request to run an eye lightly over a single page of costings a week before the announcement. His sinister minister, Nick Minchin, revealed that the proposal had not even gone to cabinet, and sniffed that in the total budget context $10 billion was a pretty pissy sort of amount anyway, which was not quite the impression his Dear Leader was seeking to deliver.

It quickly became obvious that the figure of $10 billion had simply been plucked out of the air; after all, it was a nice big round number, eminently suitable for a tabloid headline. Detailed costings were simply not available. The National Farmers Federation, which might have been expected to call for a week of thanksgiving at the size of the handout, said it might take a full year to work out the detail, and it wasn't giving the Great Big Splash so much as a tentative tick until the work was done. And the Labor state premiers, having originally made cautiously approving noises, went into reverse. At a hastily convened water summit, only the New South Wales premier, Morris Iemma, facing an election which he planned to keep free from distractions, was prepared to sign up, and even he had reservations. Victoria's Steve Bracks and Queensland's Peter Beattie wanted guarantees that their states would not lose out; such guarantees could not be given. South Australia's Mike Rann, whose state of South Australia is most dependent on the Murray, insisted that the new Murray-Darling Authority be made independent of the government, along the lines of the Reserve Bank; Howard indignantly refused.

In the meantime an examination of what detail there was in the plan revealed that some $3 billion was destined as a handout to irrigators to improve their efficiency. Well, that was jolly nice for the irrigators, but one might have thought that if the technology was available to improve their efficiency, and therefore their productivity and their profits, they might have paid for at least part of it out of their own kick. Not only was it to be a gift from the taxpayers of Australia, but the irrigators, unlike the rest of us, would continue to receive their water free, gratis and for nothing. Agrarian socialism has seldom had it so good. Incidentally, one of the efficiencies the big irrigators can look forward to is to have their canals lined, in order to reduce seepage. Again, goody goody for them, but it is just this seepage which fills the watertable, which in turn supports the smaller irrigators who cannot afford canals. Get big or get out.

Which is, of course, what the government was planning for. The irrigators don't have to pay for their water, but they will now be able to sell their rights to it to the highest bidder, which is likely to be the government itself. The hope, indeed the expectation, is that a lot of smaller, marginal producers will agree to sell up, so that the spare water can be returned to the river system – a popular idea. But what if the producers, seduced by their share of the Great Big Splash, decide to hang on? Would pressure be put on them to leave? Would they even be subject to compulsory acquisition? Under no circumstances, screamed the rugged individualists of the National Party who had negotiated the handouts for their well-cosseted constituents. Private property was sacrosanct. The land was sacred. It could never be taken from its traditional owners, never, never, never. Well, rejoined Aquaboy Malcolm Turnbull, hardly ever. Certainly not unless all other approaches failed, and of course they wouldn't. The government's terms would be so generous that farmers would sob with gratitude as they accepted them. So compulsion would not be necessary – except, of course, as a very last resort ...

This, of course, was precisely what the Nats feared, that this smart-arse little urban playboy was taking over their traditional territory and teaching his grandmother to suck eggs. And to revert to Sir Humphrey Appleby, it must be said that Turnbull is indeed a courageous choice for the delicate role of salesman-mediator. Turnbull is hugely intelligent, prodigiously energetic and almost insanely ambitious: his macrocephaly is not just physical. And, those who have spent time with him would add, he is an arrogant, abrasive, bumptious little bastard. Irritatingly, he pronounces 'nuclear' as 'nucular', in the manner of George W. Bush. Not only that, he has lousy political judgement: at the 1998 Constitutional Convention, Howard played him off a break, manoeuvring him into an unwinnable position which Turnbull was only too eager to take. Anyone with the temerity to try and point this folly out to him was either ignored or, more usually, abused. I reported at the time that by the end of the week the only motion which would have passed the convention by universal acclaim was one describing Turnbull as an arsehole.

But defeat at the subsequent republic referendum did not soften the man; he had now brought his messianic temperament into the ministry, this time with Howard's enthusiastic support. His sky-rocketing promotion to cabinet, and to a portfolio which was already proving vital in an election year, showed Howard's touching faith in a fellow megalomaniac. When he remembers to use it, Turnbull can exude a certain manic charm; he may be able to woo some of his fellow city-dwellers. But it is a lot harder to imagine him working the suspicious locals in an outback pub. Even in the Billinudgel, a place sophisticated enough to serve salt-and-pepper squid on alternate weekends, Turnbull is regarded as just a bit too spivvy. As the number-one spruiker for the Great Big Splash, he would have his work cut out – if, indeed, anything remained of the Great Big Splash by the time of the election. A fortnight after its proclamation, its future looked as dubious as that of the rivers it was supposed to save.

Rudd, showing a chutzpah Howard and Turnbull must have found well nigh unbearable, generously offered to help. The issue was so important, he said gravely, that he would roll up his sleeves and get together with the premiers to help allay their misgivings. He had, he reminded the fuming government ministers, already announced that he was calling a real water summit, not just a cosy chit-chat about the Murray-Darling Basin but a super-dooper get-together of the best brains, the most qualified experts in the country, to thrash out the whole business of what was happening to our water, what was causing it, what we could expect in the future and what we should do about it. Apart from driving Howard to apoplexy, Rudd was driving home the highly relevant point that Howard's Great Big Splash, or at least the trickle that was left of it, was only there to treat a symptom of climate change, not the cause; and on that cause the government seemed as hesitant as ever.

There was a real danger that if it did nothing at all, it would be left hopelessly behind. For instance, Howard had made a political virtue out of declaring the coal industry off-limits: nothing must be done to disturb Australia's comparative advantage as a producer or put at risk the jobs of the miners. And besides, if we didn't sell coal to China, someone else would (the eternal excuse of the arms salesman and the drug dealer). But the industry itself was taking a longer view: its leaders saw that if they ignored the rising tide of public concern, one day it might engulf them. Thus, some of Australia's largest miners were already calling for carbon trading, if not for an actual carbon tax or mandatory limits to emissions; and even the relevant union, the same CFMEU which Howard had so successfully exploited over the logging of Tasmanian forests back in 2004, accepted the need for action. Moreover, the states were talking about setting up their own emissions-trading scheme if the commonwealth refused to take the lead. Western Australia was even considering a carbon tax.

With great reluctance, Howard – now calling himself a climate-change 'realist' – performed another back flip and announced that he would start to initiate the commencement of preparations to consider the theoretical possibility of an inquiry into the desirability of carbon trading. The government, in due course, would act promptly. Trading had been Labor policy for some time, so Rudd and his colleagues could legitimately claim that Howard was just playing catch-up. Their line was a simple one: Howard was really a climate-change sceptic, always had been and always would be. The only way to make sure that the subject was treated seriously, as the public clearly wanted it to be, was to change the government.

It seemed to prove their point when, in reply to a question in parliament from Rudd, Howard replied that the jury was still out on the link between global warming and man-made greenhouse-gas emissions. Several hours later he returned to the house to say that he had misheard the question: he thought Rudd had been referring to the drought, not to man-made emissions, and while he believed the jury was still out over whether the drought was directly linked to climate change, he certainly believed that man-made emissions were, he honestly, truly did. His apologists said the mistake came because he is somewhat deaf. Well, maybe, but 'drought' and 'man-made emissions' are hardly homophones. And in any case, the idea of deafness did not sit well with Howard's desire to portray himself as still basically young and energetic and open to fresh ideas. It was a costly slip that confirmed that Labor was setting the agenda on climate change.

But, like Howard, Labor regarded the whole issue of coal as basically just too difficult. Rudd made it clear that while he supported all possible efforts to clean the industry up, Labor had no plans to shut it down or even phase it out. However, the Greens, unburdened by the prospect of having to implement their policy decisions, had no such inhibitions. Bob Brown hit the airwaves to urge the major parties to use the next parliamentary term to come up with a policy aimed at phasing out coal exports – which, in practical terms, meant the industry. Or at least that was what he meant to say; what came out was more ambiguous, and could be taken to mean that the entire industry should be phased out within the next three years.

In a frenzy of anti-Green glee most of the media took it to mean just that, and went on to brand Brown, yet again, as a lunatic zealot, an extremist whose real aim was to destroy industrial society and take humanity back to the caves. Interestingly, the same tabloids reported a truly demented idea from the US absolutely straight: some deranged (so-called) scientists were proposing to reduce global warming by putting a large number of reflective fragments in orbit around the Earth. At the same time they admitted cheerfully that they weren't really sure what the side effects might be, but hey, it was worth a try. Yeah, and so was the cane toad. In comparison, Brown came across as quite boringly rational.

By a pleasing coincidence the Greens leader was making a public appearance in my area the next night, so I turned up at the Byron High School auditorium, curious to see how he would handle the furore. I was not alone; the car park was packed with huge gas-guzzling four-wheel drives, showing the Green rank and file had also arrived in force to demonstrate their solidarity. Actually, it was more like idolatry: they hung on his every word, although there was a frisson of disappointment when he explained that his actual plans to phase out coal exports involved a decade or even two. It rather took the drama out of the situation. I was tempted to interject that by that time there was every chance that technology would have developed a way to clean up the industry anyway, so a phase-out would be unnecessary, but decided the consequences at the hands and feet of the rest of the audience might be unpleasant.

Apart from that, I found Brown a bit of a let-down; the legendary charisma wasn't there, and he had nothing new to say. The only time he perked up was when he described the impending fate of the flightless Tasmanian stag beetle, doubtless a worthy creature but one lacking the popular appeal of the koala. And his view of his party's prospects was, in all senses of the word, pathetic: if only the major parties could be stopped from using their resources to persuade people to vote for them, he mused, then people might vote for the Greens instead. I left the meeting unconverted and unenlightened, but with a rather better idea of why Peter Garrett had decided his political future lay with a major party.

Still, the ALP's giant phallic symbol was clearly feeling his way. The most effective bits of Labor's attack on the Great Big Splash had come not from Garrett but from the man whose job he had assumed, Anthony Albanese. Garrett, in a head-to-head television debate with Turnbull, had been boring, and so had Turnbull; both were so scared of sounding narky that they failed to add anything to the sum of human knowledge.

But at last there was some good news on the climate-change front. In response to global warming, or possibly the drought (no one seemed to be quite sure which), the air conditioning in parliament house had been turned up by two degrees. Think globally, act locally. Perhaps we could make a difference after all.

> *Don't dance or ride with General Bangs – a most immoral man.* —RUDYARD KIPLING

★ 4.

WHILE CLIMATE CHANGE was still a matter for debate in early 2007, political change was becoming hard, undeniable fact. In the second week of February the ground trembled: according to the opinion polls, Kevin Rudd overtook John Howard as preferred prime minister. Six years earlier Kim Beazley had briefly achieved the same feat; Simon Crean and Mark Latham never did. The same polls showed that the primary Labor vote was finally locking in at over 40 per cent, while the Coalition vote was frequently below that number; after preferences, Labor was looking at a landslide. Moreover, Rudd himself was sailing along on a little pink cloud, popularity at undreamt-of heights, totally unsullied by anything the Coalition could throw at him.

And it wasn't as though they hadn't been trying. Peter Costello's sarcasm about Rudd's career in Queensland, Tony Abbott's sneers at his religious convictions and Howard's tut-tutting at his lack of experience had all gone straight through to the keeper. More junior critics received the same treatment: Greg Hunt suggested improbably that Rudd's policies were being written by Noam Chomsky, while Chris Pyne warned that behind Rudd lurked a mob of screaming socialists preparing to drive the nation to either totalitarianism or anarchy, which he seemed to believe were the same thing. Those on the government benches bayed and jeered but Rudd sat through it all apparently oblivious, writing incessantly without so much as raising his eyes to his tormentors.

This, of course, infuriated them still further, which was probably Rudd's intention. It was in this context that he dropped the throwaway line that he would rather enjoy playing with Howard's mind for a while – a line not quite as menacing as Paul Keating's famous threat to do John Hewson slowly, but sufficiently ominous to reinforce the by-now-frantic efforts to cut short Rudd's political honeymoon.

But the government simply couldn't get to grips with him; every time Howard tried to pin the agenda down on his own terms (national security and economic management), Rudd skipped away to a different area. The government complained that he was being slippery and evasive, a complaint often made of Gough Whitlam when he took control of the agenda; but now as then, the punters seemed to find the fancy footwork a refreshing change from the brick-fight that question time had become under Howard.

They also showed no apprehension about Rudd's intellectual prowess, in spite of repeated attempts to characterise it as smugness or self-superiority. When the great American Adlai Stevenson was accused by his opponents of being an egghead, he coined the memorable slogan, 'Eggheads of the world, unite: you have nothing to lose but your yolks.' Rudd did not show quite that panache, but his composure and politeness continued to win him points with the public. A report that the Liberal machine had reconstituted a dirt unit headed by past president

Tony Staley to try and do the same job on Rudd as had been done on Latham came as no great surprise, but there was a general feeling that Rudd would have rather fewer skeletons rattling around than did the bovver boy from Sydney's west.

Rudd's immediate success rubbed off on his colleagues. Under Beazley, Labor's frontbenchers, when not warring among themselves, had often seemed to be doing little more than going through the motions; at times they had been positively torpid. This was at least partly because Beazley insisted on hogging question time for himself and for whichever shadow minister fitted into the plan of the day, but it was also partly because of the government's unquestioned psychological dominance. Now the real prospect of a portfolio of their very own seemed to have sharpened the shadow ministers' minds wonderfully; the party seemed united and enthusiastic in a manner not seen for many years.

There were slip-ups, of course: Julia Gillard's common-sense observation that a full-time political career was incompatible with raising young children produced howls of outrage from the conservatives. But in the public mind this was probably less serious than Howard's decision to have a VIP aircraft drop him and his wife off for a holiday in Broome on his return from a conference in the Philippines. When the story broke he hurriedly repaid the extra cost. But the self-indulgence smacked of the very hubris he was constantly telling his party room to avoid. And it gave substance to the growing feeling that the government had, perhaps, been there too long; it was growing tired and arrogant, and it just might be time for a change.

This was the message that the cautiously optimistic were reading from the opinion polls, both public and private. The swinging voters seemed to be getting ready to dump Howard; at the very least they were becoming bored with him. What they needed was assurance that they could do so without too much risk. They liked what they had seen of Rudd, but they certainly weren't totally convinced, and unless something dreadful happened (like another couple of interest-rate rises, for instance), they could still be scared or bribed back to the fold. When I put this scenario forward in articles in the media, I was depressed to find the humourless Howard-hugger Gerard Henderson agreeing vigorously. To win, Rudd would still need not only a lot of skill, but a slice of luck as well.

The importance of this should not be underestimated. Some politicians are lucky, others are not. Whitlam was an unlucky one, his carefully wrought program derailed by two oil-price shocks. Hawke was lucky, hugely aided by brawling among his conservative opponents. And in office Howard had been lucky: the *Tampa*, the War on Terror and the commodities boom underpinned his twin appeals to security and prosperity. But in 2007 there were the first signs that the luck was beginning to turn, in concert, perhaps, with his judgement; fittingly, it was the great misadventure of Iraq which provided the backdrop.

★

Desperate to move the political debate onto his own ground, Howard went back to what he thought was safe: Labor's policy to withdraw Australia's combat troops from Iraq as soon as was practicable. After all, that was a goody three years ago. But the world had changed, even if Howard had not; that policy was now endorsed by a large majority of Australians and also Americans, including a leading Democratic contender for the presidency, Barack Obama. When informed of this, Howard went slightly mad: Osama bin Laden, he spluttered, would be praying for a win for Obama – or, indeed, for any Democratic candidate.

Perhaps he thought that this was a way of repaying his mate George for slagging off Mark Latham last time around; perhaps he was just being consistent – after all, he used much the same line about Rudd. Whatever the case, jaws on both sides of the Pacific dropped. Obama replied neatly that if Howard really believed that keeping troops in Iraq was so vital, he might like to contribute a few more of his own. Rudd said it was now clear that it was Howard, not himself, who was the real threat to the American alliance; what if Obama became president, as was perfectly possible, or indeed any Democrat, which was more likely than not? Several influential American politicians and commentators told Howard to butt out; more woundingly, rather more laughed contemptuously. Meanwhile, the *Australian*'s foreign editor, Greg Sheridan, proclaimed solemnly (and presumably from a far-distant planet with only rudimentary communication with our own) that it had been an excellent week for Howard. Well, it could conceivably have been worse – and then it was.

As Howard promised extra military trainers for Iraq and continued to rant about how troop withdrawal would be a catastrophe for Iraq and the West and a huge triumph for terrorism, Tony Blair announced that Britain was about to start pulling out of the country. Once again, Little Johnny was the one out of step. The spin-doctors tried valiantly to insist that black was white: the British withdrawal, which they refused to call a withdrawal, was actually a sign of success; the job was getting done. Then why couldn't the Australians start coming home? Well, there weren't enough of them. The contingent was too small to split up. Then why couldn't they all come home? Because we couldn't desert our allies, as it would damage the American alliance.

And then the great architect of the Iraq war, Vice-President

Dick Cheney, arrived in Sydney and said that withdrawing Australia's token presence would not affect the alliance in the slightest. Howard responded bravely that Cheney was just being diplomatic and avoiding getting involved in Australian politics, which coming so soon after his own Obama outburst was either the wildest hypocrisy or early onset Alzheimer's, take your pick. Cheney's visit might have seemed like a good photo-op when it was planned, several months previously, but the timing was, to put it mildly, somewhat awry – or unlucky. Apart from that, the Veep gave one platitudinous interview to Greg Sheridan, who inexplicably did not ask Cheney how much he personally had profited from the war, and caused great disruptions to Sydney traffic before returning home, where he was not very welcome either.

A new poll suggested that Howard could lose his own seat of Bennelong, as well as the government; a glamour candidate, the media star Maxine McKew, offered to contest the seat for Labor. Howard said that the adverse polls only made him determined to work even harder for the benefit of the Australian people; he sounded rather like Boxer, the horse in *Animal Farm* consigned to the knackery by his ungrateful colleagues.

But the real urgency was to find something – anything – to take the spotlight off St Kevin. Policy, or rather policy gimmicks, had been tried and failed: the Great Big Splash was now just background noise and announcements on everything from roads to light bulbs had barely touched the inside news pages before disappearing without trace. And there was at least as much bad news for the government as good: the trade deficit continued to rise despite the commodities boom, tourism had collapsed, Brendan Nelson lost the RSL vote by equating Iraq with the Kokoda Track and Amanda Vanstone released her words to a new national song to be sung, unbelievably, to the tune of 'Land of Hope and Glory'.

George Brandis tried to revive everyone's flagging spirits by ordering that ministerial correspondence be addressed not just to 'Dear Prime Minister' but to 'My Dear Prime Minister', but it wasn't enough. What was needed was a really good smear, a silver bullet that would clip the saint's wings and bring him tumbling back to the pack, something to prove that the new Opposition leader was really just another politician, perhaps not as brutish and dishonest as Howard himself – that would be too big an ask – but at least not the Great Young(er) Hope that the voters craved. And at last the gutter trawlers came up with something: not much, on the surface, but with a bit of puffing and with the aid of an acquiescent press gallery, it could be blown up into a monster.

★

To those of us fortunate enough never to have met the disgraced Western Australian politician turned lobbyist Brian Burke, the real mystery was how he managed to exert any political influence at all, let alone set himself up as a sort of premier-in-exile. Yet three ministers of the current Western Australian government had fallen into his clutches and been sacked as a result. Their naivety seemed incomprehensible.

You would think even those unaware of Burke's criminal record would be warned off by his appearance. The slightly too tight dark suit with the open-necked white shirt, panama hat and dark glasses simply screamed spiv, shonk, sleazebag. If you saw him walking down the footpath towards you, you would hastily cross the street, keeping a hand on your wallet. If you had him in your home or office, you would count the teaspoons after he'd left. Yet his friends (and he still had plenty, something which should alarm federal politicians on both sides) insisted that Burke was a bundle of charm, a charismatic con man in the style of Peter Foster. And what was indisputable was that he, in partnership with the equally unlovely Julian Grill, got results. His list of clients was an impressive one and extended well beyond the usual run of dubious developers and Labor Party cronies.

On his home turf he was certainly loathed and feared, but he was also accorded a perverse admiration and respect. As the ongoing investigation into his activities revealed, he demanded to be taken seriously. But it must be said that he was not, as John Howard and his attack dogs sought to portray him, Satan himself, the lord of all evil whose very presence corrupted everything it touched. It was a measure of the government's failure to lay a glove on Kevin Rudd in the past three months that his encounters with Burke were given such exalted status.

Rudd, two years ago when his leadership aspirations were still in the formative stage, had thrice run into the ex-con, a friend of a friend. Well, one might legitimately ask, so what? It was perhaps a little indiscreet, given that there was at that stage a ban on state-government ministers meeting Burke, but no one seriously suggested that any favours were sought or given. The results spoke for themselves: if Burke was supposed to tout for caucus votes for Rudd in the leadership spill, he did an unusually ineffective job, because Rudd ended up with just two out of the nine Western Australian votes on offer. Politicians meet scores of people every week, and it's a safe bet that among them are many more unsavoury than Burke. Dick Cheney springs to mind.

But Burke was in the news and the connection with Rudd could be made, so the heavies went in with all guns blazing. Tony Abbott's line, pinched from one of Crikey's more excitable commentators, was that Rudd had supped with the devil – not once, but three times. Peter Costello said that everything and everybody who associated with Burke was morally and politically compromised and that Burke never did anything without wanting something in return, implying that Rudd was now somehow in Burke's debt. Alexander Downer said baldly that Rudd was lying about it all. Howard, assuming his role as firm but fair Elder Statesman, mused that Rudd had huge amounts of explaining to do but that whatever he said wouldn't make any difference to the fact that he was now hopelessly compromised.

This was hyperbole on a grand scale, but that was the point: it put Rudd in the position of having to give a detailed reply to charges that were so wide-ranging, so general as to be effectively unanswerable. And Rudd bit; he spent three days floundering, with the dancing bears in the Murdoch press chortling that the honeymoon was finally over – Rudd was back in the pack as just another politician whose judgement and honesty were under question, who was clearly too naive and inexperienced for the job.

It was all good clean healthy fun until Burke's office contacted the *Australian* to say that Brian Burke had also met one of Howard's ministers, Ian Campbell, and what about that, then? Campbell, sprung, rang Howard; Howard promptly accepted his resignation, whether it was offered or not. As Campbell quite openly pointed out, he hadn't actually done anything wrong, but the important thing was to win the next election. If his presence was some kind of impediment to Howard and the gang throwing dirt at Rudd, he was quite willing to get out of the way, the unspoken rider being that it would only be for a little while: the political and moral corruption would undoubtedly dissipate straight after polling day.

Campbell's noble gesture allowed Howard to insist that Rudd should stand down; it was now a matter not just of judgement and honesty, but of that mysterious American concept, character. Rudd replied by challenging Howard to call an election based on honesty and see where that got him. But he had clearly been bruised by the week; he had overreacted and overexplained, suggesting that he might be vulnerable under sustained pressure. The government had got a fair slice of what it wanted.

But there was a price to pay, which extended beyond Ian Campbell, grinning happily in the expectation of a lavish payback. Burke's clients were not too happy about Abbott and Costello; they did not feel that they had supped with the devil or that they were morally and politically compromised, and resented the implication that they were little more than a pack of orcs to Burke's Sauron. Among them were quite a few Liberal Party supporters, even Liberal Party donors: for example, Howard's close friend and valuable contact Andrew 'Twiggy' Forrest, of Fortescue Metals, attended the same notorious dinner as Rudd. Costello said that they didn't matter, because they weren't trying to become prime minister, which was true as far as it went; but Abbott had explicitly included Burke's clients in his own sinners list. Given that there were two seats in the west that the Coalition was desperate to hold and another two it dearly wanted to win, there was a bit of urgent fence-mending for Howard to do.

★

The initial polls suggested that Rudd had weathered the onslaught pretty much unscathed, but the more sober commentators realised that these things take a while to filter through and that most punters would remember vaguely that Rudd had once done something a bit dodgy, even if they couldn't remember exactly what it was. But there was comfort for Labor, too; if that was really the worst that the Coalition muck-rakers could come up with after three months of digging, then there wasn't too much to worry about. There was even a positive for Labor out of the whole sordid exercise: when Rudd stumbled, ranks closed around him in a display of solidarity not seen in the parliamentary party for a long time. Swan and Gillard, the two most senior frontbenchers who had no particular reason to love their leader, were particularly strong in his defence. Then there was the re-emergence of Paul Keating, dismissing Burke and Grill as the Arthur Daley and Terry McCann of the west, deriding Howard as a little desiccated coconut and Costello as all tip and no iceberg. Preposterously, Costello claimed that this proved Keating would join Burke in the role of Rudd's puppet master.

And although the opinion polls continued to run for Rudd – one had Labor's primary vote standing at an unprecedented 50 per cent, rising to 61 per cent after preferences, a figure which would have reduced the Coalition to around twenty seats were it to be realised in an election – the government decided not to let up. Howard himself, apart from continuing to mutter gravely about Rudd's lack of judgement, stayed more or less clear of the cesspit, but his mud-men – Costello, Abbott and Downer – plunged in headfirst. Disturbingly, the media followed: while editorials tut-tutted about mud-slinging and demanded an immediate return to debate about policy rather than personality, the investigative journalists of the press gallery went back to Rudd to ask the same questions again and again and again, apparently for no reason other than that Costello told them they should.

The Coalition finally claimed a victim: Labor's effective shadow attorney-general, Kelvin Thomson, was found to have signed a reference for Fat Tony Mokbel, a major drug-dealer and suspected murderer on the run from the law. Mokbel had not been quite as notorious at the time of the reference, but he still had a string of convictions which should not have been overlooked by Thomson or anyone else. In more sober times this carelessness might have been forgiven, but in the mounting hysteria about character it was clearly a hanging offence. Rudd duly hanged him; Downer, poisonous as ever, spluttered that he had always thought there was something grubby about Thomson. Presumably the assumption of grubbiness, along with carelessness, poor judgement and dubious association was now to be considered a capital crime. If so, there was going to be a lot of space on the frontbenches of both sides of the house as the great cleansing proceeded.

Downer then headed straight for the bottom, picking up a tabloid beat-up about the circumstances of Rudd's childhood. Rudd's account was that when his sharefarmer father died, his family had been evicted from their property; Rudd junior was just eleven at the time. The son of the property owner appeared to say that the Rudds had not really been evicted; rather, another sharefarmer had taken over their allotment. Downer, pontificating from the heights of three generations of wealth and privilege, said the public had a right to know the truth.

Tony Abbott, nastier still, dug up the sordid detail of Rudd senior's death and suggested that the son was telling self-serving lies. Accused of giving muck-raking a bad name, he replied that Rudd himself had started it: in the previous month the Opposition leader had asked Howard about a phone call the prime minister had received from Ron Walker, a prominent businessman and a former treasurer of the Liberal Party. Walker had informed Howard that he and two other businessmen with strong links to the party, Hugh Morgan and Robert de Crespigny, were starting up a company to exploit nuclear power. This was just two days before Howard set up his own pro-nuke inquiry into the industry.

The suggestion was that the men were working in cahoots: a fairly tenuous proposition, given that Howard's enthusiastic promotion of nukes was already well advanced, but at least it was a matter of public concern, certainly as much so as the attacks on Paul Keating's business interests had been in the times when Howard was leading the Opposition. To equate it with the shit Costello, Downer and Abbott were throwing at Rudd was simply fanciful. And, promised the mud-men, there would be more to come: The Public Had a Right to Know.

It quickly became clear, however, that the excruciatingly high moral standards Howard had rediscovered since hastily abandoning them in 1997 were to be applied selectively. When it was revealed that his minister for the ageing, Santo Santoro, had sat on an undeclared packet of shares allotted to him by a company which made drugs for the ageing for six months before selling them at a handsome profit, Howard said that this was not a breach of his code, a conflict of interest or even a lapse of judgement; it was mere oversight, the kind of mistake any busy minister could make. After all, many had in the past, not least his old roommate Warwick Parer, a minister for coal who dabbled extensively in coal-mining stocks. Parer had been forgiven and so would Santoro be, not least because Santoro had donated his gains to charity. Well, actually he hadn't; when sprung and forced to sell the shares, Santoro had passed the profits to a right-wing political lobby group which campaigns against abortion and homosexuals, which he described as a good cause. Good enough for Howard, anyway – until it turned out that the oversight was just one of 72 share tradings which Santoro had inadvertently forgotten to declare.

Howard sacked Santoro forthwith and said he was very angry; but really he had no one to blame but himself. For ten years it had been open slather; not a single minister dismissed and all kinds of misdemeanours forgiven and forgotten, up to and including Santoro's first 'oversight'. Then there was the appointment of Santoro in the first place: as everyone in Queensland and many outside could have told the prime minister, Santoro was a hard-right-wing enforcer, a successful party bagman (prospective donors seldom refused him) and a ruthless factional warrior. Appointing him to a sensitive portfolio was always going to be a risk – dare one call it a lack of judgement? Grilled on the *7.30 Report* Howard was querulous and blustery; he sounded uncannily like his old nemesis, Joh Bjelke-Petersen.

But then, ever since the Joh for PM debacle of 1974, the Sunshine State had proved difficult for Howard. There was also a bit of a problem with three of his Queensland backbenchers, Andrew Laming, Ross Vasta and the sacked minister Gary Hardgrave, who had been raided by the federal police under suspicion of defrauding their electoral entitlements. There was nothing much Howard could do about this except invoke the presumption of innocence and keep his fingers crossed, but it did make the high moral ground on which he was attempting to perch just that little bit more slippery.

And, as the polls continued to show, the public wasn't buying it – at least, not so far. It seemed that the voters really, truly wanted to believe in Rudd, and they weren't happy about the vicious campaign against their pin-up boy. Quite a few did not believe that Rudd had been completely honest about his meetings with Burke; after all, it beggared belief that a politician as ambitious as Rudd would attend any gathering of movers and shakers without trying to turn it to his advantage. But they were apparently prepared to forgive him, especially in view of Howard's own record of deceit over rather more important matters, such as taking the country to war.

★

The Coalition's hard men still believed that they were making an impression; sooner or later Rudd's honeymoon with the electorate had to come to an end, and when it did the doubts they were planting would start to bloom. And anyway, they really hadn't much else to do at present, and playing in the mud was kind of fun. Even the revelation that John Howard had been seen at a dinner also attended by a violent criminal pornographer did not faze them, although the *Courier-Mail*'s front-page headline – 'Accused torturer attends Howard fundraiser: PM HAS LUNCH WITH PORN KING' – was pretty much the stuff of nightmares. Wayne Swan said that Howard could have lunch with a porn king if he wanted to, and he was sure the prime minister would have a perfectly reasonable explanation. Actually he didn't, but Peter Costello said that the porn king had been a ring-in, not on the original invitation list, so Howard couldn't have known. He did not say whether handshakes and pleasantries were exchanged, or whether the party would return the porn king's $2000 admission fee. And Costello, Abbott and Downer promised that the campaign against Rudd would continue unabated. As they might have put it: we're down in the shit, but we remain undeterred.

Yet if the big boys in their safe seats remained blasé about the polls, the backbenchers in the marginals certainly weren't. Howard felt the need to respond: yes, he said, the polls were a bit dodgy, but as always he would resolve to work harder (on behalf of the Australian people, of course) and run faster: Run, Johnny, Run! Not only that; he had a strategy which went beyond spreading stories about Rudd kicking cats and farting in lifts. The problem was, our Dear Leader confided to his close friend Alan Jones and anyone else who happened to be listening, that Rudd had conned the public into believing the economy was no longer a real issue; that both sides agreed on the basics, so the good times would continue whoever was in power – after all, they had been going on for so long that most people by now took them for granted. The voters had to be reminded that their prosperity was not due to blind luck; it was the result of good economic management, something not to be put at risk by placing the steering wheel in inexperienced hands. The trouble with this argument, as a letter-writer to the *Sydney Morning Herald* pointed out, is that if you took it seriously you could never again have a change of government – never, ever. Well, Howard might answer, so what?

Howard's new line – which he clearly liked, because he repeated it several times – was that the economy does not run on autopilot. But actually it just about does, or at least it has since the reforms of the Hawke–Keating era. Most macroeconomic factors are beyond Australia's control; whether they are helpful, like the commodities boom, or a hindrance, like the Asian economic downturn, they are simply things we have to live with. Governments can make the effects better or worse: Tim Fischer's push for markets in the Middle East meant that we escaped the worst effects of the Asian slump, while Howard's electoral profligacy and failure to spend money on infrastructure has meant that we have not capitalised on the current boom. But we are simply not a big-enough player to set our own terms and conditions in the world economy.

Thus most economic management tends to be about fine-tuning, and most of that is done not by the politicians but by the gnomes in Treasury, particularly when the treasurer is Peter Costello. Costello has always been more interested in politics than in economics, and more interested in a comfortable life than in either; all tip and no iceberg, indeed. Almost all of the government's important spending decisions are made not by him but by Howard, and the only real challenge to the madder ones comes not from Costello but from Finance Minister Nick Minchin.

As treasurer, Wayne Swan would almost certainly be as reliant on advice from Treasury as Costello, so there would be no sudden switch in policy; and in fact, the overall quality of economic management would probably improve because, unlike Howard, Rudd would not feel compelled to hurl pots of money at any interest group which threatened to vote against him. Even at the micro level the only immediate change would be the end of WorkChoices, which in hard economic terms might not make that much difference.

John Howard, it will be recalled, boasted that WorkChoices was not a device to lower wages but to raise them; under WorkChoices there would be the option to trade off terms and conditions for higher pay. Yet from the few statistics the government was prepared to release, it appeared that while conditions were certainly being lost, pay was actually declining. Howard implicitly admitted this in one of his attacks on Rudd: getting rid of workplace agreements, he said, would allow wages, and therefore inflation and interest rates, to rise. But then, of course, interest rates had already risen four times since he promised to keep them low.

Howard's economic credentials, it seemed, were no longer what they had once been – at least, the tough boys in the New South Wales Labor Party thought so. With two weeks to go before the state election, they started including his image in advertising attacking the hapless Liberal leader, Peter Debnam. It was another association that Howard could have done without.

> *Oh give me new figures!*
> *I can't go on dancing*
> *The same that were taught me*
> *Ten seasons ago.*
> —THOMAS HAYNES BAYLEY

★ 5.

AS JOHN HOWARD'S SUMMER of discontent segued into an autumn which he desperately hoped would provide a bit of mellow fruitfulness, he would have been heartened to read 'Bipolar Nation', the *Quarterly Essay* by Peter Hartcher. Hartcher is the political editor of the *Sydney Morning Herald* and one of the more independent thinkers in a torpid Canberra press gallery; it was he who first identified 'Keeping Interest Rates Low' as the big lie which would win Howard the 2004 election. His 2007 essay named Howard's successful political weapons as luck, which we have already mentioned, and fear: according to Hartcher, Howard invoked largely imaginary terrors so that he could then exorcise them from a grateful electorate, in the manner of a mother who sticks her child's hand in the fire so she can then comfort the infant. Hartcher's gloomy conclusion was that Howard had perfected this technique to such a degree that Rudd would find it almost impossible to counter it; hence, a fifth term loomed as all but inevitable.

By the end of March I tended to agree, although with one important caveat: the interest rates on which Howard had relied three years earlier were coming back to bite him on the bum. With four rises in his fourth term, Howard could hardly revert to his former promise, and although the base rate of 6.25 per cent was still comparatively low, the cost of mortgage repayments was now far higher than it had ever been under Labor, because the punters had been seduced (at least partly by Howard's assurances) into borrowing hugely beyond their means. A lot of them were now hurting and one or two more rises would push them over the edge, and the prospects were for at least one more before polling day. Howard's grip on the issue of economic management was not as firm as it had been, and if that dissolved, so, almost certainly, would his government.

But not yet, and if you viewed the news from a certain perspective (Howard's), it was not all bad. Santo Santoro had finally resigned from the Senate, blathering about his integrity remaining intact, and Alexander Downer whimpered that the senator had suffered enough and should be treated like a human being. He had not yet found an overseas post for Amanda Vanstone, but at least she was off the frontbench. The payout of $4.6 million to discredited executives of the Australian Wheat Board had unfortunately been made public, but the point was that they were now paid out, gone, finished. Tony Abbott and Bronwyn Bishop had appeared incongruously dressed as Fred Astaire and Ginger Rogers at a fundraiser – but, well, no one took either of them seriously anymore, so it hardly mattered.

All trivial incidents, really, when taken individually; together, they added up to a distracting background noise as he prepared to re-emerge as the great war leader with a speech on Iraq. But once again that little bastard Rudd upstaged him. Just hours before Howard was due to climb to his feet, Rudd came out with a proposal to broadband Australia with a fast, all-but-universal service in a public–private partnership kick-started by the sale of some of the Telstra shares gathering dust in the Future Fund. The headlines were set by the time Howard got around to his heavily promoted major speech.

In the event it wasn't major; it would barely have made lance-corporal. Several commentators noted the contrast: the fresh young leader with a visionary and up-to-date plan for the future against the tired old man once again justifying the failed policies of the past. It made Peter Costello's bombast about Rudd raiding the Future Fund look more like desperation than effective politics, although some of the media's dancing bears went along for the ride (but not too enthusiastically; the media moguls have been the most severe critics of the Howard government's constant procrastination in modernising telecommunications and especially of the dithering over universal, fast broadband).

In fact there could be few better uses for at least some of the billions locked up in the Future Fund, aptly described by Lindsay Tanner as a solution in search of a problem. Apart from the social benefits, investing the fund in projects of this kind is good economics: not only do you get your money back in direct dividends, but the flow-ons from decent infrastructure add hugely to productivity, and thus to the gross domestic product. Real economists applauded the initiative, which left our treasurer looking even sillier than usual. The final blow came when both Communications Minister Helen Coonan and Finance Minister Nick Minchin admitted that the Future Fund was filling up faster than expected anyway, so there would be money to spare.

★

In something of a huff, John Howard took himself off to New South Wales for the last week of the state election campaign, where it was confidently predicted that the Libs, under the hapless Peter Debnam (Howard's choice), were in for yet another hiding. Addressing a small crowd of the faithful, the prime minister declared, 'After twelve years, we need a new government.' As jaws dropped he added '... in this state,' but quite a few of those listening felt that his words had a wider significance.

For weeks now Howard's parliamentary performances had been, at best, lacklustre; he was querulous and tetchy, he misheard questions and rambled in his answers. Peter Costello, in contrast, had consistently gone in with all guns blazing. His critics complained that it was all bullshit; maybe, but it was quality bullshit. After Howard's protégé failed to win a single Labor seat in New South Wales, the rumblings came into the open. Paul Sheehan, a conservative commentator with the *Sydney Morning Herald*, was unequivocal: 'The people have spoken. John Howard should go. Now.'

One of the problems was that the victorious premier, Morris Iemma, said that his somewhat spurious promise to defend the workers of New South Wales from Howard's WorkChoices had been the key issue in the election. This could have been dismissed as propaganda, except that the view was also held by a lot of Liberal candidates, including Howard's close friend Pru Goward, who struggled to win what should have been a safe Liberal seat. And WorkChoices was clearly not going the government's way. In order to try and humanise the concept, Howard had replaced the saturnine Kevin Andrews as the relevant minister with Joe Hockey, whom he described as 'a great big bear of a man'. Unfortunately, ursinity was proving insufficient as a sales mechanism; indeed, the amiable Hockey was emerging as a bear of very little brain.

For months Labor's feisty shadow minister, Julia Gillard, had been demanding that the government produce statistics to show the effect of Australian Workplace Agreements on the terms and conditions of those who had signed them; the limited data available suggested that these employees were consistently worse off than those on collective agreements and had lost one or more benefits, such as penalty rates or holiday pay, in the process. The government, relying on no evidence at all, insisted that they were in fact better off. Eventually Hockey said that no figures were available and they never could be, since there was no valid way of comparing the two systems; to which Rudd replied reasonably that the government should therefore stop saying AWAs were a boon to employees.

Howard's line was that overall wages had risen and unemployment had fallen over the first year of the new system. Labor answered that this had nothing to do with WorkChoices and a lot to do with the mineral boom, and that wages would have risen a lot faster under the old system (which would have meant that interest rates would have too, although neither side wanted to mention that). Labor added that the rate of increase in productivity had actually slowed under WorkChoices, and even the Australian Business Council agreed that it was 'a very long bow' to suggest WorkChoices would improve productivity. A survey of small business produced the surprising conclusion that 40 per cent of those surveyed believed WorkChoices was an unfair system. And in parliament, Gillard was all over Hockey, so much so that by the end of March Howard was pushing his minister aside and taking her questions himself. It didn't really help: whenever he tried to get back to the broad sweep of economic reform, Gillard was able to come up with a specific example of people who had been dudded. Netballers, slaughtermen, casuals in a chocolate factory: the list seemed inexhaustible. Most insiders agreed that WorkChoices by itself would not win or lose an election, but no one except Howard was still claiming it as a positive for the government.

And then there was climate change. A flying visit by Sir Nicholas Stern of the Stern report had put this back on the front page, in the very week Rudd was to hold his own Climate Change Summit. In spite of Malcolm Turnbull's wild claim that no country in the world had done more about climate change than Australia, the event made it clear that Rudd, not Howard, was leading the debate; indeed, his plans to go to China for discussions on clean-coal technology and to produce Australia's own Stern report on the economic effects of climate change looked positively prime ministerial.

But the biggest plus was the quality of the delegates whom Rudd, through his business-liaison man Sir Rod Eddington, was able to attract to his summit. While the government tried to stretch its boycott as widely as possible, an impressive array of national and even international scientists, academics and business leaders attended. Whether their presence was due to a genuine concern for the issues or simply a desire to take out insurance in case of a Rudd victory, it was a potent political image. The best Howard and Turnbull could manage in reply was the promise of $200 million to a fund to slow deforestation in Indonesia, a worthy objective indeed, but one which was somewhat at odds with their relaxed approach to deforestation in Australia.

★

Howard must have been mightily relieved that Rudd's triumph, like everything else, was eclipsed in the media by his old nemesis, David Hicks. After more than five years, things suddenly came to a head; and with one bound, the dangerous terrorist, the treacherous enemy combatant, the worst of the worst, was free – well, almost.

In the end it hardly mattered whether the Australian government conspired with the Americans to fix the David Hicks case. John Howard and his ministers had behaved so deceitfully, so hypocritically and so dishonourably for so long that if they didn't, then they probably should have, finishing off what they started. The belief that they did was perfectly justifiable: the links from Howard to Dick Cheney to the 'convening authority', his former employee Susan Crawford, and between Downer and US Defence Secretary Robert Gates, while circumstantial, were pretty damning. It was only appropriate that when Hicks finally got his day in court, the whole thing was a sham, a charade conducted apparently as much for the benefit of the military commission itself as for the edification of the general public. After the judging colonel dismissed Hicks's civilian lawyers because they refused to accept that the judging colonel could make up any rules he liked as the case proceeded, it seemed we were in for another long delay, unacceptable to either side; and it was at this stage that the fix went in.

Hicks pleaded guilty to a vague and essentially undefined charge which did not even exist at the time he was alleged to have committed it; this allowed the prosecuting colonel to claim that he had admitted everything and should be nailed to the wall. Both in America and Australia there was much huffing and puffing about the so-called confession, a carry-on that deliberately ignored the very core of the idea of plea bargaining, which is that it is a deal, a connivance where both parties give ground in order to achieve a quick and easy compromise. To suggest that Hick's plea was to be taken as the truth, the whole truth and nothing but the truth is not just to miss the point; it is by definition arrant nonsense.

In the very same week Faye Turney, a British sailor captured under disputed circumstances by the Iranians, appeared on Iranian television to say that yes, her ship had indeed been trespassing in Iranian waters, a contention vehemently denied by the British navy. Turney's lead was quickly followed by other captured sailors, and no one claimed either that their admissions were true or that they should be charged with perjury for making them. This was a deal, a plea bargain for better treatment or, hopefully, for release. But we were supposed to believe that when Hicks went through the same process he was guilty, not only as charged, but of all the other allegations Howard, Downer, Ruddock and Co. chose to peddle.

From the fabricated plea, the military commission descended into farce. The prosecuting colonel argued passionately that Hicks should serve another seven years, the maximum allowable for a plea bargain (another illustration of the fakery of the process: if Hicks was really guilty as charged, under the law he faced life imprisonment). Hicks's remaining counsel, the redoubtable Major Michael Mori, asked for a more lenient twenty months. After much deliberation the sentencing colonels agreed on seven years, only to be told by the judging colonel that the secret plea-bargain deal included a custodial sentence of just nine months. Then, presumably, they all went back to doing whatever it is that colonels do, having achieved nothing except to show that the military-commission system is not only monstrously unjust, but ultimately absurd.

Hicks would come home, if a high-security Australian prison inhabited by violent criminals who believe he is a terrorist who deserves summary punishment can be described that way, and would remain incarcerated and gagged – unable to speak to the media in any form – until after the federal election. Howard hoped the voters would now forgive, or at least forget. They might, although initially they showed little sign of it; in particular the gag order, which would have been unconstitutional in America itself, was seen as just a little bit too convenient for Howard, even by the arch-Tory David Flint. But whatever the short-term benefit for our Dear Leader, history will forever record him as the prime minister who betrayed and abandoned one of his own citizens to arbitrary imprisonment and maltreatment by a foreign power.

★

By this stage it was amply clear that Kevin Rudd, whatever his other qualities, did tend to take himself very seriously indeed. His single-minded determination to get to the top of the greasy totem pole had certainly been the main factor in his success to date, but there was a price. Many of his colleagues felt alienated by the sheer force of his ambition; they had no doubt that if they got in his way, however accidentally, they would not survive. His insistence on running the whole show by himself irked them; whenever there was something important to announce, the leader took it over, leaving the relevant shadow minister to nod and smile in the background. In an election year this was probably good strategy, but it didn't mean Rudd's frontbenchers had to like it, and after three months of it they were starting to feel unappreciated.

Perhaps more worryingly, the press gallery, which had initially greeted the new man with unfeigned enthusiasm, was getting tired of being taken for granted. Rudd was seen as becoming too manipulative, something of a control freak; almost – God help us – another Howard. His heavy-handed staffers did not help; after they went in boots and all to try, unsuccessfully, to kill off an admittedly tacky story querying Rudd's account of his childhood, relations cooled even further.

Senior gallery members noted that while Rudd was happy to do regular appearances on television and radio chat-shows, where the hardest question he was likely to be asked would be about what he thought of the latest opinion polls, he refused to submit to a grilling by the experts and hardly ever held a proper press conference.

At the beginning of April the government's constant complaint that he was avoiding any real scrutiny of his program was starting to bite, at least within the gallery itself. Not that the government was in any position to criticise; but then, the government was the government, with all the resources of incumbency. The Opposition needed all the help it could get. The problem was underlined by the first poll of the month: Labor and Rudd were still comfortably in front, but for the first time they had gone backwards. Gleeful government members talked of a developing trend and remembered previous election years. Perhaps the old man still had enough tricks up his sleeve to pull off one last win. Time to ratchet up the fear.

The old bogeymen were still the best bogeymen. Over the years some of them had had a bit of a makeover: the Red Menace of the previous century was now the Muslim Terror, and doing very nicely, thank you. The Yellow Peril had slipped down the charts a bit, but was still useful from time to time as the Unlawful Boat People. However, one of the golden oldies required very little repackaging: the threat of Union Domination could be, and was, trotted out at regular intervals, and 2007 was to be no exception. What made this year slightly different was that the threat could be linked to the Great Labor Takeover: with Labor now in power in every state and territory, only the thin blue line of Howard and his doughty colleagues in Canberra stood between Australia and Total Labor Rule. If they should somehow disappear, Kevin Rudd would weakly submit to the demands of the premiers, who as everyone knew were in the pockets of the unions, and we would be left with ... yes, you got it, Trade Union Tyranny.

It wasn't the best of arguments, since tensions between Rudd and the unions were already considerable, but it was about the only one remaining, so it would have to do. Once again the attack dogs were called into action to warn of the looming menace, a task made more difficult by the undeniable fact that union membership, after a brief boost under the threat of WorkChoices, was again on the decline. This was precisely what WorkChoices had been designed to achieve: union officials were shut off from possible recruits, and indeed from the non-government workforce as a whole. Still, the leadership continued to mount a well-funded and effective campaign, which the government now claimed (with its customary penchant for round figures) would cost $100 million, an exaggeration of about 400 per cent. In this context it should be, and in fact was, noted that the government had spent some $55 million of taxpayers' money flogging WorkChoices before the legislation was even passed, and then another $2 million in a secret survey to find out whether the initial advertising had worked (if the opinion polls were any guide, it hadn't).

Howard now ruled out further raids on the Treasury as inappropriate, and called on the business community to advertise on the government's behalf instead. Unsurprisingly the business community told him to do his own dirty work; after all, it already contributes lavishly to Liberal Party funds and with the polls looking the way they were, businesses were not about to lay themselves open to charges of blatant political partisanship with the prospect of a terrible revenge if Labor actually got up.

And business was not the only institution which was starting to feel uneasy about the way things were going. In the first week in April the *Financial Review* published an extraordinary speech made by the head of Treasury, Ken Henry, to his department in which Henry attacked the government's approach to water policy. Treasury, it will be recalled, was left high and dry during the preparation of the $10-billion Great Big Splash, and Henry made it clear he thought the policy was a bad one, that it could have been a lot better if Treasury had been consulted and that, it being an election year, we could expect a lot more bad decisions and his staff should be on their guard.

It wasn't quite as blatant as that, of course, and Henry said rather unconvincingly that it should not be taken as an attack on government policy or process. But the leak, the first of substance through the iron curtain Howard had constructed around the public service, could hardly be seen as accidental. While Treasury is no longer the pre-eminent force it once was, it still sees itself as the key policy-maker within the public service, and Henry is generally regarded as the service's incorruptible doyen. His speech was more than a ritual complaint, or a sigh of resignation; it was a clear warning to Howard that the ad-hockery had already gone too far, and that Treasury now demanded a seat at the table whenever major economic decisions were being made.

And if it did not get it? Well, John Howard is old enough to remember 1974, when the Whitlam government left Treasury out of the loop while planning to borrow $4 billion in petrodollars to build a national pipeline grid. When the Treasury head, Sir Frederick Wheeler, failed to persuade the government to abort the project, or at least run it through conventional channels, a mysterious source known as Mr Williams became a serial leaker to the Opposition. Mr Williams was later named in the senate as Des Moore, then a deputy secretary in Treasury and now head of a conservative think-tank. Moore denied the allegation, but whatever their origin, the leaks were incredibly damaging to the government, and eventually what became known as the Loans Affair triggered the blocking of supply in 1975 and Whitlam's subsequent dismissal.

The circumstances were slightly different – for instance, Howard's $10 billion was less than half of Whitlam's $4 billion in today's money – but the parallels were still clear enough to worry Howard, if not his Aquaboy, who in response sneered dismissively that Treasury would not even know the cost of replacing a Detheridge wheel with a computerised flume gate. It may not, but like Malcolm Turnbull it can learn; and it does know a thing or two about making life very uncomfortable for bumptious young ministers. Turnbull was not exactly cowed; within a month he was back demanding the damming of the Clarence River in New South Wales, so that water could be pumped to south-eastern Queensland – an idea that provoked outrage in the front bar of the Billinudgel. Howard told everyone to think of themselves as Australians and reiterated that the Victorians should sign up to the Great Big Splash. Kevin Rudd said that if we only had Labor governments everywhere we could end the blame game and all these kinds of dispute would be magically solved. The Labor premiers continued to glower at one another.

★

It was time for some light relief and, quite unintentionally, Kevin Rudd stepped up to provide it, appropriately enough through his preoccupation with silly media. Rudd has few natural advantages: he is average, greyish, bespectacled and, as he freely admits, a bit nerdy. But he is also a fluent talker with an easy manner, a good smile and a highly convincing family – fuel that keeps the talk-back shows, day-time television and the less pornographic women's magazines going. He would be mad not to exploit what he's got, and he shows no signs of insanity, much less diffidence.

It could be argued that his diligent appearances on Seven's *Sunrise* had done more to make him acceptable to the public than all of his policy statements put together, and his other forays into pop radio and commercial television (like *60 Minutes*) reinforced the image of a straightforward sort of bloke with nothing to hide, always available and not too up himself to talk to real people, rather than just the prima donnas of the Canberra press gallery. It had been a carefully controlled strategy, and as the polls showed, it had worked.

But there had been a price to pay – two, in fact. The first was that the prima donnas of the press gallery became miffed; they expected to be treated with a certain amount of reverence, especially by media-hungry Opposition politicians, and to be ignored in favour of their lightweight cousins was simply not on. And the second, more serious price was that the silly media were by definition silly. The shows were full of people called Kochie and Mel and Daffy and Muffy. Few of them had a clue about what happens in Canberra, and even if they had, they wouldn't let on for fear of offending their dumbed-down audience, who just wanted to be entertained. They were prepared to acknowledge that Rudd was a politician, but their enquiries about actual policy were at best cursory; it would not have been surprising to hear Muffy ask winsomely, 'Oh Mr Rudd, it's all so fascinating, but please will you tell me: just what is a politic?' Their ignorance might have been blissful, but to a politician surrounded by sharks waiting for the slightest slip, it could also be very dangerous.

And thus Rudd was caught in a trap not of his own making when the creative minds at Channel 7 decided it would be pretty cool to do an Anzac Day cross to the battlefield of Long Tan featuring their very own Kevin Rudd and Joe Hockey. Hockey, whether by good luck or good management, pulled out swiftly; his place was taken by the indefatigable Bronwyn Bishop. In the meantime someone at 7 (perhaps the weatherman) realised that there was a time difference: as *Sunrise* went to air on the east coast, it would be just 4 a.m. in Vietnam. Nevertheless, perhaps something could be stooged up ...

And so, inevitably, came the tabloid headlines about how Rudd was offering an insult to the diggers by promoting a fake dawn service to get himself, yet again, on television. His denial that he had anything to do with it failed to end the matter; it turned out that his office had indeed been warned of the risks, not by his old Department of Foreign Affairs, which passed on its assessments to the government, which gleefully waited for Rudd to become mired, but by an honest broker in Veterans Affairs. The warning never reached Rudd, but he copped the flak in any case; he had little choice. And the news that his enforcers had once again behaved like thugs in their attempts to kill the story did not help either.

Hockey, to his credit, at first refused to blame Rudd for the shemozzle, but after a few days he joined in the general government baying. Channel 7, no doubt working on the theory that in the world of commercial television there is no such thing as bad publicity, treated it all as a bit of a hoot; but for the more serious commentators, it was further evidence of bad judgement, and Rudd was accused of not being careful enough, which at least made a change from the charge of being a control freak. And of course the prima donnas pounced. It had done Rudd huge damage, they gloated. His credibility was trashed. His arrogance had finally undone him. The man would never be the same again.

Rudd did have the grace to appear mildly chastened; he reluctantly gave up *Sunrise*, though not silly media – he was rumba-ing away with Kerri-Anne Kennerley before the week was out. And he told the National Press Club that the business had been handled badly and he would make sure it didn't happen again. Howard, meanwhile, took the lofty approach: it had left, he said, a nasty taste in the mouth. Which meant that when the polls came out and showed that the punters didn't give a stuff about it, he must have felt really nauseated.

> “*They need a calculator, but it was a dancer that got it.* —Pierre de Beaumarchais

★ 6.

The Newspoll of 17 April was enough to raise the gorge of any Coalitionist. The public's infatuation with Rudd was now clearly beyond the honeymoon stage; we were talking about a full-on romance, with the former lover, one John Winston Howard, cast aside like a worn-out sock. Labor's primary vote was sitting on 50 per cent, with the Coalition languishing on 35; the two-party-preferred vote was running at 59–41. This was a couple of points down from the March peak, but since then Rudd had gone through a series of beltings by both the government and the media; apparently they had been almost completely ineffective. Rudd's performance rating – the difference between those who liked him and those who disliked him – was a solid 50-plus. Howard's was minus seven. And Rudd was preferred as prime minister, by a score of 48 to 36. No Opposition leader in history had hit such consistent highs; it was no longer sufficient to speak, as some of the cynics in the media did, of St Kevin. Deification was obviously in order.

The only solace for Howard lay buried at the bottom. Newspoll had also asked the punters how they felt about the prospect of Labor governments across the board: in every state and territory, and federally as well. Actually, most didn't feel much at all; 55 per cent thought it was unimportant, with, surprisingly, Coalition voters even more blasé about it than their Labor counterparts. But of those polled who did care, slightly more thought it would be a bad thing: 42 to 37. It wasn't much, but it was the only straw worth seizing, so Howard seized it.

On the same day Rudd performed at the National Press Club, and for the first time released some details of his industrial-relations policy. Unfair-dismissal laws were back, but with a generous buffer period: in big companies they would not apply for the first six months and in smaller ones for a year, giving employers ample time to weed out any obvious misfits. Still, with a bit of a stretch this could be translated as a win for the horrible Faceless Union Bosses, and Howard so translated it. The trouble was that the other bit – no right to strike without secret ballots – was undeniably a win for employers, and no amount of spin could make it anything else. The best Howard could do was dismiss it as a sop, a subterfuge to conceal the full extent of Rudd's capitulation, which would be made clear (he fervently hoped) in coming weeks.

Even this line of attack was seriously undermined by a leak to the *Sydney Morning Herald* revealing that in spite of Hockey's denials, statistics had been collected about the effect of WorkChoices, and that the anecdotal stuff peddled by Labor had, if anything, understated the reality: almost all the AWAs examined knocked out at least one of the conditions which had been trumpeted in the taxpayer-funded advertisements as 'protected by law', and nearly half of them knocked out the lot. Hockey protested that even if this were true (and he still didn't know), there were compensations, because the AWAs contained extra 'family-friendly' conditions. Alas, the same leak showed that the vast majority didn't.

To put the icing on Labor's cake, Peter Costello repeated the mantra that AWAs were the only thing holding down interest rates; to end them would cause a wages explosion. Well, for starters interest rates had already increased three times since WorkChoices had been introduced, so the supposed panacea wasn't doing much of a job. But in any case, simply going from individual contracts to enterprise bargaining, which was essentially Labor's plan, would not allow for any across-the-board wage breakout, which is what would really put pressure on interest rates. It would, however, allow some workers to regain some of the wages and conditions which had been ripped from them.

The example of a middle manager who had been sacked, and then seen his job re-advertised with a substantial cut in salary, seemed to sum up the case against WorkChoices. At first Howard expressed dismay: this was not what his reform was supposed to be about. But then he decided that maybe it was if the company involved felt it wasn't making enough money. Quite.

Rudd then left the country to make a ritual visit to the US in general and Rupert Murdoch in particular; the *Sun* King responded with a sort of quasi-endorsement, which was welcomed with gasps of relief by Labor supporters but which had no effect at all on the ferocious campaign being waged by the *Australian*. The day after Rudd's Press Club speech the paper had run a total of seven news stories, two comment pieces, two features and an editorial, of which all but one story and one feature were in full attack-dog mode. This did not seem to signal a surge of support. The common view was that if a Rudd victory appeared inevitable Murdoch would come on board (he likes backing winners), but these days he isn't all that concerned about the land of his birth anyway. In the meantime those who Paul Keating described as the 'middle-of-the-road fascists' of the *Australian* would be given a free run.

Apart from that, Rudd's visit was mainly about chatting to old acquaintances in the state department, but the fact that he made it at all, leaving Julia Gillard to sell the newly released policy, was an indication of his confidence in their partnership. If the polls were achieving nothing else, they were at least restoring unity and euphoria to the Labor Party.

★

The Libs, on the other hand, were starting to look seriously rattled. In an apparent attempt to change the subject back to an old favourite, border protection, Howard announced a truly bizarre scheme whereby we would swap our refugees with those of our great and powerful friend. Thus a group of Sri Lankan asylum seekers, found to be genuine refugees but presently incarcerated on Nauru, might be exchanged for a similar number of Cubans languishing at Guantanamo Bay. The rationale for this expensive exercise was that it would deter future boat people in both hemispheres by sending them somewhere they didn't want to go, at best a piece of petty sadism and at worst just plain stupid; surely if those involved are genuine refugees it would be less trouble for both sides just to accept them, rather than to pay a fortune to swap them for a group of malcontents. Howard – still obsessed with his old mantra about *we will decide*, etc. – couldn't see the absurdity.

The prime minister then donned his trusty Akubra for a photogenic visit to the Murray-Darling basin, where he discovered that there was no water left and would be none for irrigators in the coming year. His reaction to the crisis was to imply that somehow it was the fault of the Victorian government for not signing up to the Great Big Splash; until that happened, there was nothing that the commonwealth could do, and his advice to the desperate was to pray for rain. Farmers, who had been hoping for something a little more active on the secular side, were understandably disappointed; but by then Howard had moved on to attempt to placate various small-business groups, including the entire local-government sector, which could not make sense of the WorkChoices pay scale. Hockey threw an extra $5 million at the Fair Pay Commission and told it to explain.

Howard paused briefly in his electioneering to announce that yes, Amanda Vanstone was going to Rome and that Rod Kemp, affectionately known to his fellow senators as Elmer Fudd, would be joining her on the continent; Kemp was to end his undistinguished public career as ambassador to Paris, and that would teach those bloody French. Costello confirmed his leader's fatalism about the weather: 'Droughts will come and droughts will go,' he mused, dismissing the concerns of the bush in a phrase that vindicated the rural view of him as a citified pissant. There were large rallies against WorkChoices across the land and the venerable British medical journal the *Lancet* urged its readers to vote against Howard for being anti-science. It was not a good lead-in to what was promising to be a very full week.

The first big event, which turned out to be little more than a curtain raiser, was another major prime-ministerial address. This one was called 'Australia Rising', a title which – his critics said, tongues firmly in cheek – was Howard's best since 'Incentivation', a slogan dating from the '80s. Like previous efforts, it fell flat, being notable mainly for the preposterous assertion that Howard was the only politician who could be trusted to deal with climate change, because it was not the greatest moral challenge confronting us, as Rudd claimed. The economy was, and he had the experience and Rudd didn't. He heroically refrained from adding that both global warming and interest rates would always be lower under a Coalition government.

The speech was poorly received across the board: the *Courier-Mail*'s front-page headline was 'DISHONEST JOHN'; the *Daily Telegraph*'s was 'PM'S HOT AIR.' Oh well, at least there was Anzac Day to follow: Howard cheekily spent it in Rudd's own Queensland electorate, while Rudd played it safe in Canberra, not, as planned, Vietnam. He still found time to introduce a new policy on innovation and research, once again jumping Howard's still-struggling agenda.

But it was only a lead-up to the main attraction: the long-awaited ALP National Conference, the great gathering of movers and shakers (not to mention has-beens and never-would-bes) who make up Labor's supreme policymaking body. The Liberal equivalent is the prime minister, whose every whim becomes policy; John Howard's reign had already demonstrated both the strengths and weaknesses of this system. But at the glitzy convention centre at Darling Harbour the media had no doubt what was necessary: to succeed, Rudd had to do a Howard, dictate and dominate, run roughshod over any opposition, grab any recalcitrant delegates by the throat and shake them until their teeth rattled. The *Australian* declared it yet another Big Test; in fact, the paper's breathless scribes identified a whole series of tests – uranium, industrial relations, logging, water, the colour of Rudd's ties. It was bigger than the Ashes. If this was to be a circus, they wanted to see blood on the sawdust.

But actually it didn't work out like that at all. Conferences in the past have indeed had their memorable blues, especially over uranium, which has been described as the Labor's own political kryptonite. But the big question – to mine or not to mine – was settled in 1984. The question in 2007 was whether to stay with the so-called three-mines policy or not; in other words, whether to continue to mine quite a lot or to open the way to mine even more. The answer might, and in fact did, excite some residual angst, but it was hardly a great moral dilemma. The debate was good humoured and tightly managed, the result predetermined by the judicious use of proxies. This resulted in a win–win situation: Rudd carried the numbers, but the Left could say it had a moral majority. Anthony Albanese, who ran the Left's opposition, could claim, in an echo of Billy Snedden after the 1974 election, that he hadn't won, but he hadn't actually lost either.

Rudd won everything else easily, was fluent if not particularly rousing, paid due respect to the party's history and traditions, rebuked a fiery unionist for calling John Howard a skid mark on the bed sheet of Australian politics, and did not fall off the stage. In other words, by the standards the *Australian* had set, he passed the test. This left Murdoch's flagship no choice but to shift the goalposts, which it promptly did: Rudd had failed because the *Australian* did not like his industrial-relations policy.

Certainly it turned out to be a much more thorough dismantling of WorkChoices than had been anticipated – although not, if read dispassionately, a particularly radical one. The long-sacred Industrial Relations Commission, already knackered by Howard, was to be disbanded, along with the other new agencies set up under WorkChoices. In their place was to be a one-stop shop called Fair Work Australia, which was in fact the old IRC writ large: it would provide information, interpret the law, handle disputes and set penalties for breaches. Critics leapt on this, claiming it would be a tyrannical monolith, law-maker, prosecutor, judge and jury in one – something, incidentally, Labor had complained of vigorously when the Americans set up a similar body to run trials at Guantanamo Bay.

But in fact it was not very different from the role the Conciliation and Arbitration Commission and its successors had played between 1904 and 2005. Most of Howard's 'protected by law' conditions were now to be in fact protected by law as a reinforced safety net for employees; and workplaces where a majority voted to be represented by a union were to be represented by a union. The *Australian* screamed that this was undemocratic: it could lead to a situation where the rights of 49 per cent of workers were ignored. The paper found the WorkChoices position, where the vote of 100 per cent could be ignored and usually was, perfectly satisfactory.

And it wasn't all one-sided; much of the red tape which had bedevilled small business was to go, and business was invited to continue to negotiate the fine-tuning of the proposals. It was, to put the worst gloss on it, not unreasonable – certainly no more than would have been expected from a party which, in the last analysis, is supposed to represent the interests of labour against those of capital, and the more rational observers saw it that way: Peter Hartcher in the *Sydney Morning Herald* pointed out that profits as a share of the GDP had been increasing at the expense of wages for years, so business really had no justification for playing the victim.

Mike Steketee, one of the two serious commentators left at the *Australian* (the other is George Megalogenis), suggested that business had overreacted to the policy, partly because it had not been consulted over the detail and partly because it had been egged on by the government. But most of the urging was coming from Steketee's colleagues. Paul Kelly and Dennis

Shanahan shook, steamed and frothed. The paper also ran five successive editorials blathering about Labor being in thrall to Faceless Union Bosses: surely a record. And business responded; not only the ACCI's Peter Hendy, a Liberal Party mouthpiece since his days working for Peter Reith, but the Australian Industry Group's more reasonable Heather Ridout. The idea of a business-run advertising campaign, rejected when Howard had suggested it, suddenly gained traction.

Julia Gillard didn't help by suggesting that businesses who entered the political fray could get injured: this was gleefully interpreted by Howard as a threat of retaliation. Rudd held the line, prepared to compromise at the edges to maintain the position of highly paid mine workers on AWAs but not to back down on the overall principle. But some of his colleagues suddenly went weak at the knees. They felt that they had been doing just fine with business, pissing into every well-tailored pocket that offered itself, and now they were once again being spurned. The blame fell not on Rudd but on Gillard, who had done most of the legwork. Nervous Nellies recalled her 2004 creation of Medicare Gold, a fairly minor factor in the ensuing electoral disaster, but bad and unthought-out policy nonetheless.

Suddenly Gillard was very bad news – until, that is, Mad Bill Heffernan repeated an old line about her being unsuitable to lead because she had chosen to be barren. It was a stupid crack that had absolutely no relevance to Gillard's political ability, but such is the mood of today's press gallery, which sees everything in terms of points for and against, that it was seen to get Gillard – and Labor – off the hook. Indeed Ross Fitzgerald suggested in the *Australian* that Heffernan was only saying what Howard believed; Howard replied in a personal letter indignantly denying the accusation, which a number of readers took as confirmation that it was true. In the end

Howard told his hatchet man to apologise, which he grudgingly did, and that was the end of it; but it gave Labor a breather in which business (and especially the miners) could be soothed, if not placated, and the political scene could regain some equilibrium.

★

And then it was Howard who blinked. Faced with yet more incontrovertible evidence that although some miners and professionals were doing quite well out of AWAs the vast majority of lower-paid workers were getting screwed, he announced that there would be a mechanism whereby some of them, under certain conditions, could be repaid with some form of compensation if they signed away certain conditions. As a concession it was pretty stingy, surrounded by a morass of ifs and buts; but the point was that it showed Howard was for turning after all; the man of steel once again flopped in the face of bad opinion polls. The media dancing bears praised the tactic and its timing: just as Labor was getting into trouble with its own IR policy, Howard emerged as fair and compassionate, the battlers' friend – what a clever man he was. The Labor people agreed that Howard was clever – and also mean, tricky and desperate.

And, of course, there was a useful side benefit. Howard had said that it would be inappropriate to spend any more taxpayer funds advertising WorkChoices. But now WorkChoices had been changed, so naturally it was the government's duty to inform the public, at length and ad nauseam. And if the taxpayer-funded advertising blitz about the change happened to mention that WorkChoices was the best thing since sliced bread, a reform without which civilisation as we know it would come to a halt, well, what an amazing coincidence that would be. Clever, mean, tricky and desperate, and utterly unscrupulous – even, as Gough Whitlam had pointed out at the weekend, corrupt.

But then, Howard had to do something. While the industrial-relations brawl meant that Rudd could not declare his weekend at Labor's big tribal get-together an unalloyed success, there was no doubt he had gone further ahead on points. The other big set-piece of the conference was climate change, with Rudd promising to subsidise the greening of households with solar panels, water tanks and the like; it was a smart and popular idea which brought climate change (now not only the greatest moral challenge, but the greatest economic and environmental challenge as well: Rudd was taking the fight back to Howard) into everyone's backyard.

Howard's response was, once again, an atomic wedgie: plans for nuclear power plants were now to be placed firmly on the front burner, and if Labor refused to accept them, that only showed it was still mired in the past, while he was Mr Fission, the man of the future. Some of his colleagues were less than impressed; even Malcolm Turnbull, morphing briefly from Aquaboy into Serious Environment Minister, said that it remained to be seen whether the nuclear option stacked up financially and economically: 'Nuclear power plants may never be built ... I'm certainly not predicting they will be.'

Even the most sycophantic commentators described Howard's line as courageous, in the Humphrey Appleby sense. The realists thought it was plain foolhardy. While not all Australians are scared witless of nuclear power, a very large majority are unhappy about the idea, and nobody, but nobody, wants to live next door to a reactor. Howard's plan envisages not one, but 25 of them dotted around the coastline. Asked just which towns would be the recipients of the glittering prizes, Howard passed the buck: that would be up to private enterprise. The populace was not greatly reassured. Deliberately or not, Howard, who knows a thing or two about scare campaigns himself, handed Labor the opportunity for the mother of them all: the Coalition wants to turn your suburb into Chernobyl. Perhaps, just perhaps, the stories spread so assiduously by Rudd and his spinners had substance: the old man was losing it. While not everyone fully appreciated Paul Keating's splendid intervention calling Howard a 'pre-Copernican obscurantist', most gathered it had something to do with the idea that Howard was getting out of date and out of touch.

Veterans of past defeats at Darling Harbour fervently hoped so, but it was with more hope than conviction. The divide between those who saw the glass half empty and those who saw it half full was neatly illustrated by the reaction to Gough Whitlam's remark that the situation in 2007 was remarkably similar for Labor to the one he had faced in 1969. The pessimists noted that 1969 was the year in which Labor had scored a mammoth swing, but still fell agonisingly short of victory; the optimists noted that in 1969 Whitlam had won seventeen seats and in 2007 Rudd only needed sixteen, and a lesser percentage swing.

The problem was, as the realists pointed out, that those sixteen were a huge ask. Queensland was looking good, with Rudd's local-boy factor helping, especially in and around Brisbane, where the mood was pretty buoyant anyway. As many as eight seats could be in play: Bonner, Moreton, Blair, Wright, Petrie, Bowman, Longman and Dickson. Outside Brisbane, Herbert and Hinkler were, as always, on the wishlist, but no one was particularly sanguine: the Queensland provinces were always difficult. Still, the deep North could put Rudd halfway home on its own.

Unfortunately the rest of the country wasn't looking as cooperative. South Australia might contribute three (Kingston,

Wakefield and Makin) with Boothby as an outside chance. Tasmania should return Braddon and possibly Bass. There wasn't much left to win in Victoria, although Deakin was an outside possibility, and then there was Solomon in the Northern Territory: a total of twelve likely and another four possible, with two states to go. Looking good. But this assumed no losses, and in Western Australia both Swan and Cowan were hanging on by their fingernails. Without the reassuring presence of Kim Beazley to prop them up, either or even both might go. On the other hand, if the swing took hold, Labor could win Hasluck and Stirling, but you wouldn't want to back them.

Which brought us to New bloody South bloody Wales, federal Labor's perpetual albatross. The premier state had consistently refused to deliver its share of seats, and there was no reason to think that was about to change. In fact there was one compelling reason to suppose that it wouldn't: in March the cornstalks had closed their eyes, held their noses and eaten a big shit sandwich by re-electing the state Labor government, a noisome and discredited bunch of goons who were nonetheless considered marginally preferable to the pitiful alternative. This result not only demonstrated the immeasurable advantages of incumbency, in which Howard was revelling; it also provided voters with the perfect excuse to vote conservative federally. The Coalition in Canberra would help neutralise the gang in Macquarie Street, and in any case they had surely done enough for Labor for at least three years, if not a lifetime.

There were possibilities: Labor could hang on to Parramatta, now notionally a Liberal seat since the redistribution; Malcolm Turnbull's seat of Wentworth had become marginal; Lindsay was not out of the question; even Howard's own seat of Bennelong was being eyed wistfully. Then there was the bellwether seat of Eden-Monaro, always held by the party in government, and Dobell on the Central Coast. Rudd's people were also talking up Page on the Northern Rivers, but as a quasi-local I couldn't see it: if they were depending on Page they were in deep trouble.

I was also uncertain about the strategy of pushing celebrity candidates into some of the marginals; this might work in city seats, where no one knew the local member anyway, but regional areas tend to be jealously parochial. Maxine McKew in Bennelong made sense; I didn't think she'd win it, but she'd certainly distract Howard from the national scene. But rushing a distinguished retired soldier, Mike Kelly, into Eden-Monaro could be sending the wrong signal: a known and trusted local might have been a better bet. And it was hard not to notice that when the celebrity just happened to have a trade-union background, like Greg Combet in Charlton or Bill Shorten in Maribyrnong, they were delivered a lifetime of safety.

Still, the decisions had been made and the possibility of a win was there; but the arithmetic suggested that it would take a genuine national swing to achieve it, and this was far from guaranteed. The rider, from the optimists, was that Howard had not had a really big win since 1996; even when everything was running for him, economically and politically, it had been fairly close. Now the tide was undoubtedly turning, politically at least, and it could just be enough. It could, but as yet I was not prepared to put money on it.

★

Meanwhile, in the lead-up to the budget, there was some light relief from the man whom his erstwhile diplomatic colleagues call contemptuously 'our room-temperature foreign minister', Alexander (call me Lord) Downer. Downer's public image is as an unctuous buffoon, but actually there is more to him than that: he is also a bully, as those underlings unlucky enough to have been the victims of his petulance will attest. He is also impervious to irony: having just described Kevin Rudd as the vainest man he had ever met, Downer now sold himself as the subject of the ABC's *Australian Story*, which gave birth to a double episode after the filming coincided with the Indonesian air crash in which three Australians died. My impression was that Downer emerged as an arrogant and posturing upper-class twit; but then, I had already made up my mind.

If you feel my judgement of one of the most senior and trusted members of Howard's inner circle is a trifle unkind, I ask you to recall his handling of the wheat-for-weapons scandal, with particular attention to his appearance before the commission headed by Mr Justice Cole. Here is a transcript of the evidence he gave on 11 April 2006. It has been lightly edited by Hal Judge (to whom thanks) but nothing of substance has been omitted.

> It could have been it may have been I don't specifically recall I can't precisely remember I don't recall I don't recall I couldn't rule it out it is possible I don't know I'm not sure I have only a very distant recollection I don't recall I don't think I did I'm pretty sure I didn't make a note I don't recall I could have done I don't recall it I don't recall I simply do not recall.
>
> I would have made a note of it and been quite focused I might have turned out to be wrong I don't recall I don't recall I don't recall I don't recall I wouldn't use that language I don't remember precisely it didn't mean anything to me it doesn't mean anything to me I wouldn't recognise him nothing at all I don't read the summaries unless I'm stuck on a plane I have no idea I have no idea.

> I can't recall I gave no such direction I don't recall I didn't make any notes I just don't recall I can't answer that question I can't recall my state of mind I don't recall I simply do not recall I do not recall I can't quite find the place I don't recall I simply do not recall I don't recall I don't recall I don't recall I'd have to reflect on that.
>
> I don't recall I don't recall I'm not sure I don't know I don't recall it is sketchy very sketchy I can't tell you I wasn't aware there is so much intelligence it's a very major challenge to deal with intelligence I have no recollection of it I just can't recall it at all I have no recollection I have no recollection information flows appear to be very imperfect I was not aware.
>
> I don't know I don't know I can't recall I'm not aware I can't recall I don't know I don't recall I assumed I don't recall we had no knowledge I can't specifically recall I can't recall I just can't specifically recall it's very difficult to recall I'm not sure that I'm not sure I wasn't sure.
>
> I can't specifically recall I don't recall I don't know I can't say I just don't know I don't have any specific recollection I'm not aware I wasn't aware I had no knowledge I wasn't aware I wasn't aware I wasn't aware I just can't recall.

To add to the fun, Howard's newly appointed minister for the ageing, Christopher Pyne, was reported to have told the residents of an old persons' home that he wasn't really comfortable in his job; he would rather have had Downer's gig at Foreign Affairs. The problem was that as a young person himself, he preferred to avoid aged-care events. Naturally Pyne denied that this was what he had said, or at least what he had meant, but many present took it that way. It was not quite as big a blue as that of one previous junior minister who, on receiving the unlikely portfolio of Environment, Aborigines and Arts, complained to a colleague that he had been given trees, boongs and poofters, but it demonstrated that a long term in office had given even the most junior members of the government ideas above their station.

Episodes like this gave Rudd breathing space from his industrial-relations concerns and no doubt emboldened him to an uncharacteristic display of confidence: he told a Brisbane May Day rally that victory was in his grasp, reported in the *Courier-Mail* as 'I'm taking the Lodge, says Rudd.' After pressure from Rudd's bovver boys, this was softened in later editions to 'I will win, says Rudd,' but it still appeared, at best, to be a premature ejaculation.

Still, he wasn't the only one tossing around a bit of hubris. Tony Abbott told his fellow peddlers on yet another bike ride for charity that the government was set for an August election. At first glance this seemed unlikely: surely Howard would not want to risk missing out on chairing the APEC meeting in September? But then again, perhaps appearing on the same platform as George W. Bush might not look like such a good idea by then. The forecast was generally dismissed as a bit of Abbott big-noting: almost certainly Howard had not yet made up his mind, and absolutely certainly he wouldn't tell a mouth like Abbott if he had. But it had to be factored in: if the budget was a real zinger and if the government got a bounce that was confirmed in the polls by the end of June, Howard just might break the habit of a lifetime and go early.

Over to you, Peter the Perennial Pretender.

> *If you are going to walk on thin ice,*
> *you might as well dance.* —PROVERB

★ 7.

IT WOULD BE STRETCHING THE TRUTH to say that Peter Costello approached his twelfth budget with enthusiasm. For many years he had made it clear that he would prefer each new budget to be his last; the whingeing had started after his first six-pack, and he was now up to half a slab and still counting. But at least he could say that this one was important. The budget was not, as Dennis Shanahan breathlessly claimed, the centrepiece of the political year; the annual fiscal ritual had long since lost its mystic significance, and in any case the centrepiece of an election year is the election, duh. But the government was desperately hoping that the budget would prove to be a hinge, a turning point. At the very least it was a chance to regain the initiative, and with a bit of luck it might stop Rudd in his tracks.

Although it was not reflected in the polls, the opposition was beginning to show signs of strain. The industrial-relations policy remained a problem, and Rudd was not quite as self-assured as usual: perhaps his daughter's wedding had got to him where Howard and his hit-men had failed. It was up to

Costello to land the vital punch. But it would not be easy: while the government was awash with money from the mining boom, it could not just hurl it at the voters, as it had in the past. To do so would not only appear cynical and profligate; it could over-stimulate an already buzzing economy to the point where the Reserve Bank would have to increase interest rates again, and that would be electorally disastrous. On the other hand, the government had to give at least a slice of its windfall gains back to the taxpayers if it was not to look mean and uncaring. The trick was to find a way of doling out the cash which would be both popular and fiscally responsible.

But first, as always, tax cuts. This time they had to go to the lower middle, mainly because the top end had received such unconscionable bonanzas in past budgets. The problem was that cuts towards the bottom end of the scale cost a hell of a lot, partly because there are more poor than rich but also because they flow through to the top end anyway; the income of the super-rich includes the income of the poor, and part of it is taxed in the same way. Thus, a cut of $14 a week might not mean very much to someone on $250,000 a year, but unless you increased the top rate (an unthinkable proposition), he or she was going to get it anyway. But then, $14 a week was not all that much, even to someone on average weekly earnings; it was better than a poke in the eye with a burnt stick, or than the notorious $6 cut which Amanda Vanstone had described as the 'sandwich and a milkshake' tax cut, but it certainly wouldn't cover the three interest-rate rises since the last election. In fact, over the life of the Howard government, the battlers received just one half of one cent in tax relief for every dollar they earned. Still, the record showed that the punters would be pathetically grateful for any cut at all, and more importantly would be seriously miffed if they got nothing, so $14 it had to be.

Then there were the usual, seemingly random handouts: a dollop for carers, a sweetener for superannuation contributors, a spoonful for pensioners. This was both cynical and silly; surely if pensioners and carers and the like are underpaid, they should get a proper rise rather than a one-off payment. But no one was prepared to argue that pensioners didn't deserve a present (as Howard put it) and in any case, given that the small print revealed many of the tax cuts would not come through until 2008, it was important to get at least some money into some pockets as soon as possible.

But that still left an awful lot in the kitty. A large chunk could be moved into infrastructure, which in practice meant a gigantic pork barrel from which rural electorates could be funded for roads and bridges closer to the election. But even then, after all the normal running expenses had been paid, there was still some $13.6 billion left. We had been told, over and over again, that any surplus was destined for Costello's pride and joy, the Future Fund, set up to pay superannuation for public servants – a singularly uninspiring aim. But uninspiring or not, the Future Fund was supposed to be sacred; Rudd's idea of re-investing some of the loot in national broadband had driven Costello to well-feigned apoplexy. Yet now, even as the $13.6 billion was trundling its way towards the vault, Costello reefed $5 billion off the top for a permanent Universities Endowment Fund, which at least sounded a bit sexier – and apparently that was all it had to do.

The announcement had the commentators gibbering with awe and delight next morning: it was brilliant, breathtaking, unsurpassable. With one stroke the Opposition had been sidelined, if not wiped out altogether. Dennis Shanahan was so excited that he penned three separate comment pieces for one paper: the headlines – 'A sharp lesson for Rudd,' 'Labor outflanked on policy strength,' and 'Rug pulled from under Rudd's feet' – give just a hint of their content. (In case anyone still missed his point, two days later he summed up lyrically: 'Kevin's gone from on a roll to in a hole.') The rest of the press gallery, while not quite so fulsome, was pretty enthusiastic: the consensus was that Costello had pulled off a political coup.

Well, let's just take a calm look at it. The new fund was not a limitless trough to replenish the funding the government had ripped out of the universities over the past decade; it was limited to capital works, meaning new buildings. And while the vice-chancellors loved the idea of expanding their real estate (and perhaps even getting an erection of their very own) the rest of the education establishment felt that this was not where the real crisis lay, especially as Costello had also announced the end of the limit to the number of full-fee students a university could enrol: a clear signal that if the universities were short of money for recurrent costs, they could make it up by increasing their number of rich, thick students.

The other problem was that although $5 billion sounded like a lot of money, it had to cover a lot. The idea was that it would be topped up from the surplus every year, but obviously this would depend on the economic circumstances at the time. At the start it would provide an annual income of about $300 million, to be shared among 38 institutions. Some would obviously get more than others, but none would get all that much. Labor's spokesman, Stephen Smith, put it in perspective by noting that the current building-maintenance bill for all universities was $1.2 billion a year; the Australian National University alone needed $500 million for urgent repairs. Costello's building fund was of course welcome, but it was no panacea for the problems of universities, let alone for education as a whole; and to say it trumped Rudd's Education Revolution, which covered new funding and planning from preschoolers to postgraduates, was plainly absurd. 'Costello's Masterclass' (as the *Australian* breathlessly christened the effort) deserved a solid pass, but not the high honours the media accorded it.

And the worry about the rest of the budget was not so much with what was in it – in his reply Rudd found very little to criticise, an omission seized upon by Howard – but what was left out. In the preceding weeks there had been a barrage of leaks anticipating all sorts of goodies: a return to the Commonwealth Dental Scheme, a fully revamped approach to Indigenous health problems, massive child-care subsidies, an inland railway from Melbourne to Brisbane – only absinthe drinkers looked like missing out. But on the night we got none of the above. The 43 per cent of Australians who said they couldn't afford to go to the dentist were promised not subsidised care, but more dentists. Aborigines were not offered a comprehensive health program, but instead unaffordable private housing. The contribution to child care was hardly more than tokenism. And the railway was put on the back burner, perhaps to be reheated as an election promise.

There were other interesting omissions, too: the budget made no allowance for government advertising in the coming year, which, given the increasing rate of it, had to be put down to concealment rather than oversight. And the anticipated funding for the $10-million Great Big Splash in the next twelve months? Just $52 million: barely one half of one per cent. Scarcely a drip. One final note from the masterclass: Costello's speech contained not one mention of WorkChoices. Yet the budget outlook was for both productivity and employment to fall in the coming year. Howard did not seek to explain this extraordinary discrepancy.

★

Rudd's speech in reply was low-key but positive: he announced another chapter in his Education Revolution, a trade school for every high school that wanted one. He also assured us that he was a proud fiscal conservative, a theme which was immediately picked up in a series of party advertisements. This was obviously designed to pre-empt any suggestion that he would run a big-spending election program, something he had shown no sign of doing. Indeed, if there had been criticism, it had usually been that his aims were too modest: we could do with a bit more vision. Interestingly, more people watched his speech on television than watched Costello deliver the actual budget; but then, more people watched *The Chaser's War on Everything* than watched Channel Nine's evening news. Perhaps viewers are becoming more discriminating.

And so perhaps, just perhaps, are voters. The media consensus was that budget week, and the week leading up to it, had been bad ones for Rudd: he had stumbled in parliament, he had appeared confused over fee-paying students, and there were rumours of a rift with Julia Gillard as he tried, unsuccessfully, to mend fences with the miners in Western Australia. More disturbingly, he finally seemed to be running out of puff. And the budget had been given a near-rapturous reception by the media and its Canberra-based commentariat. Howard had always said that he did not expect any immediate bounce in the opinion polls, but would it be too much to hope for at least a slowing of the Rudd bandwagon?

Well, yes. On Monday the Galaxy poll and on Tuesday the Newspoll, generally considered the bible, showed that Labor, far from stalling, had actually moved further ahead. Newspoll had Labor's primary vote back to 50 per cent, with an 18-point break on the two-party-preferred, and Rudd now led Howard by 12 points as preferred prime minister. And the weird bit was that the bastards had actually liked the budget. Sixty per cent said it was good for the economy, as opposed to 11 per cent who thought it would be bad, but those figures could be ignored as a reflection of what people had seen in the media. However, 36 per cent thought it would make them richer and only 14 per cent thought it would make them poorer; only 31 per cent thought Labor would have delivered a better budget, against 44 per cent who thought it wouldn't have. To confirm these findings, the consumer-confidence index lurched upwards by an unprecedented 7.5 per cent. So why then, why oh why, did 25 per cent say it would be more likely to make them vote Labor and only 17 per cent say it would be more likely to make them vote for the Coalition?

No one could really say; Howard, grinning uncomfortably on television, muttered something about the Australian public's sense of humour. Any thought there might have been of an August election was promptly abandoned: while the Coalition still hoped for better polls as the budget's benefits became clearer (or the voters came to their senses), the ground was far too slippery to trust. Richard Farmer, a commentator on *Crikey* who is a veteran of the Labor campaigns of the '80s, pronounced flatly that it didn't matter when the election would be held: the Coalition was now past recovery, and Rudd would become prime minister. The fact that the government still had heaps of money to spend (another $8.6 billion in the surplus with barrow loads unspent from last year: $89 million in funds for climate change alone) seemed irrelevant. As the *Courier-Mail* summed it up, with another memorable front-page headline: 'Can't Buy a Vote.'

If Rudd was not home and hosed, he was certainly riding high in the voters' esteem. So why did the press gallery keep getting it so wrong about him? The honeymoon was supposed to have ended back at the beginning of March, when his visits to Brian Burke were revealed. Then the doubts over his account of his childhood were meant to have trashed his credibility. The Anzac Day *Sunrise* affair should have damaged him beyond repair. His industrial-relations policy made him unfit for office. The budget had knocked him out of the game. Again and again the gallery had put him down and written him off, and every time he had bounced back bigger, brighter and better than before.

It was obvious that the gallery didn't particularly like Rudd personally; I had seen their hostility at the ALP National Conference, where there was a concerted attack from the whole media pack. Nothing wrong with that; Rudd could be devious and evasive and just as hard to pin down as Howard or any other politician. But it was puzzling that the gallery seemed determined to seize on any piece of trivia which they believed would bring him down and then insist, contrary to all the evidence, that it had in fact done so. I'm not just talking about Dennis Shanahan, who is as rabidly partisan as any Piers Akerman, Andrew Bolt or Janet Albrechtsen. Veterans like Laurie Oakes and Paul Kelly were guilty of the same lack of judgement, leaping on unashamed beat-ups in what turned out to be futile and embarrassing attempts to take the gloss off Rudd. Not only was the public unconvinced, but it reacted the opposite way, to the bewilderment and fury of the pundits.

There was a splendid example of this over the weekend after the budget, when the *Australian* resurrected Rod Cameron, Labor's polling guru from the Hawke–Keating days, to lambast Rudd's industrial-relations policy. It was bad politics, Cameron said, because it brought the trade unions back into the game, and everybody hated the unions: 'You can't go back to the regulated workplace environment of a generation ago and most people don't want to return. The majority of voters are anti-union and they don't want the unions back in their lives.' Actually Rudd was not proposing a return to the regulated workplace environment of a generation ago; he was talking about the deregulated environment post-Keating, with only slight modifications to the system which prevailed before the recent introduction of WorkChoices. But Kelly, instead of correcting Cameron, took the misdirection as yet another excuse to pontificate.

'Labor is deluding itself on a huge scale,' he thundered. 'It has misread the public mood, created a false sense of political reality, fooled itself into thinking that people don't want a flexible labour market and fallen into the trap of an alliance with the trade unions on IR policy.' Hang on a minute: had he read the opinion polls lately? Labor's policy was precisely the reason people were flocking to the party. Private polling by both parties revealed that WorkChoices was political poison; voters might not be great fans of the unions, but the mere mention of WorkChoices scared them rigid. Howard realised this, even if Kelly didn't: that very week the word went out that the name was to be expunged from the vocabulary of the government and all its servants. The new term was to be 'Workplace Relations', which was nice and neutral. The excuse for this piece of semantic acrobatics was that since Howard's flip-flop it wasn't really WorkChoices anymore, but something still more wonderful: the red gold had been gilded and the lily painted white. Whether the punters would be fooled was yet to be seen, but it was another illustration of just how far Labor's industrial-relations policy had put it ahead. If Labor had misread the public mood, so too had Howard, in spades; but neither seemed to think so.

★

A week later Kelly tried to claw his way back to relevance by inventing a new theory of the cosmos. There were, he explained, two competing realities at work. One was the 'inside the beltway' (whatever a beltway was) reality, where everything was going swimmingly for the government and the Opposition was floundering. This was the world according to Kelly. But in the 'outside the beltway' reality, the voters were deserting the Coalition for Labor. 'These two political realities are both valid,' Kelly blustered:

> Within the engine room of politics the Coalition is now dominant but abroad in the nation Labor has a commanding grip. The truth, however, is that only one reality will prevail. Only one version can triumph on election day 2007. Either the logic within the beltway will take the country or the mood in the country will overwhelm the beltway's logic.

There was just one problem with this scenario: the two so-called realities were not equivalent. The second was grounded in actuality, and involved factual measurement and analysis. The first existed only in Kelly's head and those of his mesmerised colleagues. Public opinion might indeed change, but if it did it was unlikely to be just because Paul Kelly thought that it should.

Howard certainly wasn't relying on it. Yet again Treasury was raided for another round of advertising to tell people all about the wonderful new safety net he had placed under WorkCh ... er, workplace relations. This, we were assured, would be strictly non-political, just the facts, no spin. Howard seemed unaware that this virtuous guarantee amounted to an admission that at least some of the other $1.7-billion worth of government advertising he has inflicted on us during his regime was in fact political and therefore an improper use of taxpayers' money. And his refusal to tell anyone just how much more the latest exercise was going to cost suggested that even it was not completely above-board. Kevin Rudd took the opportunity to promise an end to the rort if he was elected: government advertising of more than $250,000 would have to be tested by an auditor. It was a worthy idea, and we will watch its implementation – or not – with considerable interest.

But the fact that The Policy Formerly Known as WorkChoices had now become The Policy That Dare Not Speak Its Name did not mean that Rudd was completely in the clear with his own industrial-relations policy. It didn't matter particularly that employer groups were still prophesying doom, destruction and the end of the world as we know it if the policy was not junked altogether; the more the bosses whinged, the more they convinced the workers that the policy must be good for them; and since there were a lot more workers than bosses, Labor's brains trust was losing neither votes nor sleep. In any case, anyone who thought about it knew that business had been doing very nicely indeed before WorkChoices, so claims that the end of the legislation would lead to a massive collapse were simply baloney.

But it did matter that the policy should appear coherent and workable, and the more Rudd and particularly Julia Gillard struggled with the transitional arrangements for those on AWAs, the knottier the problems became. The line they fell back on was that AWAs had to go, but if an employee was happy with the arrangement it would be allowed to carry through to its demise – which in practice could mean five years, plenty long enough to come up with some equally satisfactory arrangement. So far, so good; but what about employees who were not happy and felt that AWAs had been forced on them against their will? If anecdotal evidence was to be believed, there were an awful lot of those in the retail and hospitality industries, and more every day.

Gillard's response was that they would somehow be allowed to get out of the AWAs: in other words, to break a binding contract which, in legal terms, had been freely entered into. At the very least this was opening a tin full of worms that Labor could have done without. By contrast, her fellow frontbencher Craig Emerson, beavering quietly away with small business and independent contractors, appeared to be winning hearts and minds at a surprising rate; the independent contractors actually put out a statement saying they preferred Labor's position to that of the government, a turnaround as unlikely as the timber workers backing Howard in 2004.

★

Howard now made another attempt to regain the initiative, with a second Australia Rising speech, this one to be a comprehensive look at schools. The advance publicity suggested that it would be the complete and final answer to Rudd's Education Revolution. What actually emerged was a promise to attack bullying in schools, just like the promise he made in 2004. Rudd endorsed it with unexpected passion, but when you think about it, of course he would; like Howard, Rudd was surely a victim of bullying in his schooldays – or if not, he certainly looked as if he should have been. Having been a victim myself, I sympathised, but a war on bullies hardly constituted a visionary reform to the secondary-education system. Like Howard's previous Australia Rising speech – the one about, er, I forget – this one promptly sank without trace.

He took out his frustration on the television networks: not only had the government's traditional Aunt Sally, the ABC, shown *Bastard Boys*, a compelling dramatisation of the 1998 waterfront dispute in which the government and the bosses had conspired to break the maritime union (a typical piece of left-wing bias, screamed the Howard-huggers), but the usually reliable Channel Nine had screened an episode of a soapie in which a wicked employer had misused his powers under WorkChoices to offer an employee a take-it-or-leave-it AWA. Howard unleashed his enforcers, but for once the networks refused to grovel. Perhaps they too sensed the winds of change.

The only thing that went according to plan was the decision to get his beloved cricketers off the hook by forbidding them from touring Zimbabwe, a decision which reeked of hypocrisy (Howard opposed sporting boycotts of South Africa during the apartheid days, and wouldn't dream of imposing them on China, whose human-rights record remains one of the worst in the world) but which went down a treat with a public thoroughly conditioned to loathe President Mugabe. Rudd retaliated with an equally populist move: a Labor government would not only prosecute Japan in the International Court of Justice for its illegal whaling, but would consider direct action against whalers operating in Australian waters.

Through all this the opinion polls barely moved; there was a statistically insignificant movement back to the government which could not be called a post-budget bounce, and was nothing to set the pulses of increasingly nervous backbenchers racing. Some Liberals were now openly bemoaning the fact that they had not changed leaders when they had the chance last year; it was now far too late, but Costello, for all his over-the-top political hamming, was now looking a far stronger performer than the old fellow, particularly in question time.

Howard went close to admitting this when he mused to the party room that the fact that he, Costello and Downer had all been in their respective positions since 1996 could be interpreted as a weakness as well as a strength. He had no rabbits to pull out of his hat, and the way the polls were going the government faced not just defeat but annihilation; it would be months before things started looking better, if in fact they ever looked better at all. On this cheerful note he told his fellow Liberals that yet again he was abandoning his free-enterprise principles to cave in to the Nationals on a monopoly sales organisation to replace the Australian Wheat Board.

Actually, things were not quite as bleak as he made them out to be. While the polls showed the government trailing Labor on almost all the important issues – education, health, climate change and, most notably, industrial relations – Howard still led convincingly on the vital subject of economic management, and was also still ahead on national security. The latter had pretty much dropped off the radar, as neither side was now all that keen on mentioning the war, but the former indicated that the nation's hip pocket remained, as always, the most sensitive part of its anatomy. If Howard could somehow turn the campaign into a referendum on economic management, to the exclusion of all else, he could be back in control.

Rudd was acutely conscious of this risk, and was attacking it from two angles. The first was to run a constant series of distractions: keep the focus on climate change, industrial relations and education, which were already grabbing the attention of the electorate. If the voters could be persuaded that these were the things that really mattered if they were serious about protecting their hip pockets, then Howard's rhetoric about his record and experience could be turned against him as an obsession with the past and a lack of concern about the future. The second line was to continue to assert his own credentials as an economic conservative in the Howard mould, only more so: not only would Rudd not compete if Howard set up a pre-election spending spree, but he would spend less than the government – a courageous stand, given the well-demonstrated insensate greed of the electorate. At the same time Howard was to be portrayed as reckless with public money, unscrupulous when it came to spending it for political advantage and self-indulgent when it came to his own comfort. This exercise could not only be devastatingly effective if the media took it up; it could also be a lot of fun. Rudd's troops approached it with unfeigned enthusiasm.

First there was the advertising. Penny Wong, the frontbencher responsible for (among other things) government accountability, came out with the news that government advertising in the Howard years had cost no less than $1.7 billion, with plenty more to come. Notable campaigns included the initial promotion of WorkChoices ($55 million), superannuation ($69 million) and boosting private health funds ($19 million). Before that, of course, was the mammoth GST effort: $120 million before legislation had even been drafted, let alone passed by parliament. This brought to mind the current Son of WorkChoices campaign that was pushing safety-net provisions which, as yet, did not exist. While the government refused to put a figure on the exercise, it was revealed in the Senate estimates committee that the cost so far was $4.1 million, or $25,000 per hour. Malcolm Turnbull, franker than his colleagues, admitted that a climate-change ad series that he had in the pipeline would cost $53 million – slightly more than the total which would have been spent on the Murray-Darling Great Big Splash for the entire year, if the Victorians would only come to the party, which they still hadn't. There was also to be an apparently uncosted education campaign to counter claims that the government was underspending on government schools, by any standards a blatantly political effort. Indeed, so crowded were the commercial airwaves with government propaganda that it was getting hard for legitimate commercial advertisers to book space.

Howard continued to claim that it was all perfectly legitimate, just necessary information for the public, no political spin; but as Julia Gillard pointed out, that was as silly as pretending that advertisements for Pizza Hut were not aimed at selling pizza. Peter Hartcher, in the *Sydney Morning Herald*, attacked the abuse of public funds, as he had in the past; and surprisingly, he was joined by Steve Lewis in the *Australian*. Like the government's longevity, the newspaper's reliance on publicly funded advertising could no longer be seen as an unalloyed advantage.

★

Howard's self-indulgence provided even more colourful copy. In the Senate estimates committee hearings it was painstakingly established that maintenance of his two residences – Kirribilli House and the Lodge – had cost a cool $20 million for the year. As Penny Wong pointed out, we only had one prime minister: why did he need two houses? Moreover, he did things in style. Wong issued a summary:

TOP TEN LIST OF THE PM'S RENOVATION RESCUES

1. $540,000 to renovate the prime minister's private dining room
2. $125,000 to relocate staircase at Kirribilli House
3. $101,272 to renovate the Lodge dining room
4. $35,000 to renovate the bathrooms at Kirribilli House

5. $29,000 for wardrobe construction at Kirribilli House
6. $64,433 for new back staircase at Kirribilli House
7. $82,000 for 20-seat table and chairs at Kirribilli House
8. $25,635 to renovate the prime minister's Sydney office
9. $19,400 for four single-seat Chesterfield lounges and six new chairs for Canberra office
10. $16,613 to replace dinner set at the Lodge

Actually, the first one wasn't for either residence but for the prime-ministerial suite at Parliament House; Janette decided the current dining room wasn't big enough, and wanted to extend it by knocking down a wall. The estimate covered that, and only that: not the new furniture, carpets and dinnerware that would also have to be bought. When the estimate was revealed Howard hastily cancelled the project, no doubt to Mrs Bucket's chagrin. Still, think what else she could have for the money: a modest third residence, for instance, one where she could keep the wine. The two existing residences had gone through a staggering $110,000 worth of plonk in the past four years. And then there were the new chairs for the cabinet room: a snap at $2885 for each ministerial bum, plus $18,000 to a consultant to select them ...

This was precisely the kind of snout-in-the-trough extravagance that infuriates the punters: here was Howard telling the battlers that they'd never been so well off, and then thumbing his nose at them. It was far more damaging than any wheat-for-weapons scandal could possibly have been. The only comfort was that the drought finally seemed to be breaking – coincidentally, just at the time that the popular ABC weatherman Mike Bailey declared himself a Labor candidate opposing Joe Hockey in the relatively safe Liberal seat of North Sydney.

Rudd, as ever, remained cautious: he still believed that in the end the election would come down to 51–49, one way or the other. Howard must have hoped desperately that Rudd was right, because 49 per cent would be enough for him to win. On the raw figures, Labor needed 51.3 per cent to pick up its seventeenth marginal: Howard's own electorate of Bennelong.

> *Then turn not pale, beloved snail*
> *But come and join the dance.*
> —Lewis Carroll

★ 8.

In mid-May, in a fit of exasperation at the difficulties of dealing with state governments, the sinister Phillip Ruddock remarked that he sometimes felt like Sisyphus. Sisyphus was a mythical Greek king of Corinth who waylaid travellers and murdered them; he was renowned for being sly and treacherous, and so cunning that he could even trick the gods. When they finally caught up with him he was condemned to roll a boulder to the top of a hill; when he got it there, it fell back to the bottom and he had to start again, and again, for all eternity.

Ruddock may have been referring to federal–state negotiations, but his observation also unwittingly evoked the frustration he and his colleagues felt at their inability to lay a glove on Kevin Rudd. The problem was that they shared with Paul Kelly the delusion that the government was doing everything right: the economic management had been impeccable, the exploitation of national security immaculate. For more than a decade they had found the perfect balance between greed and fear. Yet now, suddenly, the voters had deserted them for a nerdy little upstart whose main talent appeared to be an indefatigable ability to answer his own rhetorical questions. Not only was it unfair; it just didn't make sense. Therefore, they must be on the right track: it was just a matter of going on doing what they'd done before, only this time even more stridently. Second verse, same as the first – a little bit louder and a little bit worse.

But there was to be one tactical refinement. Rudd himself was apparently invulnerable; no matter how clearly the government and the media pointed out his manifest failings, the public only embraced him further. So if they couldn't get at the man directly, perhaps they could do so through his wife. Thus the spotlight was switched to Therese Rein.

One way or another, the wives of political leaders had been a bit of a problem for most of a century. They didn't mean to be; almost invariably they set out to play the role of loyal and supportive helpmeet, being there when the public demanded it and, more importantly, making themselves scarce when it didn't. But sooner or later they found themselves newsworthy in their own right, and usually to their own detriment and that of their spouse. Therese Rein, the first of the breed not to adopt her husband's name, was simply the latest in a long line of embarrassments. In this context it is important to note that the prime minister's wife is not like the American president's wife: she is not the nation's First Lady. That distinction belongs to the wife of the governor-general, so Lady Major-General Whatsisname is the one who really should be out there doing it for Australia. But in practice this has never been the case: She Who Occupies (or Seeks to Occupy) The Lodge is the one the public wants to know about, and the one who, willingly or not, must suffer the exposure.

Some manage to remain private: Ben Chifley's wife was supportive to the extent of allowing him to live with his secretarymistress when in Canberra, and Pattie Menzies and Bettina Gorton were equally content to live in the shadows of their more flamboyant husbands. Others have been more outgoing: Zara Holt famously redecorated the Lodge and proudly paraded her three handsome daughters adulterously fathered by Harold Holt during her first marriage. Sonia McMahon became famous for wearing a slit dress to dinner at the White House. Enid Lyons valiantly defended her rather dim husband against undermining from Robert Menzies, and eventually became a politician in her own right, ending up as Australia's first female federal minister. And of course Janette-Hyacinth Bucket-Howard long gloried in the perception that she played something of a Lady Macbeth role in the partnership. On the Labor side, things have often been more iffy: Margaret Whitlam became an icon in her own right, but caused something of a scandal by accepting a government appointment to the board of Commonwealth Hostels. A cruel joke claimed that Gough Whitlam had to take her overseas with him as she was the only woman capable of push-starting a Boeing 707. Hazel Hawke became an object of public sympathy after loyally enduring her husband's infidelities for most of her life, only to be deserted at the end. Anita Keating hung on through her husband's rise and rise, helping to win the 2000 Olympics for Australia in the process, but left to pursue her own life when the crash came.

Given this, it was entirely understandable that the Rudds should view their marital future with a certain amount of trepidation and should seek to sort out as many of the problems as possible before Kevin's actual tilt at the Lodge. The Rudds are in many ways a conservative couple: steadfastly Christian, devoted to their nuclear family and promoters of good old-fashioned values. But in other ways their marriage is a thoroughly modern one. Not only does Therese Rein have her own career, but in financial terms at least it has been far more successful than that of her husband. Moreover, until the government dirt squad got to work there was never the slightest suggestion of any breach of ethics on her part; on the contrary, her companies specialised in placing clients considered too difficult by the mainstream employment agencies, and were widely praised for their contribution to the social good. Rein was rightly considered a model businesswoman, and the fact that she had combined her career with a successful marriage, including bringing up three well-balanced children, made her a model to the wider community as well.

Her mistake was that staff at a company she had taken over had underpaid some workers. To make it worse, the workers were not under a collective agreement but on individual contracts – though not AWAs. Although the government tried to portray it as a case of ruthless exploitation, in reality the mistake was minor and forgivable; when it was detected, she dealt with it swiftly and honourably. Under normal circumstances there would have been no problem. But the circumstances were not normal: Rein was the wife of a putative prime minister – a putative prime minister, moreover, who was making his running on precisely the sort of ground her mistake covered. It highlighted his difficulty in sorting out his policy over AWAs and individual contracts by exposing even more confusion in what was already a fairly muddled area. And it suggested, ominously, that there could be further problems ahead.

The government pounced, screaming about hypocrisy and double standards. Almost every day the Opposition raised another case of hapless employees being dudded by ruthless bosses under what used to be WorkChoices; now here was their leader – well, his wife, but let's not split hairs – guilty of the same offence. Actually, it wasn't. What Rein had done was illegal, because her workers were employed under common-law agreements, based on the relevant award. When sprung, she had to correct the error. If the workers had been employed on one of Howard's AWAs, there would have been nothing anyone could have done about it – that is, before the introduction of the still-invisible safety-net provisions. But the government relied on this distinction being too subtle for the general public, as it was too subtle for the entire editorial staff of the *Australian*, who once again pronounced the pricking of the Rudd bubble. 'Rudd Cornered By Wife's IR Deals,' gloated the front page.

Well, no; but it did suggest that Therese Rein's business interests could become a serious political liability. The dilemma was entirely new: while prime-ministerial wives in the past may have taken part-time jobs or run hobby boutiques, there had never been a genuine businesswoman, let alone one who competed for federal-government contracts. Reluctantly, Rein acknowledged that in an election year a choice had to be made. Rudd says he left the decision entirely to her, and there is no reason to disbelieve him. There were those who said she should have hung tough; but in the end she chose to sell off the domestic side of her operation rather than risk further embarrassment to her husband. It was an act of loyalty, of course, yet it also showed a deal of public spirit.

In announcing her decision Rein insisted that it was made not just to help Rudd; in a wider sense her concern was the country as a whole. This might have sounded pompous and sanctimonious, but she was so obviously sincere that it carried conviction. Along with her other virtues, Therese Rein was clearly a true believer. She was also bloody good on television, bringing out the best in her husband as well as winning hearts and minds herself. To the consternation of the government, the media consensus (apart, of course, from the usual recalcitrants) was that after a nasty few days once again Labor had emerged from the cesspit smelling as fragrant as ever.

★

That was certainly the view in the front bar of the Billinudgel, where Therese Rein was unanimously declared a Good Sort, not at all like that snooty bitch of Howard's who looked as if she'd forgotten where to put it, if she ever knew. The Billi was in a political mood: a government audit had just reported that the former dynastic local member Larry Anthony had used his ministry to channel community grants to National Party electorates, particularly his own. Anthony was cheerfully defiant about it, and the patrons at the front bar had no great objection to him pork-barrelling his constituents – wasn't that what local members were for? The problem was that none of the loot had found its way to Billinudgel.

There was also a mild sense of betrayal that Anthony was not attempting to regain the seat of Richmond but had instead put his hand up for preselection to the neighbouring, safer seat of Page. When the Nats in Page said they weren't interested in Richmond's rejects he once again retired from politics, muttering about ingratitude. The consensus in the front bar was that he ought to go and get a proper job: one he could actually manage, like working as a fencepost on the family farm. Given the number of nervous Coalition backbenchers considering their futures, he might have to move quickly. There was even a report that Janette Howard had been sprung checking out nursing homes on Sydney's North Shore. She said it was for her mother, but then she would, wouldn't she?

Lending substance to the stories, Howard appeared to have gone into a state of unreality. Everyone knew that there was a big climate-change advertising campaign in the offing. Departmental officials had admitted it in Senate estimates. Leaks to Labor had provided not only the cost but even some of the scripts. As sure as Christmas, it was coming. But Howard kept denying it. Or not quite denying it; unable to break the habit of a lifetime, he used a series of weasel phrases to leave himself a way out when, inevitably, the ads appeared. He had not seen them; they were not signed off; no campaign could exist because no minister had approved one. Sixteen separate and detailed questions failed to shake him. As Michelle Grattan wrote in the *Age*, the whole process made him look devious, stubborn and slightly crazy: what was the point of the pretence, unless of course he was planning to cancel the campaign, which he clearly wasn't. The old charge of 'mean and tricky' was revived.

Other ministers seemed equally flaky. Asked why he thought the polling showed the government in so much trouble, Workplace Relations Minister Joe Hockey replied jovially that it was because he wasn't as pretty as Julia Gillard. Foreign Minister Alexander Downer announced that he was off to America for a holiday as a guest of his old, close and dear friend, Condoleezza Rice. The secretary of state responded, with a faint air of bewilderment, that she was always happy to see Mr Downing.

Labor took advantage of this scattiness to try and underline its image as firm but fair, especially on the industrial front. It had now been established both officially and unofficially that WorkChoices was screwing vulnerable workers; there were even stories of employers who claimed that they had been forced against their will to cut wages and conditions to keep pace with their more ruthless competitors. Gillard put in a calm and convincing appearance at the National Press Club to emphasise, yet again, the logic and justice of Labor's stand, while Rudd proved himself hairy-chested by demanding and receiving the party resignation of Electrical Trade Union boss Dean Mighell. Mighell had been the one who had described John Howard as a skid-mark on the bed sheet of Australian politics at the ALP's national conference; now an old recording popped up on which he could be heard boasting about conning the bosses into giving his members undeserved pay rises.

The *Australian* called it a good beginning, and indeed it set a puzzling precedent: whether Mighell's offence was bullying, bravado or simply bad language, it was hardly a rarity in what had always been a pretty robust union movement and indeed in the Labor Party itself. If Rudd was to apply the same standard across the board, he'd find himself a mighty lonely player at the next national conference. However, the act was clearly intended to be symbolic rather than exemplary, and as such it conveyed the idea that Rudd could indeed be trusted to stand up to the unions – to some of them, part of the time, anyway.

★

Far more convincing, and to my mind far more important, was Rudd's commitment to reconciliation, which emerged full-blown on Reconciliation Day itself, the fortieth anniversary of the 1967 referendum and the tenth of the release of the report on the generation of stolen children. For most of the Howard years Indigenous affairs had hardly been on the agenda and what little action had taken place had been almost entirely negative. Howard's very first action as prime minister had been to send the auditors in to ATSIC, a pre-emptive strike which was followed by the gradual erosion of the body's powers until its final abolition in 2004.

In the meantime there had been the stolen-children report, which Howard had handled by authorising a smear campaign against the principal author, Ronald Wilson, and then refusing to make a public apology or to take any substantive action on its findings. And there had been the High Court's Wik decision, which had led to Howard using the power given to the Commonwealth in 1967 to legislate not for the benefit of Aborigines – as was the clear intention of the referendum – but to remove some of the rights found by the High Court to exist. By 2007 the key government policy was to allow private individual ownership and transfer of communal property, a method of undermining the granting of land rights which had been one of the few concrete legacies of the referendum. It was hardly surprising that Indigenous audiences turned their backs on Howard on the rare occasions when he felt compelled to address them, or that he was heckled and abused even by the handpicked audience at the Reconciliation Day ceremony.

Labor, to its shame, had been a passive spectator throughout most of the debacle. During the Kim Beazley years Aborigines had been viewed as a side issue, a distraction from the main game. At one stage Beazley even instructed his staff that Aboriginal activists, along with gay law reformers, women's liberationists and environmental radicals, were not welcome in his office. On a personal level he was deeply concerned about the deprivation and injustice, and he actually wept over the stolen-children report. But while Labor policy was sensible and enlightened, it was kept tucked away at the back of the cupboard. Simon Crean took much the same view and Mark Latham went even further: he actually anticipated the policy to abolish ATSIC, although he did have vague plans to replace it with another representative body, an idea which Howard derided.

But Rudd went back to the days of Paul Keating, or even Gough Whitlam. To quote the great man himself: 'All of us as Australians are diminished while the Aborigines are denied their rightful place in this nation.' In Howard's presence, Rudd asked for a bipartisan commitment to clearly defined goals, but he must have known this was futile. For starters, Howard never set targets: he had a lawyer's aversion to locking himself into a position where he would be accountable. But more importantly, Howard never had and never would accept that Australia's indigenes were any more than just another disadvantaged group, with no claim to special consideration simply because they happened to be here first.

So they had lost their culture, their children and, in many cases, their own lives? Tough. He wasn't responsible and he wasn't going to lose sleep over it and he certainly wasn't going to apologise for it. If the survivors wanted to become real Australians now, and look after their houses and bring their children up decently and get proper jobs, that was fine and he'd send someone like Mal Brough around to help dismantle what was left of their traditions. This was what he meant by 'practical reconciliation', and they could take it or leave it. He was certainly not going to match Rudd's eminently reasonable proposals to eliminate the seventeen-year gap in life expectation within a generation, or halve the infant- and childhood-mortality rates within a decade, or halve the illiteracy rate in the same time. No special treatment.

Rudd's program was both detailed and costed, which was unusual in itself; experts in the field, including the Australian Medical Association, said it wasn't nearly enough, which was of course true. But the point was that Rudd, in a clearly heartfelt speech, was prepared to make it a front-line policy commitment. Like Howard, he must have known that there were no votes in it. Unlike Howard, on this issue he allowed himself to be ruled by conviction rather than the opinion polls. If Rudd became prime minister, reconciliation might again become possible. For veteran believers like myself, it was a long overdue bugle call, and all the more welcome because it came from an unexpected source. Rudd's campaign to date had been shrewd, calculated and tough-minded – nothing wrong with that, but it was an enormous pleasure to confirm it had heart and soul as well as brain.

★

In contrast, John Howard's offerings seemed to emanate more from an upset liver than any other organ. He was becoming increasingly irritable about the Victorian premier, Steve Bracks, who still refused to sign up to the Great Big Splash. Increasingly it appeared that he would have to make concessions to Bracks, which would then enrage the other premiers, who had signed up without making similar demands. But at least he could place himself back in the climate-change debate from another angle: his handpicked 'task group' of compliant public servants and industrial polluters was ready to hand him the result he had requested over an emissions strategy. It was, as he had known it would be, pretty piss-weak, but even so it required a stupendous about-face on his part. Howard had always rejected carbon trading for Australia: if and when an international scheme emerged, then we'd have to have a look at joining it, but until then it was in the nation's best interests to stand back and emit like buggery.

However, business and even the miners tended to look a little beyond the next election, and needed some form of certainty. They actually wanted a trading scheme, albeit one on their own terms. So suddenly Howard announced that he was preparing to make the most important economic decision of the century, and give them one; or sort of. From being a distraction, a virtual non-event, one of the ALP's ideological fantasies, climate change became the Crucial Issue. Some time around the end of the term of the government after next, something or other really ought to be done about it.

Howard chose to announce his conversion at the Liberal Party's annual conference, an affair so lacking in drama that he himself was televised nodding off during an early session. Unlike its Labor counterpart, the Liberal conference does not even pretend to have a policy-making function; it is simply a social get-together where the members can hear rousing speeches from their leaders and, if so inclined, present their gripes, secure in the knowledge that absolutely nothing will be done about them. This is confirmed by the fact that the gripes are always the same: there is too much filth on television and not enough discipline for the young. Sub-branches can be relied on to move motions demanding the return of conscription and capital punishment. Vast quantities of tea and scones are demolished and in the evening strong drink is frequently taken, and by and large it is a nice weekend's entertainment.

The grand finale was Howard's speech. Given his dismal history, it was a brave effort. After all, in spite of increasingly urgent warnings from the scientists and against the example of most of the other industrialised nations, Howard had spent the first decade of his prime ministership doing exactly nothing. The past six months or so had been a little more productive, but not much: the centrepiece – joining George Bush's AP6 group – was supposed to present an alternative to the despised Kyoto, but in fact it was little more than a sideshow: the other four members (China, India, Japan and South Korea) had all ratified Kyoto and made it clear they saw that as the main game, while Bush himself had failed to secure any funding for the venture. Apart from that there had been some money to save Indonesia's forests while continuing the destruction of our own, and Malcolm Turnbull's proposal to change light bulbs (how many politicians and how long does it take?). To call the action dilatory would be like saying that Alexander Downer is unlikely to trouble Carl Lewis over a 100-metre sprint.

But as always, Howard was not about to apologise. He was, he trumpeted, a climate-change realist, intent on finding practical solutions to the problem. This in itself was an ominous signal: 'practical' is Howard-speak for doing nothing – see practical reconciliation, for example. But Howard had always been an expert at spinning nothing – or at least very little – into a grand plan of action, and his task group had given him the very little he needed. Yes, there would be carbon trading. That was the positive bit. But look, it would be so unobtrusive that you'd hardly notice it. Indeed, if you were getting on in years you probably wouldn't notice it at all, because nothing would happen for at least four years, more likely five. That period would be devoted to the study that should have been taking place for the previous five years or longer, but there's no point in rehashing the past. What matters is that Treasury is finally getting on with it, and we can expect a result any year now, although certainly not this one. But rest assured that eventually we will get the announcement of some (unspecified) emission cap, and some (unspecified) carbon price, followed by an (unspecified) reduction target. As one of his predecessors so neatly put it: the government, in due course, acted promptly.

And the cost of this exercise? We thought you'd never ask. As Peter Costello had perhaps prematurely pointed out, there will indeed be a cost, because that's what market solutions are all about. Electricity prices would rise, but not by much and not until long after Howard's retirement. And when we say not much, we mean not in the same ballpark as prices would rise if the fanatical ideologues of the Labor Party had their way, by taking all the cars off the roads and shutting down all the factories and driving us back into the caves. Recession? You don't know the half of it. And we're talking not just about a nerdy little Kevin Rudd recession; we mean a ginormous bug-eyed, bald-headed deep-green Peter Garrett recession. Have a think about that before they come and turn the lights off forever. So now, who do you trust? And remember, the weather will always be better under the Coalition than it would be under Labor.

The point of it all, of course, was not the policy itself, so vague as to be effectively meaningless, but the scare campaign it could generate. The problem was to give the scare campaign legs. The only solid fact Howard had to play with was Rudd's target of reducing emissions by 60 per cent by 2050, a target widely accepted internationally and one even the Australian business roundtable said it could live with, without undue cost. Howard's mutterings about Australia being different and not wanting the Europeans to set our targets for us sounded more chauvinistic than convincing. He had also exhumed a throwaway line of Garrett's about a possible 20 per cent reduction by 2020, but Garrett immediately denied that this was Labor policy, so that didn't fly either. In the end it came down to the old formula: *I'm the only one who knows how to manage the economy, so trust me.* It had worked in 2004, but three years and four interest-rate rises later it was looking a bit shop-soiled.

★

Given the vacuity of Howard's speech, it was probably fortunate that it was overshadowed by the latest Galaxy poll, which showed a sudden lurch back towards the Coalition. The figures said that while Labor would still win an election, the Coalition was now back in the hunt. Perhaps the long-awaited Budget

Bounce had arrived, or perhaps the relentless smear campaign against Kevin Rudd and his colleagues was finally taking effect, or perhaps the sheer weight of taxpayer-funded advertising had bludgeoned the voters into submission. Perhaps; or maybe there was a bit of an aberration in there. On the face of it, it did seem unlikely that three-quarters of a million voters had switched straight from Labor to the Coalition in just a fortnight. However, it lifted the spirits of the government wonderfully, and even the more realistic of the Labor strategists gave a gentle sigh of relief. The two-party-preferred result, 53–47, was a margin they could understand, and so could their supporters; it meant that there were two sides still in the fight and that smugness was an indulgence they could no longer afford.

Not that the news was all bad: the federal police had now raided the Liberal Party's Queensland headquarters in relation to the case of Hardgrave, Vasta and Laming, and this time the warrant carried the name of Howard's own handpicked state director, Geoff Green. Rudd once again moved to the high ground, announcing another step towards bipartisan appointments in high places: not only would the judges or commissioners or mediators or whatever in his Fair Work Australia bureaucracy be chosen by agreement with the Opposition, but the same would apply to the ABC board, traditionally the home of the cultural warriors of whichever party was in government. This had been Labor policy for some time, but it still made front-page headlines in the *Australian*, giving welcome relief from industrial-relations tirades.

Meanwhile cabinet had yet another go at resolving the standoff between Telstra and the ACCC, resulting in yet another committee to try and work out a way to counter Rudd's promise to broadband the continent. Actually, it was not so much an answer as a copy: the idea was to open the profitable cities market up to tender by the private firms, while using public money to extend fast broadband to the regional and rural areas. Given that Rudd's proposal was to use much the same amount of public money but lump it all into one scheme, the difference was at the margins, although the Labor plan was obviously simpler and neater. Telstra responded by sacking a net 500 workers, which was not quite what the government intended. But omelettes and eggs ...

A report came through from Geneva that the ACTU president, Sharon Burrows, had succeeded in having Australia placed on the International Labour Organization's shame file – smearing her country, as the *Australian* put it. This turned out to be yet another beat-up, but it was one Rudd could have done without. Again he asked Gillard to try and do something about her mad union mates, and set himself to defuse yet another scare campaign. At least there was some light relief: another round of taxpayer-funded government advertising made its way into the press, but this one was a bit different. Authorised by the Department of Industry, Tourism and Resources, it was headed 'Collective Bargaining – making it easier to do business.' Hang on: wasn't collective bargaining the aim of the Faceless Union Bosses, the very thing WorkChoices had been designed to wipe out? Well, yes; close reading revealed that the ad was actually encouraging collusion among businesses to put pressure on their suppliers, not the rights of workers to organise. Still, it made a change from the blitz reassuring the downtrodden and oppressed that they'd never had it so good.

Then Joe Hockey appeared on the Kerri-Anne Kennerley show doing a Shrek impression, complete with green pointy ears which he asked to keep. And it was still the first week of June. The long pre-election winter had only just begun.

> “*If I can’t dance, I don’t want to be part of your revolution.* —Emma Goldman

★ 9.

On 11 June the ABC’s *Four Corners* showed a program called ‘Ghost Prisoners’, detailing the American policy of secretly sending suspected terrorists for interrogation in countries where torture is accepted practice. In particular the reporter, Sally Neighbour, examined the case of Mamdouh Habib, an Australian captured in Pakistan, sold to the Americans and then ‘rendered’ to Egypt. There, Habib was viciously tortured: apart from standard treatments like having his fingers broken and nails torn out, he was sealed in a lightless chamber with water up to his chin; only by constantly rising on his toes was he able to avoid drowning. Unsurprisingly he eventually broke down and confessed to anything his interrogators demanded, however improbable; among other things he claimed responsibility for helping to organise the September 11 attacks. He was then taken to Guantanamo Bay, from which, after protracted incarceration, he was released without any charges being laid. He is now back in Australia.

Throughout this appalling saga the Australian government failed to lift a finger. Initially Alexander Downer said, predictably, that he had no idea where Habib was. Eventually Downer admitted that Habib was in Egypt; but, he was assured, being well treated. Either it did not occur to our dilettante foreign minister to ask why Habib was sent to Egypt if not for torture or (more likely) he didn't give a damn. *Four Corners* included interviews with high-ranking US officials who said it was inconceivable that the Australian government had not been informed of the truth – if, of course, anyone had bothered to ask. It was, one would have thought, an explosive story, especially coming from Sally Neighbour, a highly reputable journalist whose expertise in the area is admitted even by the *Australian*, which is normally contemptuous of the ABC: the paper employs Neighbour as a special correspondent. Certainly the program deserved following-up in the next day's press.

But, barely a mention; instead, the headlines were all about a plan by the dreaded ACTU to campaign against the government (Shock! Horror! Who'd have thunk it?) and Howard holding a piss-up for his mates at Kirribilli House (Honest John misusing public funds? Well, stuff me up a dead bear's bum). Oh, and yet another opinion poll, showing Labor may have lost a bit of ground in Queensland: the projected avalanche might turn out to be a mere landslide.

This last emphasised not only the press gallery's preference for the trivial, but also the hypocrisy of the pundits: they frequently criticised the politicians for being poll-driven, but were themselves totally obsessed with psephology. The obsession seemed to have grown with each election, and to have reached a climax in 2007, presumably because the polls weren't behaving as the pundits thought that they should. For them, this was a mystery of metaphysical proportions, which might have helped to explain why they were so keen for the party leaders to meet the Dalai Lama. After some shilly-shallying, both did, but as far as is known neither achieved enlightenment. Certainly their performances as parliament moved into the last session before the long winter break suggested they both had a bit to learn about renouncing worldly ambition.

It was, of course, shameful for the mainstream media to have ignored the Habib story; but in a sense they could claim to be showing sound editorial judgement. In politics, it's not the big things that are the problem. As John Howard has shown, you can declare war, bring in a swingeing new tax, subvert the public service and abandon your citizens to torture, and the people will grumble for a week (if they even bother to do that) and then prepare to vote for you again next time around. But make a bad joke, interrupt the footy grand final or slip into a pair of fishnet stockings and you may never hear the end of it. And worst of all is the trousering of a few extra bucks of public funds for self-indulgence. You can get away with subverting millions in taxpayer funds to promote your party's policies: this corruption – and there is no other word for it – is now enshrined in Australian tradition. But don't, whatever you do, snaffle a lazy thousand and spend it on drink. Well, not if you're likely to get sprung.

Howard must have felt safe enough inviting a few business mates home to Kirribilli for a few drinks, especially as he had already taken the precaution of charging the Liberal Party a trifling amount for its own delegates. Certainly he would not have expected this unobtrusive piss-up to develop into what some wag christened the cash-for-canapés affair. It swamped parliament for a whole week, largely negating the government's efforts to make something sinister out of the fact that the unions were running a sophisticated election campaign – admittedly a bit of a non-story to begin with. And from the start, Howard mishandled the matter, changing his story about who and what the token charge was meant to cover, nitpicking over whether the function could be called a fundraiser (the businessmen invited had just contributed $8250 each to Liberal coffers) and denying that there could be anything wrong with the practice, because he had been doing it for years and so had Bob Hawke. Hawke promptly replied that yes, he had done something similar, but realised it had been inappropriate; he regretted it, and really Howard should recognise that two wrongs don't make a right.

From here on things deteriorated: it was revealed that Howard had also held what he termed an official function, a piss-up for the Young Liberals, this time at the Lodge. This reopened the question of why he was still at Kirribilli House at all; when he originally misappropriated it, the excuse had been that his kids were still at school in Sydney, so he had to live there too. Nine years after the last of the young Howards was loosed upon the world, the old couple were still firmly in residence, an expensive exercise in itself. Howard's supporters loyally denounced it all as a smear campaign, a distraction, a cynical device to take the attention of the electorate away from the big issues, like the fact that Kevin Rudd really had horns and a tail. *Get over it*, they implored, *let's move on*. But what the punters heard was, *Who cares? It's only taxpayers' money, and there's plenty more where that came from.* Not the right message for an election year.

Therefore the message had to be swamped, and fortunately there was another piece of frippery around to do just the job. This was the so-called Unions' Dirty Tricks Manual, an election primer for union organisers to use during the forthcoming campaign. There was nothing either new or interesting in it; the instructions on how to go door-knocking reflected what all politicians had known, and done, for millennia. But Howard and Costello clutched this straw with the enthusiasm of men who have nothing left to lose. After all, it tied in with the line about how the unions would run the country if Rudd ever became prime minister, and there was enough naughty stuff in it (like not always telling the whole truth about your opponents) to dress it up as the most sinister and dangerous document since the Communist Manifesto.

The only problem was that Labor also had a document, this one being the blueprint for an equally grisly strategy from Big Business, which involved coercing Rudd and Gillard with the threat of a huge and horrific advertising blitz if they refused to cave in on industrial relations. It then transpired that Big Business was to go ahead with the blitz anyway, and that it was to be handled by the fine old firm of Crosby-Textor, Mark Textor being the American who introduced the Liberals to push-polling and had run their surveys and much of their black propaganda ever since, and Lynton Crosby being the former director of the Liberal Party who once described John Howard as 'dull as batshit'. Crosby-Textor, in other words, is the agency of the Liberal Party, run by the Liberal Party for the Liberal Party. Its involvement rather took the gloss off the idea that business wanted to run an independent, non-partisan campaign aimed purely at improving the IR laws.

Howard and Hockey were placed in the embarrassing position of having to guarantee that no taxpayer-funded research would be made available exclusively to the business campaign. Both indignantly did so, but it was impossible to see if they had their fingers crossed at the time. They then announced that employers would be forced to hand out IR 'fact sheets' to all their employees and would be fined if they refused or failed to do so. Presumably later in the year they would also be compelled to distribute how-to-vote cards. The Howard government continued to set new standards for the corruption of public office.

★

It is hard to know what the punters made of all this; needless to say, they weren't asked. But statistics showed that increasing numbers of them were hurting in one way or another. Personal insolvencies had jumped by 15 per cent in the past nine months. Bankruptcies had more than doubled during the Howard years. The early release of superannuation for those in financial hardship had risen from $32 million in 2001 to $135 million in 2006. There were other straws in the wind suggesting that Howard's mantra about the workers never having been better off simply did not compute; the four interest-rate rises since the election were still casting a long shadow, and ominously the Reserve Bank chief, Glenn Stevens, had refused to rule out another just because it was an election year.

With mortgage rates now absorbing nearly 10 per cent of disposable household income – the highest in the Keating years was just over 6 per cent – and house prices becoming even more unaffordable, the outlook was not rosy. More immediately, petrol was on the rise again, with Labor promising a full-time commissioner to monitor it and the government forced to respond by promising an inquiry. It would take more than bluster inside parliament and propaganda outside it to fix these problems. Nonetheless, until the budget benefits kicked in at the start of July, these were all the tools the government had, so they got on with it.

Rudd had made a slip of the tongue during a radio interview, when he appeared neither to know nor acknowledge that after a long period of stagnation, productivity was starting to rise again. Worse, he left at a speaking engagement some notes his staff had prepared on the subject; they were borrowed by a passer-by and a copy handed to Costello. Productivity was the basis of Rudd's economic attack on the government; if it could be shown that he really wasn't the full bottle on the subject, then, said the Howard strategists, he could be crushed like a bug and the argument about economic management would be over. They pounced.

Actually Rudd did understand productivity – the basics of it, anyway. Crudely, productivity is simply the ratio of output to input, input being the cost of labour and investment and output being the value of the finished product. The larger the difference – what Karl Marx used to call surplus value – the greater the productivity. For simplicity, most employers measure productivity as output per worker, and it follows that the more skilled the worker, the greater the value of the output and hence the greater the productivity. The boom, driven by the mining sector, led to a decline in productivity, because it attracted lots of unskilled employees into the workforce (hence the low unemployment rate) and also because much of the investment in mining would take some time before it actually resulted in increased production. Thus a slow-down in productivity in the past few years was inevitable and, on balance, no bad thing.

But that was not the whole story. As Glenn Stevens pointed out, while the mining boom explained some of the slow-down, it did not account for all of it. This was obvious anyway: the slow-down pre-dated the boom. From 1993–97 productivity growth averaged 3.3 per cent; from 1998 to 2003, 2.1 per cent; and in 2007 it was now running at less than 1 per cent. In fact, the budget forecast was for no productivity growth at all in the coming financial year. This was the long-term trend Rudd had been hammering on with his talk of an Education Revolution and Universal Fast Broadband, the challenge of a skills shortage and a failing infrastructure.

However, Howard and Costello judged, probably rightly, that this was too technical for the masses, and that it would be far simpler and more understandable just to go on belting Rudd for not admitting that there had been a marginal rise in the past two quarters, even if Stevens had warned explicitly against making anything significant out of a single set of figures. It certainly worked for the *Australian*, which gloated, 'Rudd Cornered on Economy,' an adaptation of the previous month's zinger, 'Rudd Cornered by Wife's IR Deals.' If they kept trying, surely sooner or later they would corner the bastard. Rudd obviously didn't feel cornered; he tried to bring on a parliamentary debate on productivity and, rather surprisingly, Howard refused. The economy was meant to be Howard's ground. If he didn't feel safe fighting on that, where would he feel safe? Well, Total Trade Union Domination, obviously.

Fortunately the unions were being co-operative. Having set an impossibly high standard for behaviour in the case of Dean Mighell, Rudd now felt compelled to follow it through. Thus when a video surfaced showing the CFMEU's Joe McDonald behaving badly on a building site, Rudd demanded and received the union heavyweight's suspension from the ALP. Two down, several thousand still to go. Clearly this could not go on; as several exasperated officials pointed out, building sites were not exactly the lingerie department of Myer, and a certain amount of uncouthness went with the job.

Luckily for Labor, the Liberals went equally over the top: someone got hold of another CFMEU pamphlet, this one urging migrant workers to become Australian citizens so they could vote against the Howard government. The Libs cried foul but, given that they had run yet another advertising campaign urging migrants to take out citizenship, it rang a bit false. Admittedly their own campaign had not suggested voting Labor; but still, any new citizen, the material indicated, was a good new citizen. When another video surfaced, this time showing a boss bullying workers, the issue was neutralised, at least temporarily. This did not stop Howard from repeating his predictions about total union domination, by which he meant the end of civilisation, but it did mean people were getting a bit bored with the subject. Even the appearance of the New South Wales union supremo John Robertson, threatening to pull Rudd on following the election, could not give it new legs; after all, as Robertson pointed out, it was his job to pull on governments of all persuasions, and he had been pulling Howard on for years.

And privately Robertson's supporters acknowledged that he could expect no more from Rudd than he had received from Howard. Rudd was committed to getting rid of AWAs, but he was never going to return to the days of pattern bargaining, which was what the Faceless Union Bosses really wanted. That had gone out with Paul Keating. The miners continued to complain that getting rid of WorkChoices would put projects worth squillions at risk, that the economy would collapse and we would all be rooned, but no one believed them; after all, mining profits had been running at record levels for many years before WorkChoices was introduced. When Rudd talked about getting the balance right, he sounded far more convincing than Howard ranting about a return to the days of union domination, which in any case existed only in his own imagination.

And apart from all that, things were looking pretty good for Labor. The government's plans for an Access Card had quietly collapsed, due mainly to dissatisfaction within its own ranks. Reports from the auditor-general continued to uncover underspending, pork-barrelling and what looked very much like downright rorting, this time in the highway black-spots program. Ross Vasta, one of the three Queenslander Liberal MPs under investigation by the federal police, quietly paid back $24,000 in printing costs, the result, he said, of an error; Andrew Laming and Gary Hardgrave didn't. And at the Press Gallery Ball's charity auction, dinner with Kevin Rudd went for $15,000, $5000 more than a day at the cricket with John Howard. The bidders might have had in mind that by the time the cricket season came around, Howard just might not be.

Rudd then won few new votes but some admirers by publicly congratulating the writer Salman Rushdie on receiving a knighthood; Rushdie, declared the Opposition leader, was not only a great writer but a man of rare moral courage, having survived and defied the fatwa called against him by fanatical Muslims. It was one of those gestures which reassured the doubters that there was more to Rudd than the smart and ruthless, but often irritating, politician. And the polls seemed to have settled down: all of them had Labor's two-party–preferred lead at somewhere between 10 and 14 per cent, and Rudd comfortably ahead of Howard as preferred prime minister. More disturbingly still, an unusually high proportion of voters said that their minds were made up; it would take something remarkable to swing them back. Howard started to cast around for something remarkable – and found it, of all unlikely places, in Aboriginal policy.

★

Aboriginal affairs had undergone many changes in the Howard years. The call for an apology for the stolen children had become muted as a result of Howard's blunt refusal and the old ideas about reconciliation were firmly on the backburner. But a new and media-savvy indigenous leader had appeared in the form of Noel Pearson, whose campaign against what he saw as his people's welfare dependency struck a responsive chord in Canberra. At the same time the *Australian*, defying the old dictum that stories about Aborigines do not sell newspapers, had been running a series of reports about degradation in the settlements which had emerged as part of the out-station program through which some tribes had returned to their traditional homelands. Many of the stories highlighted violence and abuse against women and children. The ABC's *Lateline* program contributed other graphic and disturbing examples.

The problem was not new or even newly exposed: the first serious report on the sexual abuse of children in outlying communities was handed to the federal government in 1991, and there had been many others since then. Howard himself had held a so-called summit on the issue in 2003, little publicised and quickly forgotten. But since then the media and Pearson had revived interest and Howard's new Aboriginal Affairs minister, Mal Brough, a muscular Christian who had done a stint as an army officer before becoming a salesman of hair products, was pawing at the ground, eager for action. The area, so long neglected (especially by Howard), might just be ready for exploitation – if the right trigger could be found.

And it was. In April the Northern Territory government had received a report on the protection of Aboriginal children from sexual abuse. The report had gone to the printer in the usual manner, and found its way to the federal government six weeks later. After brief consideration it was released on 16 June under the emotive title *Little Children Are Sacred*. Five days later Howard and Brough called a press conference to announce that they had just discovered a national emergency that required swift and radical action. Rudd, caught entirely by surprise, committed the Opposition to in-principle support and was jeered by government members for doing so. From the start, the exercise was dragged down to a partisan political level.

But John Howard's compulsory acquisition of Aboriginal land in the Northern Territory and the declaration of martial law on its inhabitants was not just an election stunt. It was something much more sinister: a massive piece of social engineering whose eventual aim was the total assimilation of the Aboriginal race. It was quite true that the breakdown of order in quite a lot (though by no means all) of the territory's settlements and the consequent degradation of many of the people, particularly of the children, had become a national disgrace; but it was hardly a national emergency. An emergency is something sudden and unexpected, like a flood or an earthquake. The plight of Australia's indigenes had been obvious for decades – some would say for centuries. The Howard government had seen and ignored report after report on the issues involved during its time in office. The fact that it was only now responding and that its response looked both hasty and opportunistic was a matter for shame rather than congratulation.

As with Howard's last surprise initiative – the $10-billion Great Big Splash to save the Murray-Darling – the plan to tackle child abuse in the settlements was announced without planning, costing or consultation. The territory government, the public service and Aboriginal leaders were all left out of the loop; even Noel Pearson, the spiritual father of the tough-love prescription, was only informed fifteen minutes before Howard made his announcement. Howard himself made a virtue out of the lack of any serious preparation: 'What matters more, the constitutional niceties or the care and protection of young children?' he demanded. In fact no constitutional niceties were involved; while the Great Big Splash depended on the co-operation of the states, the commonwealth had a free hand in the Northern Territory.

Of course, some established laws would have to be dropped: Howard's plan was clearly race-based, if not downright racist, so the *Racial Discrimination Act* had to be overridden. Still, that was not really a problem; it had been done to pass Howard's Wik legislation, removing Aboriginal rights, so there should be no problem this time. Kevin Rudd, securely wedged, could seek to amend some of Howard's legislation, but he could hardly oppose it unless he wanted to be accused of aiding and abetting child abuse, which he didn't: it was bad enough being called a supporter of Saddam Hussein for opposing the invasion of Iraq. So there were, for the moment at least, no legal or political obstacles in Howard's way.

The problems would come with the plan's implementation. For starters, there were around 600 Aboriginal settlements in the Northern Territory, with populations ranging from about twenty to more than 1000. Most would be ignored. Howard and his starry-eyed minister planned to concentrate on about 60 of the larger ones. The idea was that the military would bring in civilian police to impose law and order and enforce bans on alcohol and pornography, many of which were already, theoretically at least, in place. Doctors would follow, to provide compulsory health check-ups for all children. Civil servants would oversee the quarantining of all welfare payments, which would henceforth be linked to school attendance. The permit system by which communities could decide who was allowed on their property would be abolished, as would customary law; the land itself would be expropriated by the commonwealth.

No one was really pretending that all this was other than draconian, punitive and paternalistic, a virtual recolonisation of the territory. It would be intensely humiliating, as much to those who were already victims as to the perpetrators of violence and abuse. It would effectively abolish 35 years of land rights and remove any vestige of self-determination from the territory's Aborigines. It would almost certainly lead to the breaking up of many of the settlements with their population drifting into the cities, which was one of Howard's unstated long-term aims. There would be much despair and not a little suffering as a result. The only possible justification for such a ruthless upheaval would be if it worked, if the cycle of violence and abuse was broken for good. And here it was hard to be optimistic.

The sheer scale of the problem was daunting, and the provision of just 60 (if all the states agreed) extra police for the job, most of whom would have no experience at all of the kind of work expected of them, seemed totally inadequate. Health checks were probably a good idea, but what was to happen next, both to victims of abuse and the perpetrators – if, of course, they could be identified? Where were the nurses, the counsellors, the social workers, the psychologists supposed to come from? Most importantly, who was going to undertake the mammoth task of re-building confidence and self-respect among those who would become, overnight, not just second-class citizens but actual non-citizens, deprived of their rights and property and subjected to the same so-called protection as they suffered in the pre-1967 era? There was no sign that any of this had even been considered. But then, if the real purpose of the exercise was to eradicate Aboriginal culture completely and assimilate the survivors into the mainstream, perhaps it didn't need to be.

★

As the timing of the announcement showed, the Howard takeover was all about action, ending the parliamentary session with a huge bang and taking the political initiative away from Labor. Along with the constitutional niceties, the strategy to make it work would have to wait. Yet Howard's supporters in the media insisted that this was not another *Tampa* or, worse still, a Children Overboard. This time the man was sincere: the *Little Children Are Sacred* report and Noel Pearson's exhortations had produced an epiphany. Well, perhaps; but it was hard to forget that this was the same prime minister who squeezed the maximum advantage out of incarcerating the helpless children of asylum seekers behind razor wire, and then refused to act as they went catatonic and insane as a result. He had a lot of ground to make up before nominating as father of the year.

But after a week of frenzied preparation, involving advance teams going to the settlements to reassure them that this wasn't another excuse to steal their children and that no immediate mass jailings were contemplated, it appeared that by and large Australians were prepared to give John Howard the benefit of the doubt. They knew him to be cunning and devious, mean and tricky. They noted that he had lied to them before, constantly, and especially in election years. They realised that he had been getting increasingly desperate for an issue – any issue – which he could use to wrest the initiative back from Kevin Rudd. More than half those polled thought the election was the most important motive for Howard's onslaught. Nonetheless, most commentators and voters seemed prepared to concede that he was at least partly sincere in his desire to tackle the sexual abuse of children in Aboriginal settlements. And even if he wasn't, they didn't really care; it was about time something was done, and if this was the only way to do it, well, let's get on with it.

The melancholy truth behind this acquiescence was that most Australians had never thought very much about the plight of the Aborigines, and they were not about to start now; it was a lot easier to feel indignant about the problems that had emerged than to feel shame about what caused them in the first place. Howard hoped to gain ground from the exercise not by appearing compassionate but by appearing tough. However, one substantial group of Australians remained unconvinced: the Aborigines themselves. They, after all, had been at the sharp end of Howard's reforms all too often. They remembered his support for Pauline Hanson, his endless vendettas against ATSIC, his refusal to apologise for the stolen generations, his legislation to nullify the High Court's Wik decision, his undermining of respected leaders like Pat Dodson and his contemptuous dismissal of the idea of a treaty, let alone any form of self-determination. Unsurprisingly, they generally greeted the latest mobilisation with healthy scepticism.

One of their first reactions was to denounce it as an excuse for repealing native title; the Howard strategy included the leasing back of the settlements for five years, as well as the abolition of the permit system. Howard immediately denied that his actions constituted a land grab, which should have prompted the immediate question: If it's not a land grab, why are you grabbing the land? It apparently took the Canberra press gallery a week to ask it, and when the answer came it was hardly reassuring: it was necessary, Howard said, to make sure the troops had total control. If they decided to build houses, or for that matter to knock them down, they did not want be held up by any need for development approvals or the like. Essentially, they were doing it because they could. But, said Howard, after five years the land would revert to the old community title, cross his heart it would. Well, up to a point, corrected Generalissimo Mal Brough: of course, if the community could be bribed or bullied into accepting individual title instead, the way some of the Tiwi Island communities had, then that would be the go. A lot could happen in five years, especially five years under effective martial law ... In other words, this was not just about the sexual abuse of children at all. The agenda was far wider.

It was worth noting that the document which sparked all this, prepared by Rex Wild and Pat Anderson for the Northern Territory government, did not even contemplate the kind of blanket takeover Howard and Brough mounted; through its 97 recommendations ran a constant theme of the need for consultation and co-operation. Almost all of these recommendations had been ignored: instead we had a virtual invasion, an all-guns-blazing attack on a list of settlements chosen apparently more for their location – close to townships from which the invaders could access infrastructure and material – than for their actual problems. Already some of the potential victims were complaining that their settlements were clean, they had never had cases of child sexual abuse, but they were being shamed and humiliated by being treated as criminals. No matter. The one-size-fits-all approach, criticised even by Howard's staunchest Aboriginal ally, Noel Pearson, was the only one the government could manage. The implicit judgement was that *they were all the same* – after all, they all looked the same, didn't they?

It was also crushingly authoritarian: already the idea of compulsory health checks for children had had to be modified, not because it would have been invasive and degrading, but because it would have been actually illegal. This was all part of Howard's refusal to be blocked by constitutional niceties – or any other kind, for that matter. He himself compared the situation to the aftermath of Hurricane Katrina striking New Orleans, and the American administration's belated response to a national emergency. Once again the Coalition government, in due course, had acted promptly.

South Australian Premier Mike Rann compared it to the invasion of Iraq: Shock and Awe, devastatingly effective in the short term but degenerating into chaos and misery because of the lack of any long-term planning. The analogy was tempting: Mal Brough, impersonating Donald Rumsfeld, predicted the invaders would be welcomed as saviours. So far at least, they hadn't. It was a bad start which did not augur well for the future. Another old political dictum about Aborigines was that there were no votes in them. The first Galaxy poll after the announcement appeared to confirm this: the gap between the parties was still 10 per cent. The chill of winter was reaching even into the expensively heated bedrooms of Kirribilli House.

> *They love dancing well that dance among the thorns.* —PROVERB

★ 10.

2007 WAS NOT ONLY AN ELECTION YEAR; it was also the year after the census, a fact that had not escaped the shadowy planners who lurked in the campaign headquarters. The release of thc census figures meant that they had nearly up-to-date statistics to work with: given sufficient diligence, they could break down the voting population of each electorate by age, sex, income, ethnicity, home ownership, religion – just about everything they need to make their bribes and threats precisely targeted towards their voting victims. Alas, it was a diligence sadly lacking among most of the media, which limited coverage to the usual stuff about how we were all getting older and more female and more Buddhist.

However, the indispensable George Megalogenis did some serious number-crunching in the *Australian* to come up with a useful insight. The mortgage-belt electorates would be, as always, critical; Labor's chances of success revolved largely around winning back the so-called Howard battlers. Equally obviously, the greater the average age of the electorate, the more likely it was to stick with the government. But Megalogenis identified a third group, which could turn out to be critical: single mothers. They were on the increase, and in economic terms they were pretty much the forgotten people. Also they were over-represented in marginal electorates. They could, perhaps, be fertile ground for Labor, if Labor could stop talking about typical working families for just a moment.

The other piece of good news for Kevin Rudd and his colleagues was that the evangelical Christians might be a very noisy lobby group, but there were actually very few of them; at best they might have a marginal influence in two electorates. It would actually be more profitable to cultivate the Buddhists.

But by definition the battlers remained the real battleground. And it was at this point that John Howard's Fair Pay Commission intervened on Labor's behalf. Its minimum-wage decision of a $10.26 weekly increase was the lowest for a decade, and, coming after sixteen unprecedented boom years, arguably the meanest on record. John Howard had to endorse it; after all, the commission was his baby, a central part of the policy formerly known as WorkChoices which, he had assured workers, had helped to ensure that they'd never been better off. But privately he must have been spewing. It was not as paltry as the 2003 sandwich-and-a-milkshake tax cut, but take out a couple of pies and a beer and there wasn't much change from the one and only annual wage rise.

In 2006 the commission had been generous; the increase of $27.36 took everyone by surprise and cast doubts on the idea that it was just part of Howard's grand plan to drive wages down. But now, in an election year, it appeared that the grand plan had merely been postponed. The increase of just over 2 per cent did not even keep pace with the inflation rate; the battlers were to be well and truly screwed. Ian Harper, the commission's president, tried to explain that it was necessary to avoid pressure on interest rates and to keep the growth in employment moving, but the same arguments applied in the previous year and were ignored. Harper said nothing to justify his abrupt transformation from Santa Claus to Scrooge.

The decision confirmed the beliefs of the conspiracy theorists who saw Howard as the arch-enemy of the workers, determined to upset the traditional balance and place all power in the hands of profit-mad bosses. And the fact that the politicians' own wage tribunal had just awarded Howard and his mates 6.7 per cent didn't help either.

With one of his strengths, the economy, called into question – albeit around the edges – Howard would normally have been delighted to divert the debate back to his other one, national security. Here too, Rudd had been gaining ground; because the so-called threat of the boat people was no longer credible, Howard's attempts to pose as a latter-day Horatius holding the bridge against the barbarian hordes now seemed as outdated as the original. The image of the Man of Steel still lingered, though, and while Rudd had agreed to even Howard's most draconian security prescriptions, the suspicion remained that his heart wasn't really in it. When it came to keeping out the towel-heads, Howard remained the original and still the best. The problem was that national security was irrevocably linked in the public mind with the so-called War on Terror, which in turn led to Iraq. And suddenly the government was indeed seen to be incompetent, or at least very confused, about Iraq.

★

The immediate culprit was Defence Minister Brendan Nelson, who, like many an ambitious young hopeful before him, had been thrust into the portfolio and left to flounder. It had been clear for some time that the man was hopelessly out of his depth, and sooner or later the Peter Principle would catch up with him; but it seemed a little unfair that he should succumb by quoting from an official departmental document.

The reasons for going to war are seldom as simple as politicians would like us to think. The architects of the 2003 invasion of Iraq believed, first and foremost, that the country under Saddam Hussein constituted an unacceptable threat to American interests; but this proposition was hardly saleable to the world at large. Therefore they came up with different lines for different groups. For the visionaries, it was a chance to bring democracy to the Middle East; for redneck patriots, it was a chance to hit back at the towel-heads for September 11. For the sceptics, it was to eliminate the threat of weapons of mass destruction; for idealists, it was about getting rid of a tyrant. And for the Christian fanatics, it was God-ordained, a necessary preliminary to the looming final battle between good and evil.

But for the realists in the military-industrial complex, it was all about oil. Saudi Arabia was showing signs of instability; the West's supplies could be in danger. The best way to secure them for the future was by making sure Iraq played ball, and all the rest was window dressing. As a letter writer to the *Sydney Morning Herald* commented succinctly, we would never have invaded Iraq if its principal export had been tofu. This had always been obvious to anyone with an IQ higher than that of Alexander Downer, but it was a truth our government refused to acknowledge. So when the hapless Brendan Nelson let it slip in an otherwise-innocuous radio interview, a certain amount of hell broke loose. Fortunately Nelson was about to go overseas; he was told to leave at once and stay there until ordered to return. His senior colleagues burst into vociferous denial. Unfortunately they failed to get their story straight first, so the result was mere confusion. Rudd suggested that they were making it up as they went along. His defence spokesman spelled out the detail:

> Over the past four days, four Howard-government ministers have put forward four different reasons for our ongoing involvement in the Iraq war.
>
> Brendan Nelson last Thursday – *'resource security is one of them, and obviously the Middle East itself, not only Iraq but the entire region, is an important supplier of energy, oil in particular, to the rest of the world, and Australians and all of us need to think well what would happen if there were a premature withdrawal from Iraq.'*
>
> John Howard last Thursday – *'The government remains committed to staying in Iraq until the Iraqi security forces no longer require our support. We are not there because of oil and we didn't go there because of oil. We don't remain there because of oil. Oil is not the reason.'*
>
> Peter Costello yesterday – *'The important thing is to defend the democratically elected (Iraq) government, much more important than oil supplies.'*
>
> Alexander Downer today – *'I have made the point over and over again if you allow al-Qaeda and terrorism to be successful in Iraq, then the consequences for global security would be simply enormous.'*

The real irony was that Nelson had simply been quoting from a Defence Department update aimed largely at providing justification for Australia keeping forces in Iraq; not unnaturally, the military noted the stability of energy supplies as part of the argument. But Howard, having denied the obvious for more than five years, couldn't afford to admit it now: he continued to insist that the troops were there as part of the War on Terror – and, of course, that they made us more secure from terrorism, not less. This postscript was necessary because the GetUp organisation was currently running a TV ad featuring Louise Barry, a victim of the first London bombings. In it, Barry appealed to Howard to end the presence in Iraq, which she said was making Australia more likely to become a terrorism target. Howard's reply was that we were a likely target anyway. Which bit of 'more' did he not understand?

The government was not about to sit down and have a discussion on the subject. Indeed, it probably wouldn't have helped if it had. A Newspoll showed that only 31 per cent of respondents agreed with Howard about keeping the troops there for as long as the Iraqis wanted them – which, judging by the news from Baghdad, was likely to be forever. More than twice as many polled wanted a firm limit: bring them home now or bring them home by the middle of next year, but at least set a firm date. Coalition of the Willing no longer; the vast majority of people were now decidedly unwilling, and the same view was gaining further ground in the United States. Rudd's line that the most effective security measure Australia could now take would be to announce an exit strategy from Iraq might have been an oversimplification, but it was a model of clarity compared to the government's blathering.

★

There were, though, two failed terrorist bombings in the UK to give some substance to the Coalition's froth and bubble and, fortuitously, there was an apparent Australian link. A Gold Coast medico, Mohamed Haneef, was snatched at the airport while attempting to visit his family in India and taken away for extended interrogation. Other foreign doctors were grabbed but released. The government gratefully did its bit to gee up some mild hysteria: Downer reissued an old warning about travel to Indonesia and Howard tried to call it an upgrade, which it wasn't, and Phillip Ruddock fast-tracked another bit of irrelevant security legislation.

However, for the threat to be at all convincing, Haneef had to be a terrorist, or at least the next best thing; and from the start he stubbornly refused to fill the role. The federal police secured a number of extensions to hold him in custody, but the leaks (and there were plenty) suggested that they were getting nowhere fast. Haneef had a perfectly convincing story about why he was leaving – to see his wife and daughter in India – and the only clear link that could be established with the UK bombings was that he was the second cousin of one of the bombers. It was not good enough for the presiding magistrate, who made it clear to the police that there would be no more extensions: they had to charge Haneef or release him. So they charged him with the new and incoherent offence of 'recklessly supporting a terrorist group'.

The evidence was that a SIM card formerly belonging to Haneef had been found in the vehicle used in the attempted bombing of Glasgow Airport, driven by Kafeel Ahmed, Haneef's second cousin. Haneef said that he had given the card to Kafeel's brother Saleeb when he was in England earlier in the year, rather than wasting the unexpired portion. With a bit of legal legerdemain this could perhaps be spun as support, but it was hardly reckless, unless Haneef had known of some connection to terrorism – and if he had, the charge would have been the more serious 'knowingly support'. Moreover, even the terrorist group was a bit iffy: Kafeel Ahmed fitted the category, but there was no evidence that Saleeb was a member of anything. Indeed, the only charge against him at that stage was that he had withheld information about a possible terrorist act, which made Haneef's connection still less substantial.

This was clearly the conclusion of the magistrate, Jacqui Pearce, who refused the pleas of the police to keep Haneef in custody – which, after all, had been the point of laying the charge – and granted him bail, albeit on strict conditions. Phillip Ruddock, the first law officer of the commonwealth, fumed that this was not at all what the magistrate was supposed to do, and if the courts were actually going to uphold the law as it was written, it might be necessary to change it so that they had no choice at all. The police insisted that Haneef was what they called a flight risk, though how he was supposed to flee after surrendering his passport and having to report to the police every second day was not entirely clear. Given that he had already tried unsuccessfully to telephone the English police to explain himself, and had waited until three days after the attempted bombing before quite openly turning up for his pre-booked flight, the chances of him now becoming a desperate fugitive from justice appeared minimal. And the case against him, for what was a pretty flimsy charge, appeared very weak, even as it was presented by the police; as it was to turn out, there wasn't enough evidence to hang a brown dog. If Haneef was a risk to society, society must have been in a truly parlous state.

But not so fast. Immigration Minister Kevin Andrews, narrow-eyed and thin-lipped, simply overrode the magistrate's decision by cancelling Haneef's visa, on what were vaguely called character grounds. As is the government's wont in such cases, he refused to give any explanation but hinted darkly that there were things beyond the ken of the ordinary voter (or, presumably, the magistrate), and it was given to him and to him alone to reveal that Haneef was not a fit person to reside in

Australia. So Haneef was to remain in Australia indefinitely, at least until he was tried for something or other – it was to be hoped that the cops could come up with something better than the current holding charge – after which, whether found guilty or innocent, he was to be summarily deported. Unless, that is, the English could be persuaded to demand his extradition, in which case we'd be only too happy to have him out of our hair as soon as possible.

In Howard's Australia there was no doubt that the move was legal; but it provoked screams of outrage not only from the usual suspects, the human-rights lobby, but from almost the entire legal profession. The law Andrews was using was meant for getting people out of the country, not keeping them in: the last and most notorious example was that of the American peace activist Scott Parkin, who had his visa cancelled for undisclosed reasons and was deported forthwith. In a matter like that of Haneef, the normal procedure would have been to let the court case run its course and then decide whether to move. By preempting the court Andrews had hopelessly prejudiced Haneef's position. It might be legal, but it was undoubtedly mean and tricky, and it set an appalling precedent – a judgement shared even by the *Australian*'s reporter Hedley Thomas, who wrote a ferocious comment on the issue. In return Haneef's lawyer handed him the transcript of one of Haneef's interviews with the federal police, which suggested the case against Haneef was even weaker than previously thought. The cops and the government expressed shock and horror at this breach of convention, which impartial observers thought was a bit rich.

And then it turned out that not only had the incriminating SIM card expired two months before the attempted bombing took place, but it had not been found in the bombers' car at Glasgow after all; it had been picked up during a search of

Saleeb's Liverpool boarding house. Moreover, a forensic comparison of the transcript of the Haneef police interview with the record of the court proceedings revealed that Haneef had been seriously verballed at least twice. The prosecutor had said he had no explanation for his lack of a return ticket to Australia, but Haneef actually told the police his father-in-law was going to buy it in India because it would be cheaper. Then the prosecutor claimed Haneef had stayed with his brother in Liverpool; in fact, Haneef had explicitly stated that he had left the boarding house before his brother arrived there.

The whole thing was looking more and more like a political stitch-up; people began muttering about another David Hicks. But there was one big difference between Haneef and Hicks: Haneef's home country cared. From day one, the Indian government kicked up a major row, calling in the Australian High Commissioner and demanding explanations and constant updates. If you are to be subjected to arbitrary arrest and detention while abroad, an Indian passport is obviously of far more use than an Australian one.

★

Still, headlines about terrorism, even if they no longer reduced the populace to a quivering jelly, were at least preferable to trying to talk about the other barbecue stopper: housing. Rudd had probably been a bit disappointed when his great health initiative, a move to prevention rather than treatment, failed to take off; but he was clearly delighted with the instant success of his proposal for a housing-affordability summit. His shadow treasurer, Wayne Swan, had been plugging away at the issue for months, producing statistic after statistic about the way housing prices had been getting out of control; the average house, which had cost five years' worth of average wages in 2001, was up to seven years' worth in 2006, and still rising. Mortgage repayments now topped 30 per cent of total household income for one buyer in every four. Repossessions and personal insolvencies had hit record highs.

The government refused to admit there was a crisis; Howard said it was all the fault of the states for not releasing more land, and Costello, preposterously, denied that the eight successive interest-rate rises which had pushed average mortgage repayments up by $480 a month had anything to do with the problem. Howard even juggled the figures to try and prove that repayments were actually at an all-time low, a piece of chicanery on a par with his line about workers never having been better off, and one received with equal indignation. Swan took a more lofty stance: there was, he admitted, no magic bullet, no instant solution. And naturally he didn't really want house prices to fall, because there were more owners and part owners out there than there were wannabes. What was needed was a holistic approach – hence the summit of all interested parties, and he really, truly hoped the government would come too, in a spirit of bipartisanship. To underline his credentials as a grassroots politician in touch with the day-to-day concerns of his constituents, Rudd also proposed that the ACCC undertake an inquiry into the price of food at supermarkets, to make sure they really were competitive and not indulging in what he delicately described as unconscionable behaviour.

The government derided all this as opportunism and populism, substituting slogans for action: Rudd himself, they seethed, had refused to guarantee that house prices, petrol prices or food prices would fall as a result of it. And in any case, things weren't nearly as bad as those Labor shysters were claiming; a lot of the people Rudd and Swan were claiming as under financial stress from mortgage repayments were actually quite rich enough to manage, and others were just doing the right thing and paying off their debts before they were actually due, a prudent move in uncertain times. The Reserve Bank, whose job it was to monitor such matters, said that 25 per cent were not in big trouble; actually it was only about 5.5 per cent. So there, and how dare the Opposition run a pre-election scare campaign? Well, because it worked. And even if the Reserve Bank was right, and only one household in eighteen was in real trouble, a lot more must be on the edge and frightened of falling over it. The Rudd line might well be populism, but it was also popular. Howard should have known; he used to be pretty good at it himself.

There was some relief for Howard, though. There had been rumblings – no more than that, but rumblings – that if the polls did not improve by July, the leadership might again become an issue. Newspoll showed that he had at least clawed back some ground – or, as the *Australian* triumphantly put it, 'Howard Checks Rudd's March'. The good news was that Howard had almost caught up to Rudd on the preferred-prime-minister question. The bad news was that his improved popularity was not reflected in voting intentions: Labor's primary vote was actually up 2 per cent, while its overall lead remained at twelve points, still a potential landslide. It was the opposite problem to the one which Kim Beazley had faced for so long: the Bomber had managed to maintain his party's vote while his rating wallowed in the doldrums. It now seemed that while the mood for change was unabated, Howard himself was retrieving some credibility. Perhaps, in a perverse sort of way, there were some votes in the Aborigines after all.

Dennis Shanahan found the increase in Howard's standing, of just 2 per cent, hugely significant; and the *Australian* dug up a pollster who agreed that the preferred-prime-minister figure was really, truly important. When a couple of internet bloggers derided Shanahan, the paper went to the extraordinary length of running a full-length, 1500-word editorial defending him. My, what sensitive little plants they are, and don't they protest too much.

The next poll subdued even Shanahan: the Newspoll state-by-state breakdown, especially among marginal seats, was frankly horrific. On the figures, Labor was well ahead in every state, even Western Australia. In spite of the Iemma government, Labor had skyrocketed in New South Wales; it was looking at further gains in Victoria, would win back its Tasmanian seats, grab all the marginals in South Australia and wipe the floor in Queensland. Overall, Rudd would pick up 47 Coalition seats and lose none of his own. In strict mathematical terms this was not annihilation; the Coalition would still have a presence in parliament. But most of the present ministry, including Howard himself, would not.

To add to the general sense of woe, Howard got into more trouble over refurbishments to his VIP Boeing 737, including a bizarre episode where the long-distance fuel tanks were removed to provide more luggage space, at the request of his office, and then replaced, at the insistence of the RAAF. This non-renovation cost a neat $116,000, rather more than the new silk curtains and leather ceiling pads. Howard protested that even with the new furnishings his staff still had to endure sleeping conditions inferior to those of business class on the better commercial airlines. At every refuge for the homeless, hearts bled. Peter Costello, sensing the mood, proclaimed himself an old softy who had been known to cry in sympathy with the losers on *Australian Idol*; perhaps he identified with them. He then rather spoiled the effect by saying he had been joking, but went on to weep some crocodile tears at the news that Kevin

Rudd's lobbyist brother Greg had been forced to resign from the Labor Party after it was revealed that he had contributed to Coalition fundraisers. Costello said the story was leaked by union bosses in revenge for Rudd's attacks on Dean Mighell and Joe McDonald; if he was right, it suggested that the bosses were running scared, which was exactly the opposite of the usual line about them being firmly in control. The press gallery missed the opportunity to ask him about John Howard's brother Bob, a long-time Labor supporter.

Rudd, meanwhile, showed his grit and determination when bitten by a parrot during a walk though an Adelaide shopping mall. The *Advertiser* got the picture, but the *Australian*'s photographer missed it; so Rudd went back to the pet shop and gave the parrot a second go, which subsequently ran on the front page of the national daily. There's dedication. The best Howard could do in response was to forget the name of his candidate for Franklin, a seat he hopes to win. In other circumstances this would have been glossed over and forgiven as the sort of aberration that can happen to anyone; but not with Howard already down and writhing. The commentators put in the boot for days, seriously analysing whether the slip was in fact the start of early-onset Alzheimer's, or even the dreaded CRAFT disease (Can't Remember A Fucking Thing).

★

It was in this context that Howard decided to win back the youth vote by launching his new climate-change policy on YouTube. Some things defy parody, and this was one of them. Searching for the item on the YouTube website involved scrolling through page after page of cruel and frequently scatological satirical videos of or about Howard, all too many mocking his senility. The real thing fitted in eerily well, although it remained well down the fourth page of favourite Howard-related videos, far below the Labor Party pastiche which showed him asleep for eleven years on climate change. Once again he had only himself to blame; he had long refused to appear on any of the hip FM stations which dominated the youth market, allowing the vote of the under-35s, which he had secured in 2004, to slip back to Labor. Rudd, in devastating contrast, was seldom off the airwaves, happy to indulge in at least some of the silliness the younger commentators demanded, but never missing an opportunity to turn it to his advantage: what started as a fart joke quickly became a brisk explanation of Labor's policy on greenhouse-gas emissions. But most of the jokes were about Howard.

The continued bad press and polling finally took its toll. In mid-July Howard called a cabinet meeting to discuss the problems, which he reportedly opened dramatically by asking, 'Is it me?' Assembled ministers, reports claimed later, variously looked at the ceiling, fiddled with their notepads and feigned deafness. None actually made their excuses and left, but none rushed to embrace their leader and assure him that it was not. On the other hand, they all knew there was nothing they could do about it; Howard could afford to bare his throat, as Dennis Shanahan put it. The only obvious alternative, Costello, remained even less popular than Howard, and the outsiders simply weren't ready for it. In any case, all the signs were that the leadership was by now a poisoned chalice. The honest answer to Howard's question would have been, *Well, you're a big part of it – we should have changed leaders last year when we had the chance. But we didn't have the guts, so we've got to take the blame too.*

I was reminded of a great Bruce Petty cartoon from the dying days of Billy McMahon's government. A spoof on the terrible poem 'Casabianca', by Felicity Hemans, it showed McMahon dauntlessly manning the smouldering wreckage of a boat. The text read:

The boy stood on the burning deck
Whence all but he had fled
And a staggering piece of insight
Kept going around in his head.
When the flame of truth hits the ship of state
And the tides of time are turning
They tend to bucket the captain
But the ship is what is burning.

Howard emerged to prostrate himself before the voters in the manner of Uriah Heep: 'I have no sense of entitlement,' he moaned. 'I don't believe we are owed anything by the electors. We are there to serve them.' The problem was that the electors believed they did owe something to Howard and his team, like a great big kick up the Khyber. And Howard rather spoiled his mea culpa with his final promise to 'work very, very hard ... to be re-elected'. There were perhaps things closer to the hearts of the voters for him to work at.

The immediate program involved the resumption of the government's ad blitz. There was no longer any real attempt to pretend that the ads were not political, but even so the government's latest offering plumbed new depths. To coincide with the compulsory distribution of propaganda by all employers – the so-called fact sheet for the workers – the head of the Workplace Authority, Barbara Bennett, hit television screens to debunk what she called the myth that workers were without protection. Why, she explained, smiling sweetly, she herself was their protectress. Coming from any other source this would have been merely risible, but coming from a supposedly non-political public servant it was more than somewhat sinister. It was true that the independence of the public service had been so corrupted under Howard that the former head of the Prime Minister's Department, Max Moore-Wilton, had actually attended a party celebrating a Liberal election victory, but appearing in political advertisements was a further step to the dark side. The government's explanation – that public servants spoke to the public all the time and Ms Bennett was only doing her duty – was both perfunctory and unconvincing.

But by this time it seemed no one really cared. The situation had become so desperate that Alexander Downer was demanding that Michelle Grattan, the most venerable, staid and determinedly neutral of the journalists in the press gallery, be barred from the ABC, on the grounds that she was a dangerous lefty. Orwellian? McCarthyist? Or merely Kafka-esque?

> *Those who danced were thought to be quite insane by those who could not hear the music.*
> —ANGELA MONET

★ 11.

IT WAS HARDLY SURPRISING THAT *John Winston Howard: The Biography* was greeted with something approaching hysteria. Howard's political longevity had made it long overdue; the only previous effort, by David Barnett and Pru Goward, had been risible and was now hopelessly out of date as well. Over the years conservative commentators had complained constantly that their hero had received little attention while less-significant figures had been the subject of multiple hardbacks; there had already been a brace of books about Kevin Rudd, and even the despised Mark Latham had rated no less than three biographies.

But these same commentators were curiously reluctant to do the job themselves. Michelle Grattan had described Howard as a figure of positively awesome ordinariness; the former Liberal Party director Lynton Crosby had asserted more bluntly that he was as boring as batshit. Among the political elite there was a consensus that we already knew everything we needed to about our Dear Leader, and publishers reported no surge of enthusiasm from the wider public.

However, academics may venture where commentators can't be bothered to tread, and Wayne Errington and Peter Van Onselen showed that working in an ivory tower does not necessarily entail a disregard for profit. The Fairfax press snapped up the newspaper rights for a tidy sum and generated enough interest to make the first print run a quick sell-out. The book was never going to be a worldwide bestseller, but unlike its predecessor it was not headed straight for the remainder tables.

Actually there was nothing much new in its 400 pages: no revelations of daredevil deeds in exotic places, of passionate and illicit love affairs, even of a smoke behind the pavilion during a school cricket match. Even when the authors caught a hint of excitement, it quickly became an anti-climax: after a suggestion of a brief romance during a 1964 trip to Europe, they assured us that the real highlight was a stint of door-knocking in London's St Pancras South for the Conservative candidate Geoffrey Johnson-Smith (he lost). But what the book lacked in drama, it made up for in politics.

It was no surprise to learn that Peter Costello loathed and despised his prime minister, but it was certainly newsworthy that he was willing, and even eager, to go into the details of his contempt in an election-year book. In on-the-record interviews with the authors Costello got stuck into Howard's record as treasurer under Malcolm Fraser and depicted himself as the only real obstacle to Howard's profligacy in the present cabinet. It was a spectacular example of disloyalty, and not mitigated in the least by the claim of Costello's supporters that he did not expect the book to come out until after the election; if true, all this proved was that their man was cowardly as well as perfidious. And in spite of the headlines the story generated, the political odd couple remained joined at the hip, united in mutual hatred: if either of them had a speck of integrity Costello would have resigned, and if he hadn't Howard would have sacked him. But no, it was business as usual.

Even more revelatory was Janette Howard's encapsulation of the relationship, and in particular of Costello's insistence that Howard had promised to step down after a term and a half: 'You talk about a whole lot of things when you are trying to convince people to do things. But you don't go back and honour every one of those things unless you have made a firm commitment and John isn't into making firm commitments.' The prime-ministerial ethic in a nutshell: do anything, promise anything, lie, dissemble – it doesn't count, because it wasn't a firm commitment (or a core promise). And if people are silly enough to believe you, well, tough luck, sucker, and there's another born every minute.

Apart from that, the biography is a useful record of Howard's unrelenting capacity for treachery. From the moment of his election in 1974 he joined the forces of Malcolm Fraser to undermine the then leader, Billy Snedden. As prime minister, Fraser rewarded him handsomely, but he repaid the favour by bad-mouthing his benefactor to anyone willing to listen. Nonetheless he expected Fraser to nominate him as his successor. When Fraser, repelled by Howard's racism (among other things), went for Andrew Peacock instead, Howard moved to white-ant the new leader to such effect that he himself finally usurped the job. After Howard lost the 1987 election Peacock took the leadership back and Howard continued to gnaw away: it was in this period he gained the nickname of 'rodent'. John Hewson replaced Peacock and lost another election: Howard instantly challenged him and lost again; he resumed his role as chief saboteur. Even then the party preferred Alexander Downer. Howard went to work on him, but it really wasn't necessary;

Downer self-destructed and Howard persuaded the only other possible choice, Costello, that if he played along for a couple of years – well, maybe three or four, definitely no more than five – his turn would come.

Even as prime minister, Howard had been unable to break the habit of a lifetime: with no one above him left to betray, he turned his attention to those below. Apart from Costello, any other real or perceived threat – Peter Reith, Tony Abbott, Brendan Nelson and most recently Malcolm Turnbull – was given false expectations of advancement and after his immediate usefulness ended, sent back to the pack. And of course, Howard insisted that Costello remains the heir apparent. Of course. Pathetically, Costello's most deeply felt grudge appeared to be that he and his wife had not been invited to one of Hyacinth Bucket's candlelight suppers at Kirribilli House. And now it was never going to happen. Goodness, how sad. Poor Petey. Silly Petey. Gutless Petey.

Obviously none of this helped to restore calm to an already quivering Liberal partyroom. There was more hand-wringing over the missed opportunity for change, and much quoting of the well-worn slogan 'disunity means death.' It was left to the Mad Monk, of all people, to put the affair into some kind of perspective. Momentarily abandoning his Catholic dogma for the comforts of Zen Buddhism, Tony Abbott assured an interviewer, 'Shit happens.'

The book was something of a two-week wonder, but it achieved one unexpected benefit for Howard: by putting the government back in the spotlight, it brought Kevin Rudd's bandwagon to a temporary halt. Rudd was still hurtling backwards and forwards across the country, pausing only to chat to any available disc jockey, especially those appealing to the youth market, but he was no longer making daily headlines.

This did not mean the media gloss was wearing off; far from it. The polls remained solid, with Labor maintaining its ten-point overall lead and Rudd regaining lost ground as preferred prime minister. But this was now seen more as the status quo than a cause for wonder, something which was deeply disturbing to Coalition supporters and a source of increasing optimism to their Labor counterparts.

Certainly Rudd himself, while still warning everyone who would listen against over-confidence, appeared to be thriving on it. I caught up with him at the village of Tyalgum, in the Tweed Valley, where he dropped in for a lightning visit to assure a cheering crowd of men, women, children, dogs and horses that a Labor government would not drown their habitat by damming the Oxley River to provide water for south-eastern Queensland, as Malcolm Turnbull had proposed. This was a very different politician from the edgy control freak I had met at the ALP's national conference in Sydney; he worked the crowd like a pro and was assured, relaxed and funny – amazingly, he seemed to be enjoying it, which is more than could be said for Howard, who has never looked comfortable on the campaign trail. If Rudd could only keep it up, I thought, he just might make it.

★

I revised my odds; Howard was now, I decided, no better than an even-money bet. This was hardly an overwhelming declaration of faith in Rudd, but it was the most optimistic I'd felt about Labor for more than six years. I wasn't the only one feeling the earth starting to move; on the opinion page of the *Australian* the legendary Arthur Sinodinis (now nearly as rich as Mycenas) emerged from the depths of private industry to assure us that Howard was not really old, tired and generally past his use-by date but a positive explosion of energy. Not everyone agreed; in the Melbourne *Sun-Pictorial* the most right-wing of all the columnists, Andrew Bolt, joined the *Sydney Morning Herald*'s rather less predictable Paul Sheehan in declaring that it was time for Howard to go. Then the father of all Howard-huggers, the biographer who had judiciously awarded his hero the title of Best Prime Minister Ever, David Barnett, also jumped out of the boat: Howard, he sorrowfully stated, could not win and it was time he exited voluntarily to preserve his dignity and threw the hospital pass to Costello, who obviously couldn't win either but who didn't have any dignity worth preserving.

Meanwhile the Haneef case had unravelled completely: all charges had been dropped and Haneef had immediately returned to India, an action which Kevin Andrews (who had, after all, effectively ordered his deportation by revoking his visa) preposterously asserted was suspicious. The smearing continued: Andrews further politicised the case by releasing some (but not all) of the evidence on which he had cancelled the visa, which turned out to have already been put to Haneef by the police and then discarded. A furphy that the Indian police had found an al-Qaeda connection proved to be equally groundless. As the minister, police and prosecutor settled down to an unedifying shit-fight in which everyone blamed everyone else, Mick Keelty manfully insisted that it wasn't over; the investigation into Haneef could go on for years.

Haneef, now something of a home-town hero, announced that he would be happy to accept honorary Australian citizenship in lieu of compensation. Unsurprisingly this was not offered, and of course an apology was out of the question. Asked whether he thought Andrews might consider one, Alexander Downer snapped, 'What do you want him to do? Eat dirt?

Grovel? Come on, get real.' His frustration was understandable. The Haneef affair had revealed so many layers of incompetence and political chicanery that public trust, both at home and abroad, in Australia's security services had copped a terrible hiding. A number of commentators called for Andrews to be sacked, and Keelty's federal police were compared unfavourably with the Keystone Kops. Even Rudd, while insisting that he remained as tough as ever on terrorism, belatedly demanded a judicial inquiry.

In the end the public appeared as bewildered by the whole affair as the politicians: Newspoll showed that 49 per cent approved of the way the government had handled it, 33 per cent didn't and the remaining 18 per cent were just confused. But simultaneously, the government's lead over the ALP on who was better equipped to handle national security fell from twenty points to twelve. And Labor's lead on voting intentions actually picked up a couple of points, going from ten to twelve. Whatever the government was doing, it wasn't working.

In the circumstances it was probably just as well that business was finally ready to kick off its own advertising campaign. It had been a long time coming, with the wider business community split over whether what would inevitably be seen as partisan support for the government was a good idea, especially with the government in such deep trouble, but the dyed-in-the-wool Howard supporters had eventually kicked in for what they claimed would be an entirely non-political exercise. Just how non-political was revealed when the first ad showed a boarded-up shopfront with a sign proclaiming, 'Closed by union bosses.' In case the message still hadn't got across, the group released a piece of economic modelling purporting to show an inevitable rise in interest rates of 1.7 per cent if Rudd gained power and dismantled the policy formerly known as

WorkChoices. A superficial examination revealed that this analysis was based on the assumption that Labor would re-introduce pattern bargaining, a policy which Rudd and Gillard had specifically and repeatedly ruled out, but hey, you can't run a scare campaign without a scare, even if the scare isn't actually real.

It was doubly fortunate that the business ads were running, because the government wasn't having much luck with its own. With the taxpayers now up for more than $40 million for industrial-relations ads alone, the new series screeched to a halt when it was revealed that an actor playing a concerned father led another life as a building employer and was accused of dudding three teenagers, including his own son. That ad was pulled and Howard and his fellow ministers went back to berating Rudd for his association with state Labor governments, a tactic which had not been notably successful either.

But at least we now knew why they were doing it. As parliament was about to resume Malcolm Farr, the Sydney *Daily Telegraph*'s highly respected political correspondent, produced a genuinely sensational leak from the government's pollster, the dreaded Mark Textor. A secret poll had found that Howard was perceived by the electorate as old and dishonest, sneaky and out of touch. Extraordinarily, Howard went to air on John Laws' show to confirm it: 'There's nothing particularly new in that, I'm not particularly amazed by it,' he said dismissively.

What was certainly news was Textor's recommendation for a last, desperate strategy. It hardly mentioned Rudd himself; the inference was that Rudd had survived the worst the government could do and was now just too hard a target. Julia Gillard, however, was seen as vulnerable, especially if she could be connected to the unions. The mud cannon was to be re-aimed in that direction. But most importantly, go for the states: blame the Labor state governments for everything, and don't hesitate to intervene whenever possible. It looked like the last, best hope of a wedge.

Since Rudd had been making a point of greater co-operation with the states (the mantra of 'end the blame game' had long ago replaced the 'bridge too far' and the 'fork in the road') this at least made a point of difference. The fact that Rudd was proposing to cut down on special-purpose grants under section 96 of the constitution, and entrust the states with more responsibility in making their own spending decisions, gave the strategy a stronger focus. But it was fraught with risk. For starters, Australians tend to identify strongly with their states, especially outside New South Wales and Victoria. An open attack by Canberra could easily provoke a backlash, the more so as all the state premiers were considerably more popular than John Howard. However, no one had any better ideas, so the decision was taken to follow the pollster.

Textor's strategy was a terrific story, but almost as good as the story itself was the speculation about who leaked it. Costello, in a last strike against Howard? Howard himself, in a desperate bid for the sympathy vote? Textor, to cover himself in the event of defeat? Or some apparatchik with a grudge? Whatever the answer, there could be no doubt that there was a rat in the ranks, which would have done nothing to reassure a panicky Liberal Party.

Furthermore, when had the decision to hit the states been made? As Howard quickly pointed out, the report was months old, and he thought the position had improved since then. Well, not according to the polls, and he certainly hadn't got any younger – nor, as far as could be ascertained, more honest, less sneaky, etcetera. Textor's findings had in fact been delivered to the government on 21 June – the very day, Aboriginal critics noted bitterly, Howard had announced his decision to invade the Northern Territory in pursuit of Aboriginal child abuse. It was probably too paranoid to think that this was a test run before taking on the states themselves, but that did not prevent a lot of people from suggesting it anyway.

★

Certainly the Textor tactic made a bit of sense of the otherwise inexplicable Mersey caper. On 1 August Howard made a return appearance on YouTube to announce that he was taking over a small hospital in Devonport, Tasmania, which the state government had marked for downgrading. After two comprehensive inquiries it had been decided to rationalise the state's hospital services, and the Mersey Hospital was one of the losers. Naturally the good citizens of Devonport were miffed, and as it happened they lived in the electorate of Braddon, held by the Libs by a margin of just 1 per cent. Enter the prime minister, bearing $45 million.

The idea, of course, was hardly novel. John Winston Howard was to pork-barrelling what Elvis was to rock 'n' roll. Even in normal times he was likely to appear in the midst of a family of swinging voters in a marginal seat, grabbing a kissable baby from the surprised parent's arms and replacing it with a large taxpayer-signed money order redeemable at any government agency for a down payment on the community amenity of choice. Facing a tight election, there was no stopping him. The practice, as both the head of Treasury, Ken Henry, and Howard's own loyal treasurer liked to remind us, was both appalling in terms of policy and unsustainable in terms of economics, but Howard believed, and he had a certain amount of circumstantial evidence in support of this, that it bought votes, and that was all that mattered.

In the past Howard's porking of the electorate had included everything from a handsome rolled roast, in the form of a new football ground for the St George Leagues Club, to a few tasty spare ribs, in a cash handout for pensioners; the bill at the government charcuterie had added up to many hundreds of millions, perhaps even billions, but then, that's politics. And the point was that he had got away with it; there had been a bit of muttering about how the profligacy put pressure on inflation and therefore on interest rates, and the odd grumble about bad policy outcomes, but no one had really queried Howard's right to play Santa Claus every three years. After all, in his position most of them would have done the same.

But even in Australia there were limits, and this time our Dear Leader had exceeded them. Not only was it truly terrible health management and a blatant intrusion into the state government's constitutional role, but it was almost certain to backfire: bad policy, bad politics, bad populism. Little Johnny may have pulled off the trifecta. The initial reaction across the country was that it was just too blatant, too cynical. Throwing a heap of cash at a hospital found to be unviable by a series of painstaking inquiries, just because it happened to be in a marginal seat – what kind of a precedent was that setting? No one had been consulted about it: not the Tasmanian government, not the federal cabinet (let alone the Treasury), not even the hospital administration.

After attending to his dropped jaw, health minister Tony Abbott proclaimed loyally that the decision represented a 'seismic shift' in the way health services (and perhaps lots of other services too) were to be delivered in Australia; any community that felt itself unfairly treated by a state government should come directly to the commonwealth. Or perhaps not: Howard hastily jumped in with the qualification that he was not actually seeking a 'tectonic' shift. Abbott somersaulted vigorously in agreement: of course, the situation in the city of Devonport in the electorate of Braddon was actually unique. So would everyone please stop ringing his office, because the cheque would definitely not be in the mail after all. Education minister Julie Bishop, carried away by the frenzy, suggested that the commonwealth might also be prepared to hurl some money at schools which felt they were hard done by; after all, it was an election year, which apparently meant open slather and Rafferty's rules, so why stop at hospitals? She too had to be hosed down.

But this only drew more attention to the highly selective treatment meted out to Devonport. At this point the more rational members of the government noted that there were 150 federal electorates in Australia, and every one of them had at least one problem that could be fixed by a big squirt of commonwealth money. Alright, the majority didn't really come into the picture because they were safely held by one party or another, but for the purposes of the 2007 election at least 40 electorates could be called marginal. From now on any Howard minister who visited one would need police protection from lobby groups eager for their bit, all of whom would point to the Mersey Hospital as undeniable proof that Howard had plenty of money to hand out when it suited him. When, as was inevitable, they got knocked back, they would not be happy.

Indeed, not even all the voters of Braddon were happy. The good citizens of Burnie, whose bigger and more central hospital was meant to get an upgrade at the expense of the scaled-down Mersey, would now miss out. The inhabitants of Wynyard might well feel they were just as entitled to a hospital as Devonport. And even at Devonport itself there might be less than universal rejoicing. At least one staff member had resigned in protest at the ad-hockery of the decision and others might follow. Replacing them in the present climate would be very difficult. When the hapless Abbott was sent to Tasmania with instructions to realise Howard's promise, he was greeted with suspicion and hostility. The state health minister, Lara Giddings, said he brought no justification for the proposal, no detail and no blueprint for how the hospital was actually to operate. What started as a cynical ploy degenerated within a week into a cruel hoax, a verdict endorsed by the Tasmanian Liberal Senator Stephen Parry, who said bluntly that the decision was a disaster and the hospital should be closed. In fact, he had written a passionate letter to Ms Giddings to that effect.

From every point of view, the decision was so bad as to raise doubts about Howard's grip on reality. Now it appeared that he was totally poll-driven. Subsequent forays into other marginals, like propping up a timber mill in Eden-Monaro in New South Wales and an attempt to interfere with council amalgamations in Queensland, could be similarly discounted as mere electoral opportunism. As financial management descended into a vote-buying farce the business community, that impartial guardian of economic rectitude, maintained an embarrassed silence.

But the fact that the strategy was appalling policy didn't mean that it wouldn't buy a few votes. A stoush in Queensland could be particularly effective, given that this was the state in which Labor hoped to – had to – win a swag of seats to give Rudd any chance. Peter Beattie's plan to amalgamate dozens of broke or near-broke local councils was undoubtedly sensible policy; indeed, it was long overdue. But it was also highly unpopular: ratepayers might bag their local councillors mercilessly, but at least they were still local councillors. The idea of having them replaced by outsiders, especially in the parochial rural areas, induced widespread fear. Rudd, seeing the problems, publicly opposed compulsory amalgamations and said that it would be preferable to negotiate voluntary ones – better for him, certainly, but not for Beattie, who was sick of pussyfooting around and wanted to get the issue fixed once and for all.

Rudd pleaded with him to at least postpone the legislation until next year when the federal election would be out of the way; Beattie, exhibiting a positively Howard-like stubbornness, refused and rammed the law through state parliament. He had already refused councils the right to hold referendums or plebiscites, although some were defiantly, if pointlessly, going ahead anyway. The issue appeared closed.

Once again, enter Howard, waving the Crosby–Textor brief. It was an affront to democracy, he spluttered, and he wasn't going to see Queenslanders left voiceless. The commonwealth would tell the electoral office to run plebiscites for those who wanted them, and if they happened to take place on the same day as the federal election, my, what a happy coincidence that would be. Beattie responded by passing a law to sack any council that took up the offer, and Howard trumped him by saying the plebiscites could be initiated by community groups, private citizens, anyone who wanted one.

The idea was outrageous: apart from the fact that the plebiscites would have no effect whatsoever – the amalgamation laws had been passed and would stand – local government had always been the sole responsibility of the states. When a Labor government proposed a referendum to include local government as a constitutional entity in its own right, Howard led the opposition. For him now to pose as the saviour of shires and municipalities was nothing short of grotesque. But it could certainly cause trouble for Rudd. Several marginal seats were affected, the most worrying being Petrie, where Redcliffe was trying to resist the high-rise developers, and Leichhardt, where Port Douglas was determined to maintain its exclusivity. Even if Beattie was right, and the voters were able to distinguish between the state and the feds – and Rudd was making his opposition very public – it would make for a very messy polling day and give the Coalition canvassers a wonderful opportunity to confuse voters. The only comfort was that it at least put paid to one of Howard's more bizarre campaigns, the one where he claimed that Rudd was using the state premiers to do his dirty work for him. If this was the case, clearly no one had told Peter Beattie.

★

Early in August, Rudd, apparently stung by criticism that he was adopting too much of a Me Too policy (he had even refused to commit to reversing Howard's Mersey pork-barrel) made another lunge for the youth vote by opening a new interactive website: KEVIN 07, complete with matching T-shirt ($7, naturally, but add $8 for postage and handling). Asked whether this was just an attempt to appear cool, he replied unconvincingly: 'Oh, we're already cool.' Howard, in response, returned to YouTube to suggest that youth might like to do a gap year in the defence forces after leaving school but before going on to higher education or to enter the workforce. He had actually announced this policy at least three times already, but what the heck: this was the first time on a website. Lacking Rudd's facility with words, he failed to describe the army as 'cool'. Both leaders then moved to a different part of the net to have a discussion (debate would be too strong a word) about religious values, a cloyingly bland exercise allegedly watched by some 100,000 God-botherers.

There was no vote taken after it. But what evidence there was suggested that Howard might have needed the reassurance more than Rudd did. Undoubtedly the weirdest poll of a bizarre election year – so far at least – was the one from the left-leaning Australia Institute. Clive Hamilton and Josh Fear asked about 1000 respondents which of a list of six politicians were destined for heaven and which for hell. Given the names on the list the results were entirely predictable, but Hamilton and Fear nevertheless subjected their findings to an apparently serious analysis in terms of party, religion, age and public standing. For the record, Peter Garrett looks most certain of salvation, on 74 per cent; Bob Brown is second on 66, followed by Kevin Rudd on 61. Tony Abbott and Pauline Hanson just make it through the pearly gates, tied on 52. The only one condemned to eternal damnation is John Howard, who falls short on 47. Better luck next time – if there proved to be a next time.

> *Dancing is the perpendicular expression of horizontal desire.* —George Bernard Shaw

★ 12.

When parliament returned in August after the long winter break, the grimness of the mood mirrored the bleakness of the Canberra weather. This was it – the last chance. If the government was to make a comeback, it had to get started in the fortnight before the house rose for the APEC extravaganza. It would return for a week afterwards, but that would be a formality, a chance for ceremonial speeches from world dignitaries and last-minute wrap-ups. The serious business had to start now. There were those on the government side who still hoped that the business might include a leadership change, but that was wishful thinking. That issue had effectively been resolved when Costello wimped it in 2006. Like it or not, the Coalition's fortunes now lay in the hands of John Winston Howard, and the question was how he would face the immediate test.

There was no longer any real doubt that interest rates were going to rise on 8 August: the fifth rise since the last election and one that could only have been worse timed if it had come a month or two closer to the forthcoming election. But at least the government had plenty of warning, and some of the response had already been signalled: blame the states (naturally), stress the overall strength of the economy and insist that it was only the government's good management that had stopped rates going even higher, as they would have under Labor. Peter Costello had the script down pat, and when the Reserve Bank delivered the bad news he went in full bore.

Sure, the rise would hurt, but remember that the basic cause was the sheer, gang-busting strength of the economy: we were going almost *too* well. And look at the trade-off: unemployment at hitherto-unachievable lows, a job guaranteed to every citizen who wanted one. Remember also that while interest rates had certainly risen they were still at something vaguely resembling historic lows, certainly less than that terrible, unforgettable 17 per cent under Labor. And of course, it wasn't the government's fault; he, Peter Costello, had been the one to insist on the Reserve Bank's independence, and he couldn't help it if the buggers had gone mad. And of course, it went without saying, under Labor things would be much, much worse. Why, the wages break-out alone ... And if you didn't believe that, look at the states, irresponsibly borrowing money for fripperies like health and education and transport, while any absolutely necessary pork-barrelling the commonwealth did would come from running down the surplus, something altogether different – even if the elitist economists were too out of touch with the pragmatic world of political opportunism to see it.

It wasn't a bad story – well, actually it was, but working on the well-proven principle that bullshit baffles brains, it would have been worth a try. Unfortunately by the time Costello hit the airwaves, it was too late. Howard had blown it. After the Crosby–Textor research showing he was seen as mean, tricky, sneaky and dishonest, you might think that the Dear Leader would have broken the habit of a lifetime and admitted to a fair cop: the sloganeering at the 2004 election about interest rates just hadn't been matched by the reality since. He could still have claimed it was honestly intended, although whether he would have been believed is another matter. But he could hardly deny it was wrong. However, he, John Howard, was never wrong. So, confronted with the advertising that said, in so many words, that his government would keep interest rates at record lows, he weaselled. He *himself* had never said it: you could search through every speech he had ever made, and he would be happy to make them available. All he had said was the rates under the Coalition would always be lower than rates under Labor, and that was still true; it must be, because he was still saying it.

Of course, advertisements had appeared promising to keep rates at record lows, but that wasn't him; that was the Liberal Party, a totally unconnected entity. If people chose to believe those ads, well, he could hardly be held responsible. What he had said was what he had said, and that was all there was to it. And in any case the ads had only run for a week in 2004, after which they (and presumably the promise) 'disappeared'. Actually, they didn't; they were still on the party's website nearly three years later, but that was a matter of history. We had moved on.

As a legalistic defence, it had some merit: judges committed to black-letter law could well have come to the conclusion that while the clear intention of the accused was to mislead the public, in a strictly technical sense he had not actually done so, even if his agents and associates had. But for a public sick to death of Howard's lawyer-speak, this pig just wouldn't fly. The punters knew what they had heard in 2004, and a great many of them had acted on it; they had followed Howard's invitation to trust him and borrowed up big on the strength of it. Now they were in up to their necks and the waters were still rising;

the Reserve Bank's quarterly report, published in the same week, held out the unambiguous prospect of another rise soon enough, perhaps even before the end of the year (though not, surely, before the election).

Moreover, Howard was unrepentant; while he expressed regret that the latest rise might have hurt 'some families and some homebuyers', he was not about to mend his extravagant ways. Economists were divided about the extent to which Howard's previous profligate pork-barrelling had contributed to inflationary pressure and consequent interest-rate rises, but they were unanimous in stating that restraint was now necessary; a pre-election spending spree would make further rises certain. Howard told them they didn't know what they were talking about and that as long as his spending came from the budget surplus it would be quite okay. Yet another failure in Economics 101. But it was hardly surprising; the *Financial Review* had estimated that the government's promises to date totalled three times those of Labor, and Labor's were covered by more than $3 billion in spending cuts already identified by the industrious Lindsay Tanner, including no less than $84 million on government spin-doctors, who had proliferated like cane toads in the past three years.

Government members braced for another pasting in the opinion polls, and at first it appeared they would get it: a Sunday Galaxy poll predicted that Howard would lose his own seat of Bennelong by a comfortable margin, which suggested that things were even worse than feared. But Monday's Nielsen poll surprised everyone; the government had actually recovered ground, being now only ten points behind Labor on the two-party-preferred rating. This wasn't exactly nirvana; it was in fact precisely the same result as the previous week's Newspoll, which had been seen as a cause for despair. But the fact that it was better than expected gave the Libs a big lift, as did the accompanying survey which suggested, incredibly, that a great many voters still believed Howard: things would indeed have been worse under Labor. Perhaps, just perhaps, the backbenchers murmured, the old master of mendacity could still turn it around.

★

Certainly Howard did not lack the chutzpah to try. It was revealed that he had written a stern letter to Iraq's prime minister, Nouri al-Maliki, telling him to pull his finger out and do something about the sectarian violence, because the Australian public was getting really fed up with it. The revelation almost defied parody ... almost, but not quite:

Scene: A secure office somewhere in Baghdad. Nouri al-Maliki is seated behind a desk checking the latest casualty figures. There is a knock at the door.

Maliki: [*resignedly*] Come in.

[*Enter a small, grinning, perspiring, twitching person.*]

Maliki: And you are ...?

Howard [*for it is he*]: John Winston Howard, Prime Minister of Australia. G'day, or Shalom, as I think you people say.

Maliki: No. [*pause*] Australia, is it? The Australian ambassador told me a joke the other day. He said, 'John Hunt is a coward.' I did not understand. Perhaps you can explain ... no? Then what is your business?

Howard: Well, it's about all the fighting that's going on among you lot. I can tell you we're getting pretty sick of it Down Under.

Maliki: It may surprise you to learn that we don't like it much either. So?

Howard: Well, I'm here to tell you that unless you pull up your socks and do something about it, we'll have to take action. The opinion polls won't stand for it much longer. We'll have to consider the position of our soldiers. They might even have to leave.

Maliki: Yes, I suppose that might help. But remind me: you have soldiers here? What exactly do they do?

Howard: Well, some of them guard our embassy ...

Maliki: The Australian embassy. That's very helpful.

Howard: ... and there are others down south, in the thick of it.

Maliki: Doing what?

Howard: Well, until recently they were looking after the Japanese.

Maliki: Yes, the Japanese ... I believe they have left. So are you too planning to cut and run?

Howard: Oh no no no no no no no. Far from it. It is just that if things don't improve, public support for our presence here may no longer be sustainable.

Maliki: But as I understand it there has never been any public support. Almost from the first day the Australian people have vigorously opposed your sycophantic, token involvement. Why are you now mouthing this empty rhetoric, my little Man of Steel?

Howard: Well, I have this election coming on ...

Maliki: Ah, an election. I understand. Well, good luck to you. And may I give you one piece of advice?

Howard: Oh yes, thank you, Caliph or Sultan or whatever it is, please please. I'm a little desperate ...

Maliki: Change your name to John Hunt.

[*curtain*]

Alexander Downer delivered the punchline in a letter of his own to Maliki: if Maliki didn't smarten up and lift his game, our hilarious foreign minister threatened, it was even possible that the present government of Australia could lose office. Maliki's response to the prospect of this unimaginable international catastrophe sadly remains unknown.

Downer then told the Australian parliament that Labor's policy of phased withdrawal from Iraq was not shared by any key country in the world. Well, apart from the United Kingdom, which was implementing it; Japan, Spain, South Korea, Italy and the Netherlands, which had already implemented it; also Poland, Denmark, Thailand, Singapore, Portugal and The Philippines, to name but a few; not to mention eleven American presidential candidates, 270 Congressional Democrats and 23 Republicans, and the vast majority of the American people. Oh, and quite a lot of Australians thought it was a good idea, too.

★

For the moment at least, though, Kevin Rudd was still more interested in domestic policy. Having got huge traction out of housing affordability, he went further, with a proposal to build cheaper rental accommodation for lower- and middle-income earners who could not afford to get a foothold in the housing market. Peter Costello ridiculed it, but Howard mused that it was worth thinking about, probably because it was popular with the building industry as well as the general public. Rudd also found $100 million for innovation and $32.5 million for a pre-school program in partnership with the Brotherhood of St Lawrence, an organisation too respected for even Downer to sneer at (instead he sneered at an earnest schoolboy who dared to ask him about climate change, accusing him of being a Labor plant – paranoid as well as vicious). And for good measure Rudd promised to nominate the Ningaloo Reef for World Heritage protection.

Howard's reply was to offer a derisory $6.5 million to combat global – that's right, global – climate change. Even this pittance was too much for some of his backbench: four flat-earthers wrote a report saying they still didn't believe that people had anything to do with it. Well, Howard probably didn't either, but at least he could see that scepticism was no longer a tenable political position.

However, what he had christened Actively Pragmatic Federalism – getting stuck into the states – clearly was, and when parliament sat he took the opportunity to step up the fight with Peter Beattie over council amalgamations. Beattie had threatened to sack, fine or simply expunge from the face of the earth councils which co-operated in Howard's plebiscites. Howard now proposed legislation which would override Queensland law and remove the premier's powers. Beattie's heavily ironic response that Howard might also like to run a plebiscite about whether people wanted a nuclear reactor in their neighbourhood went straight past the prime minister, who replied that the siting of reactors would be a purely commercial decision. Council amalgamations went to basic human rights. 'Let your people be heard,' he intoned in the manner of Moses demanding that Pharaoh free the Israelites.

By now constitutional conservatives had run out of adjectives to describe just how off-the-planet, how extreme, how insupportable, Howard's interventions had become; the only hope was that they would go away after the election, like the Mersey Hospital rescue operation, which was rapidly turning into an unworkable tin full of worms. The Queensland caper broke every convention, but it was such a blatant vote-grabbing exercise it could surely not constitute a precedent. No one took it seriously; government members had trouble keeping a straight face as they held forth about the upholding of democratic principles and letting the people's voice be heard. In policy terms it was a one-off, a dirty joke.

But it was also a truly terrific wedge. It left Rudd with a no-win choice: if he opposed it, he would look as if he was pusillanimously backing away from his previous rejection of the amalgamation policy and falling in line with Beattie, but if he supported it, he would be accused of feebly following Howard into mindless populism to pick a fight with a Labor premier in his home state. In the event he took the latter option, which in strictly political terms was probably the least dangerous, but from now on it was going to be hard to claim that federal Labor was driven by sound economic and social policy. For his critics it was yet further proof that he was too weak to stand up to Howard. The prime minister had already gained mileage from Rudd's assertion that on macroeconomics there was not a sliver of difference between Labor and the government. He had even made a joke out of it: Rudd, he said, was indulging in echonomics, ho ho ho. Barnaby Joyce, more down to earth, opined that if the Opposition leader got any closer to Howard, he'd need permission from Janette.

Rudd desperately needed Howard to do something he could safely disagree with, loudly and unequivocally. So Howard obligingly gave it to him: Australia, he announced, was ready *in principle* to sell uranium to India. Having already made the same decision with regard to China he may have thought that the follow-up was logical and uncontroversial, but for Labor at least there was a huge difference. Unlike China, India was not a signatory to the Nuclear Non-Proliferation Treaty, which was the touchstone of ALP policy. Downer tried to turn the argument around: because India was not a signatory to the NPT, the United Nations was unable to inspect its facilities to make sure the Indians were not using their reactors to make weapons fuel. If Australia allowed India to buy its uranium, it could insist on the right to inspect sixteen of the country's 22 reactors. While the rest, suggested an interviewer, went on making bombs? Well, something of the kind, admitted our irrepressible foreign minister, and giggled. He added that no Australian uranium would be made into bombs, and in any case the Indians had some uranium of their own. The argument, as Labor's Robert McClelland pointed out, was spurious: by supplying India's demand for uranium for peaceful purposes, Australia was allowing India to divert its own uranium to weapons manufacture. Howard and Downer shrugged it off; the decision was basically a commercial one, based on the old adage that if we didn't sell it to them, someone else would, the excuse of every heroin dealer on his way to a just retribution.

The chaotic parliamentary session was also notable for the fact that it included Peter Costello's fiftieth birthday, the occasion for a major piss-up but not, alas, for that long-awaited invitation to an intimate evening with John and Janette. As Anthony Albanese unkindly pointed out, the date marked the 4174th day of their partnership; surely the treasurer at last deserved a guernsey? Well, no, and in case anyone had forgotten why, the sordid evidence re-emerged.

The week before Paul Daley had written an apparently innocuous piece in the *Bulletin* in which he mentioned that back in 2005 Costello had told contacts that Howard could not win another election, but he, Costello, could. Now someone asked Costello if he had made the remark, and Costello smirked it off – no, he had no idea where journalists got their stories, third-hand pub gossip, perhaps. This prompted the *7.30 Report*'s Michael Brissenden to state that far from being third-hand pub gossip, this was first-hand fact: he, Daley and another reporter, Tony Wright, had been having dinner with the treasurer when he said it. Not only that, but Costello had gone on to say that if Howard did not step down by mid-2006 he would challenge for the leadership, and if he lost, go to the backbench and carp at Howard and destroy him. The journalists had taken the braggadocio as something they could use, without attributing it to Costello; however, the next morning a Costello minder rang to tell them the comments were off-the-record. Rather than refusing to accept this retrospective decision and telling him to get stuffed, the three copped it, and there things lay until Costello told his outright lie.

Sprung, he tried to bluff it out. None of it had happened: he hadn't challenged, gone to the backbench, carped or destroyed. True, but all that proved, yet again, was that he was gutless and treacherous, Costello the Yellow. In the process he had lied blatantly both to the public and the parliament, which should have been a sacking offence, but Howard didn't care and neither, one suspected, did the public. In a brawl between a politician and a journalist, most voters would not have known which to boo most loudly. But once again, it was a distraction Howard did not need; most of the last week of the sitting was taken up with accusations and counter-accusations. While it probably didn't hurt the government much, it meant that yet again attention was diverted from the main game: smashing Rudd and his colleagues. As the pollies eventually departed to prepare for the terrors of APEC, the government was still to land a substantial blow. But then, perhaps it wouldn't need to. Suddenly John Howard got lucky again.

★

When interest rates had risen a fortnight earlier, dismayed government ministers snarled that the champagne corks must have been popping in the Opposition leader's office. This was cruel and cynical; Kevin Rudd and his colleagues were careful to assume the gravest of demeanours, assuring the punters that they were really, truly concerned about the plight of homebuyers and indeed all Australian families. But it was possible to detect a bit of extra spring in their step; perhaps, just perhaps, this was the final straw. John Howard's carefully cultivated but largely undeserved reputation as a good economic manager might be destroyed. The hope was quickly dashed: the next week's poll revealed the extraordinary news that nearly a third of voters still believed that rates would be higher under Labor and another half thought nothing would change. Only a loyal 7 per cent considered that Kevin Rudd would do better. As the waters of electoral discontent surged ever higher around him, the rock of the economy remained Howard's one safe refuge; while he could keep the debate centred on the economy, there was still hope. And even as he hoped, the world changed for him – or at least enough of it to make a difference.

The financial crisis triggered by the collapse of the American sub-prime mortgage market might or might not lead to serious problems in Australia, but there was a genuine fear among overstretched local mortgagees that it could. Economic commentators donned the sack cloth and ashes and rang their bells as they walked the streets proclaiming that the end of the world was nigh. And the great thing about it was that barely a handful of voters actually understood the issue. Indeed, even when the said commentators explained it to them, most still didn't; why should the fact that some American institutions had made dodgy loans and were now getting caught impinge on Australia's system, which we had been repeatedly assured was absolutely solid?

Our prime minister made no real attempt to resolve this apparent contradiction, but stated firmly – and for once believably – that whatever was happening was not his fault. This time, he was not part of the problem, but he was definitely the only possible solution. Only the partnership of John Howard and Peter Costello had the experience, the know-how, the tough-mindedness, to avert the looming threat. Certainly you would not go to the posturing neophyte Kevin Rudd, who had absolutely no grounding in the difficult science of economic management. Hang on: the experience that couldn't produce a single positive monthly trade balance in a six-year commodities boom? The experience that had given you record high current-account deficits while untruthfully claiming that the country was free of government debt? The experience of nine, yes, nine consecutive interest-rate rises, with the almost certain prospect of more to come? Yes, that experience – the Howard experience. And, incredibly, it was the only aspect of our Dear Leader that still appealed to us.

And it was also the reason that the government backbenchers greeted the US meltdown with ill-concealed joy and fervently hoped it could run for at least another couple of months. It was not quite the *Tampa* – you only get one *Tampa* in a lifetime – but it was the next best thing. Now it was only a matter of working out how to use it as the basis of a detailed campaign: from the sub-prime to the particulars.

Kevin Rudd's appeal, on the other hand, was broader. Voters generally believed that he'd be better than Howard at everything except the economy and national security (although the gap on the latter was narrowing), but the belief was less firmly held – at least, that was the Libs' fervent hope. Now it was time to test it again, so a story appeared in a Sunday tabloid asserting that four years ago Rudd, in the company of another Labor member, Warren Snowdon, and the notorious editor of Rupert Murdoch's *New York Post*, Col Allan, had visited a 'gentlemen's club' called Scores and may or may not have behaved badly. Shock, horror. Rudd had not been the Opposition leader at the time; he had merely been a delegate to the United Nations on a night off. He had also, he confessed, been pissed and remembered nothing; nonetheless it had been an error of judgement (yet another one) and he regretted it.

My immediate take was the same as Peter Beattie's: it was unlikely to do the uptight Opposition leader any harm at all. Those already disposed to see the man as an unctuous God-botherer who was too good to be true would have their suspicions that he was a hypocrite confirmed, while the rest of the electorate would probably think, naughty boy, but he's only human. The view in the front bar of the Billinudgel was that the only thing he really did wrong was to ring his wife next morning and apologise.

And the Labor Party as a whole breathed a deep sigh of relief. For months there had been rumours of sensationally sordid revelations about Rudd's private life simmering away in the Liberal Party's dirt unit, ready for release as soon as the election was called. I had heard several versions, the most serious (and unlikely) involving the constant use of call girls; I put this one to a trusted Canberra source and got the unanswerable response: 'Come on; when would he have the time?' Nonetheless the rumours persisted, and finally seeing them in print got rid of one more anxiety. If the worst the indefatigable muckrakers could dig up was a story that four years ago on an overseas trip Rudd got pissed and was inveigled into a girly bar, then there was not a lot to worry about. Unsurprisingly the journalist who put his name to the story was Glenn Milne, AKA the Poison Dwarf. Milne had obligingly tried to beat up the story by claiming that while in the bar Rudd had behaved inappropriately and had been asked to leave, which, according to Allan, Snowdon and the club's proprietor, was simply not true.

But at least as interesting as the story itself was the identity of its real source. Rudd had no doubt and suggested questioning Alexander Downer's office. When the ABC did so, a spokesandroid replied that they would not dignify the insinuation with an answer. Thank you, Mr Downer, we'll take that as a yes. Sensibly, other government ministers, notably Peter Costello and Tony Abbott, resisted the temptation to wallow in the prurience of it all; the subject of hi-jinks on overseas trips is not one that too many politicians would want to open up. Who could forget the tale of Memphis, and Malcolm Fraser's lost trousers? Now *that* really was a story. As in so many other fields, Rudd's alleged attempt at debauchery left him a pale shadow of the greats of the past, which in the narrow and censorious ambience of the times was probably just as well. The chastened leader then announced that he would see that the next lot of submarines on order for the navy were built in South Australia, and that he would fund kitchen gardens for primary schools so the tiny tots could learn healthy eating habits – and, perhaps, learn to throw mud at each other, a necessary life skill in Howard's Australia.

Howard, having stood loftily above the Rudd-gropes-lap-dancer scandal, as some backbenchers still optimistically hoped to portray it, now went back to basics and gave a speech about Why I Want to be Prime Minister for a Fifth Term. Appropriately there were five reasons: security, growth, fairness and balance (the motherhood formula), and then the killer, Aspirational Nationalism, a slogan no doubt brought to you by the same creative pen which all those years ago surprised with Incentivation. Aspirational Nationalism was Howard-speak for smashing the federal system: allowing the commonwealth to bypass the states at will, providing an opportunity for unlimited pork-barrelling. Howard's office confirmed enthusiastically that local councils and community groups would be able to bid for commonwealth grants for items such as libraries and sporting fields: Howard himself suggested he had bigger things in mind, such as ports and railways. But by now the principle was clear enough: sideline those Labor premiers.

In both practical and political terms Howard had arrived at a position which was the mirror image of Rudd's co-operative federalism. Rudd saw the fact that all six states had Labor governments as an unprecedented opportunity for overcoming the wasteful overlap between the commonwealth and the states, a chance to straighten out all the problems which had developed over a hundred years while maintaining the system of checks and balances. Howard recognised the lack of any Coalition state administrations as a once-in-a-lifetime opening for an uninhibited attack: the states were the enemy, and that was that. It was a total reversal of the traditional positions of their respective parties, but then, both men had spent months denying that they were hidebound ideologues. One must adapt to the prevailing circumstances, especially when there's an election to win.

★

Conveniently, on the morning after Howard's speech Peter Costello chose to announce the budget outcome, and as usual Treasury had grossly underestimated the size of the surplus. There was in fact no less than $17.3 billion to play with, which was actually a bit of an embarrassment; the government could not afford to be too blatant about adding to consumer demand at a time when everyone was so sensitive about interest rates, but you couldn't just stuff it all under the bed either. The solution? More funds. Together with the Future Fund, which would get an extra $7 billion, and the Education Fund, which would cop $1 billion, there would be $2.5 billion for a Health and Medical Investment Fund; and then there would be a big infrastructure fund, which was essentially a pinch from Infrastructure Australia, but with the important difference that it would be managed by politicians rather than by an independent board, thus maximising the opportunities for pork-barrelling. Aspirational Nationalism rules, okay?

But on the same day there was also bad news. The judge in the Haneef appeal handed down his verdict, which was that immigration minister Kevin Andrews's cancellation of the doctor's visa was invalid. The problem was not political chicanery but sheer incompetence: Andrews had applied the wrong section of the act. Howard said it was not over yet, the commonwealth would appeal and would keep on appealing, presumably in the hope that Haneef would eventually give up. But he could hardly deny that it made Andrews look like a goose. Just how goosey was made clear when Haneef's lawyers released the text of the second police interview, which made it clear that only the most dedicated paranoiac could have found evidence of guilt in it. But then, that's Howard's Australia.

However, the real blow came from Newspoll. The voting-intention part wasn't too bad: Labor had actually lost a couple of points in the primaries and its two-party-preferred lead was back to 10 per cent. Rudd's lead as preferred prime minister was up to seven points, and Howard's satisfaction rating was back in negative territory. But the cruncher was economic management: Howard had dropped six points, while Rudd had picked up three. And on keeping interest rates low, 34 per cent went for Howard and 27 for Rudd, with 22 per cent (the sensible ones) saying neither. Perhaps worst of all, for the first time twice as many people believed Labor would win as believed the Libs would hold on. It was clear that the Nielsen poll had been a false dawn; Howard's last rock was beginning to teeter. But there remained one unshakable source of comfort. The ever-reliable Dennis Shanahan pronounced that it was in fact a bad result for Labor, which should really have done much better. Howard must have been greatly relieved.

> *We are dancing on a volcano.*
> —Comte Narcisse Achille de Salvandy

★ 13.

The fortnight between the whimper that ended parliament and the bang that would start the APEC extravaganza was meant to be a breathing space, a time for both the pollies and the media to regather their scattered wits and take a sober look at the landscape. But of course it didn't work out like that; it never does. If anything, the pace increased as each side leapt forward to fill the vacuum it hoped the other would leave. Nonetheless, there was a certain amount of stocktaking, with the usual passionate-but-inconclusive results.

Labor's ascendancy could no longer be denied. The polls had stayed solid for months, and by now all but the die-hards among politicians, commentators, punters and bookmakers acknowledged that it would take something extraordinary to shift them. John Howard bravely drew comparisons with 1993, the year John Hewson lost the unlosable election to Paul Keating: then, the polls only really shifted in the last fortnight. Well, yes; but Kevin Rudd wasn't trying to sell a GST. True, said the Howard-huggers, but their man wasn't hated like Keating had been hated. Wait till the campaign proper started – then we'd see. The problem was that for most people the campaign had started long ago and they were already heartily sick of it. All they wanted now was to get it over and done with and get back to watching sport. On this reading, the Coalition was well and truly up shit creek in a barbed-wire canoe without a paddle, and it was every man and woman for themselves.

But it wasn't quite as simple as that. Although Labor's lead was substantial, it was still what the pundits described as *soft*; quite a few voters were not yet locked in either way. Moreover, the numbers reflected people rather than enrolled voters. The estimate was that there were still up to half-a-million adult Australians not on the rolls at the end of June, including some 35 per cent in the 18–25 age bracket, expected to go heavily Labor's way. In 2004 some 136,000 young voters had got themselves on the roll between the calling of the election and polling day, but since then the Coalition had sneakily changed the law so that in 2007, the rolls would close soon after Howard pulled the trigger. A large chunk of Labor's potential support would be disenfranchised. The ALP and the unions were both running frenzied campaigns to sign them up, but it would still be a bonus for the government.

More importantly, if Rudd was to march into the Lodge, the raw numbers had to translate into a minimum of sixteen seats, and suddenly the equation became a lot more dubious. Just after parliament rose I talked to Wayne Swan, Labor's indefatigable shadow treasurer and obsessive numbers man. Swan is a Queenslander, and the news from his home state was not good: the backlash against Peter Beattie's council amalgamations was more severe than most had predicted. Rudd had joined Howard in supporting plebiscites, which would go some way towards neutralising the issue, but Beattie had done little to defuse it. He had run a snap opinion poll which produced the unsurprising finding that 73 per cent of Queenslanders wanted strong, viable councils; Beattie preposterously claimed that this meant they supported the amalgamations. However, 52 per cent also supported plebiscites, so Beattie withdrew his opposition and threats of reprisals, as long as everyone understood that someone else was paying and the results would be totally ignored by his government. Labor had been hoping for a minimum of six seats in Queensland; now, Swan thought, there were only two certainties: Moreton and Bonner. Longman, Blair and Herbert were still chances, but Leichhardt would be very hard, and Flynn and Petrie were definitely out. To make up the seats that Labor needed would involve winning a smoky or two – Ryan, Bowman, Dickson, even Dawson. This was possible, but only if the swing was really on. And to make matters worse, Labor could even lose Capricornia. The only solace was that if Rudd narrowly missed out, he would at least have Beattie to blame.

On the other hand, South Australia still looked good: Labor could count on Kingston, Wakefield and Makin, and was a chance in Boothby. Tasmania looked okay now that Franklin had been sorted out: Bass and Braddon should both be won. In Victoria the only safe bet was Deakin, but McEwen and Latrobe were outside chances. In Western Australia, Labor's vulnerable seats in Swan and Cowan were both looking better, and there was a good chance of picking up Hasluck, although Stirling might be a bit too hard. Labor had been fairly confident about Solomon in the Northern Territory, but since the invasion no one could safely predict anything; Labor might even lose Lingiari. So the total to date was only eight reasonably certain with another seven possible; close, but no cigar.

Which brought us, as always, to New South Wales, where Labor had consistently under-performed. First cab off the rank was certainly Lindsay, and then the bellwether seat of Eden-Monaro, which the superstitious believed was the key to the election but was actually just another difficult marginal. Then there was Dobell, considered a serious possibility and less probably Page, further north. Labor was even looking at Cook, previously rated as a safe Liberal seat but now a little shaky after a horrendous pre-selection stoush in which the winner was accused of vote-buying and lying about his background, and was eventually replaced. But most of the drama centred around the two ministerial fortresses of Wentworth and Bennelong. Demographics had affected both, but in theory the sheer status of the incumbents – Malcolm Turnbull and John Howard – should have guaranteed them comfortable wins. But there were, as they say, extraordinary and reprehensible circumstances. Both faced celebrity opponents and serious controversies; both, it seemed, were more than a little on the nose among their normally placid constituents.

Turnbull, as the environment minister, was caught up in the furore over the proposal for a pulp mill in Tasmania's Tamar Valley. The timber conglomerate Gunns, which had replaced the Hydro as the permanent unelected government of Tasmania, had bullied and blackmailed the idea through the state parliament, and all that remained was for Turnbull to sign off on it. Normally he could have done so relatively unobtrusively and passed the buck back to Premier Paul Lennon, but suddenly Geoff Cousins, a close friend of John Howard whom the prime minister had controversially appointed to the board of Telstra, emerged as a deep greenie to challenge Turnbull's decision with a grass-roots campaign in Turnbull's own seat. The clash of the egos produced some wonderful exchanges. Turnbull snarled that Cousins was just a rich man determined to get his own way – which, coming from a multi-millionaire who had spent a motza to buy his own pre-selection in the mother of all branch stacks, showed chutzpah, if nothing else. Cousins replied silkily that he only wished he had Turnbull's money to spend. Turnbull suggested Cousins was unfit to sit on the Telstra board, and Cousins told him not to get his knickers in a twist. Howard, caught in a conflict of interest, said feebly that Turnbull was a great minister and Cousins was a great bloke, and would we please go away. Eventually a solution appeared: if Gunns would just move the bloody pulp mill somewhere else, everyone would be happy. The problem was that Gunns had already refused the proffered site because it would cost too much; however, if a major sweetener could be arranged ...? It wasn't much to ask in an election year.

In the meantime, Turnbull bought a bit of space by asking another group of scientists to recheck the figures. With any luck this would mean a decision could be postponed until after the election, or at least until the campaign, when the caretaker convention would mean the Opposition would have to be involved. Gunns, which had previously bluffed the Tasmanian government into a fast-track inquiry by threatening to pull out if it didn't get immediate approval, was now strangely silent; if nothing else, the process showed what a soft touch Paul Lennon had been. Howard, who had promised with hand on heart that he would not allow Tasmania to become a political football in 2007, as it had been in 2004, said he still hoped the mill would be built, but he wasn't pre-empting anything – well, not yet.

After all, he had troubles of his own; he had been sprung holding a secret meeting with heavies from the Exclusive Brethren, a particularly nasty religious cult known for its ability to brainwash the vulnerable and break up families. The Brethren did not actually vote, claiming exemption from the law on religious grounds. However, they had taken to interfering in elections to help ultra-conservatives combat the pernicious influence of the Left. In 2004, for instance, they had contributed a neat $370,000 to Howard's campaign, which would be very handy again this time around. In Tasmania and New Zealand the sect was under investigation for apparent breaches of the electoral act. Howard said disingenuously that he saw no reason not to meet them, they were Australian citizens, he met all sorts of people; but coming from a government that had ruthlessly pursued Kevin Rudd over a tenuous association with the Australian citizen Brian Burke, this didn't wash. The result of all this was that Bennelong and Wentworth could now both be considered winnable by Labor. The hard heads still thought the odds were against it, but the more marginals the better.

★

The diminution of Howard's authority as an economic manager had left the Coalition with no real centrepiece for a campaign. The negatives about Rudd were still there: inexperience, union domination, no serious ideology and so forth, but it was going to be hard to sell them without being able to make the comparison with their own man as a tower of strength and stability. There had been a desultory attempt to extend the contrast to the frontbench heavies on each side. But in practice Wayne Swan, Julia Gillard, Robert McClelland, Peter Garrett and Nicola Roxon did not stack up badly against Peter Costello, Joe Hockey, Alexander Downer, Malcolm Turnbull and Tony Abbott – to name only the most prominent. And in any case, in the television age elections are not won by teams but by leaders. There was really only one solution left: try to buy the election by bribing the swinging voters in the marginal seats, and to hell with what was left of economic responsibility. It might well put pressure on inflation and interest rates, but the effects would not flow through until next year, by which time it would be someone else's problem. In any case, the more outrageous promises could always be repudiated as non-core, or even *non compos mentis*.

The process had already started, of course, the Mersey Hospital being only the most egregious of many examples. It was estimated that Howard had already dipped into the pork barrel for more than $200 million for the marginals, and that was just for the big promises: it did not include numerous municipal libraries and sports fields, bridges and bypasses, war memorials and statues of the Dear Leader himself – okay, maybe not the last, but certainly any requests would be sympathetically considered. Interestingly, the Coalition appeared to be more pessimistic than the Labor strategists could have hoped: they identified 39 seats as marginal, and only a handful of them were Labor electorates which were considered winnable. And as time went on, even these few dropped off the list: Swan and Cowan in the west were still viewed as possible, along with Macquarie in New South Wales, Capricornia in Queensland and, remotely, Lingiari in the Northern Territory.

But the serious porking was about saving their own bacon, as it were. There were obviously going to be losses, but – just possibly – bombarding the swingers with taxpayers' money, of which there was undeniably plenty, might keep Labor below the magic number of sixteen seats. At the end of August, the generally agreed total for Howard election promises was $6 billion, give or take a couple of hundred million. This was considerably more than Rudd's total of $4.2 billion, and Rudd had also listed $3 billion worth of savings, whereas Howard had listed none. But the total was going to have to rise steeply if the seats were to be bought, and even after deposits to the Future Fund, the Education Fund, the Health Fund and whatever, there was still about $7 billion in the kitty. Spending it would undoubtedly put pressure on interest rates, which were already looking ominous, but there was really no choice. Peter Costello would at least pretend he did not approve, particularly as he would be the one who had to clear up the mess in the event of a victory. But even he would have to admit that if the alternative was a loss, the whole exercise could be justified in the name of ... pragmatism? Opportunism? No, let's call it Aspirational Nationalism.

Whatever this meant, it clearly included populism. Having previously declared that the siting of nuclear reactors around the coastline would be a purely commercial decision, Howard now said that of course there could be a plebiscite, no, a binding referendum among the communities involved. Challenged to name a single community likely to vote in favour, he replied that he believed things would be different by the time the plebiscites were taken; one thing that would certainly be different would be that he would not be around any more. Only a week before, the prime minister had thundered: 'Love me or loathe me, at least people know I stand for something.' Yes, but for what? It certainly wasn't either conservatism or consistency.

And nor, in 2007, was it setting the political agenda. Rudd, having broken out of the Little Sir Echo mode on the nuclear question, now came up with another Big Idea: The Great Hospitals Takeover, which was a pinch from what Tony Abbott wanted to do before he was vetoed by Howard. Abbott had been so miffed by the knock-back that he had refused even to begin negotiations for a new hospitals agreement with the states, saying he was going to concentrate on winning the election instead. He was now placed in the untenable position of having to tell the world that he had been wrong all along and it wouldn't work, to which Rudd and his supporters replied gleefully that it was a matter of political vision, will, determination and so on.

It was also, it turned out, a pretty vague idea: $2 billion would be injected into the system, and if after a couple of years the states had not got the hospitals humming, Labor would hold a referendum aiming to take control altogether. In a game of chess the move would have received the annotation !?, which is usually translated as 'bold but unsound'. The carrot was fair enough, and would provide a perfect test for Rudd's claim that wall-to-wall Labor governments could actually work to reform the creaky and redundant federal system. But the stick was more problematic: what happened if some of the states got their acts together but others didn't? Would we still have a referendum, which had to be nationwide? And what happened if, as was more than likely, the referendum failed to pass? And if it did pass, what happened to the GST agreement whereby the states got all the GST money? Would the ongoing cost of hospital funding be deducted? How would a new money-sharing arrangement work? Yes, well, it was a matter of political will ...

Moving right along, Rudd congratulated Howard on becoming a grandfather and went for the killer blow: the release of the final, detailed, locked-in industrial-relations policy. Once again, Howard was caught off-guard. Rudd, the supposed puppet of the dreaded union bosses, had clearly got his strings tangled. To switch the metaphor, he was exposed to all as a sheep in wolf's clothing. Even the *Australian* grudgingly admitted that, by and large, it was a pretty moderate document. Kevin Rudd and Julia Gillard, restored to prominence in a blaze of publicity, were pretty happy about the initial reaction. No one else liked it very much except a few of their fellow Labor politicians, and in private even these had their doubts. But the proud parents responded that this was exactly what they had hoped for: if both sides were bagging their baby with equal vigour, then it must be the perfect child. They had got the balance just about right.

When you thought about it, this was a most peculiar thing for a political leader to say. The whole point about the party system Australia shared with most democracies was that it was adversarial: you had allies and you had enemies. Naturally, you expected the enemies to disagree with your ideas and attack them by whatever means possible; there would be something wrong if they didn't. But to take comfort from the fact that your friends and supporters were equally unhappy seemed perverse. The Australian Labor Party was, after all, supposed to be the party of labour, not the party of capitalists. Obviously it had moved on from the days when it was simply the political arm of the trade-union movement – as society had changed, so had politics. But it was hard to believe that the ALP had drifted so far from its roots that it would actually welcome the news that its traditional constituency was thinking seriously about giving its first preference to a fringe party which in the past had been regarded as a haven for the fairies at the bottom of the garden. Yet this was just what was happening: tough-minded unionists were flirting with the Greens as a more union-friendly party than Labor, and the ALP leadership was taking it as a plus. And in terms of Realpolitik, they might even have been right. It is a mad world, my masters.

John Howard said that the union backlash was a pantomime, and his parrot in the Associated Chambers of Commerce and Industry, Peter Hendy, called the whole policy window-dressing; somewhere in their bunkered headquarters, the pair claimed, union bosses were chortling and cracking out the champagne. Well, no; they were grinding their teeth and preparing to try and convince the rank and file that they had not been completely sold out. The official line was that at least Forward with Fairness was better than WorkChoices – but then, almost anything was better than WorkChoices. The only thing that could be worse would be Son of WorkChoices, the monster anticipated by Finance Minister Nick Minchin when he assured business earlier this year that the whole award system and the Industrial Relations Commission were marked for destruction if the Coalition government was returned. For the unions Labor remained by far the lesser of two evils, but that did not mean it was good.

About the only aspect of Rudd's policy they really liked was the phasing out of AWAs, and even that would take far too long. But when it eventually happened, it would not, as the unions had hoped, restore their former access to workplaces. The restrictions imposed by Howard would remain, with only one serious exception: if a majority of workers in an enterprise voted to have a union negotiate on their behalf, the union would be admitted. This did not mean, as Howard claimed, that a single unionist could compel the rest of the workforce to sign up, but it did mean that employers would no longer be able to completely disregard the wishes of the total workforce, as was now the case. As they said, almost anything was better than WorkChoices.

And the other side of the equation was that business, with the exception of the predictable Hendy, wasn't too unhappy about it. The heavies would, naturally, continue to campaign for Howard; unlike Rudd, they knew precisely whose side they were on. Their advertising campaign had always been misleading, but it now became pure fiction: the scares about union bosses breaking down doors, of an inflation-fuelling return to collective bargaining leading to interest-rate rises, were exposed, as Ross Gittins pointed out in the *Sydney Morning Herald*, as outright lies. Moreover, sensible businesses, the ones where the leaders read the opinion polls as well as the government handouts, gave it, if not a round of delighted applause, at least a tentative pass mark. When BHP Billiton said it could live with the Labor policy, then you knew it couldn't be too frightening; Howard's own attempts to restart a scare campaign looked both silly and desperate. There was no denying that it was good middle-of-the-road politics that could well win the election for Rudd. But when the euphoria subsided, there were a few old Labor warriors asking each other: Is this really what we were fighting for?

Coincidentally, just as Rudd and Gillard were proudly displaying their offspring to the public, the Fairfax papers came out with a horrific series about the way foreign workers were being exploited, cheated and in some cases killed by the 457 visa system designed to fill the gaps in the local workforce left by years of government neglect. The writers produced example after example of almost unbelievable callousness on the part of Australian employers, showing that in some cases the cold-blooded and deliberate abuse of the system amounted to something very like slavery, and that the victims were generally powerless to fight back: under Howard's laws they could be sacked without notice and immediately deported at the whim of their bosses, who proceeded to demonstrate the truth of Lord Acton's axiom about power corrupting and absolute power corrupting absolutely.

The responsible minister, Kevin Andrews, lied through his paper-thin lips that the 'guests' had the same protection as other workers, and that the cases cited were exceptional; they weren't, and the only reason they had come to light was through the media and, dare one say it, the unions, which were not permitted to intervene directly but had been able to gain some publicity for the most outrageous acts. Had they the kind of access they were guaranteed before WorkChoices, they would have saved considerable suffering and at least three lives. Seen from this perspective, the fact that Kevin Rudd's government would include a high proportion of former union officials was perhaps not quite the disadvantage Coalition propaganda suggested. In Howard's Australia it was too often forgotten that trade unions are generally beneficial organisations formed by generally altruistic people for generally honourable purposes – certainly no less so than politics in general.

Politics, indeed, was getting a bad name. Even Kath and Kim, the immensely popular comedy duo, had had enough: Kath appeared in one episode to vigorously denounce WorkChoices and John Howard, and the prime minister's office appeared too demoralised even to make the usual blustering protests to the television network's chiefs. Modestly, the show declined to take the credit when the next Newspoll revealed a huge boost for Labor: the ALP primary vote was back to 51 per cent, the two-party-preferred gap was now 18 per cent and Rudd's lead as preferred prime minister had risen to 11 per cent. The only crumb of comfort for Howard was that his approval rating was now back in positive territory: plus two. Rudd's, by contrast, was plus 47. From the Libs' point of view, the figures were just too bad to be true: they implied that half-a-million voters had switched in the space of a fortnight, which was pretty unlikely. But there was no doubt that the situation was now dire, and that Howard's response – he saw the poll as a challenge and it would make him determined to work even harder – was less than inspiring.

★

It was not a propitious prelude to APEC, the greatest show on Earth. For months Australians, and particularly the residents of Sydney, had been hearing how privileged and honoured they were to have the opportunity to host a conference for no less than 21, yes, 21, of the world's most powerful leaders. Perhaps some of them weren't all that powerful; indeed, some of them were not even real leaders, since neither Hong Kong nor Taipei is recognised as a proper nation. But you still had a pretty impressive line-up, led by the United States, Russia and China, with a good back-up from Asia and even a couple from South America. Why, it was going to be almost like another Olympic Games.

Well, not quite; security might be a teensy-weensy bit tighter, with 5 kilometres of steel fencing and 3500 new clear-way signs and 5000 cops and 1500 troops and 800 private bodyguards and 35 aircraft and a water cannon, but hey, loosen up – it was only for a week or so, and there would be a special public holiday thrown in, not to mention a concert no one would be allowed to attend and a fireworks display no one would be allowed to watch. Of course, hospitals and prisons would need to be freed up for the occasion and other services just might be affected. For instance, Janette Hyacinth was organising an elaborate version of a candlelight supper for the wives at Bondi, which would completely disrupt the much-loved Festival of the Winds, but only for this year. Laura Bush pulled out at the last minute, complaining of a pain in the neck; it was generally assumed she was referring to Janette. Husband George W. then announced that he would be leaving early, but to compensate he would also arrive early, thereby adding another $4 million to the cost of the extravaganza. He was surprised to be told that the whole show was causing so much inconvenience, which was perhaps not entirely disingenuous: American tourists said they had never seen such heavy-handedness and that it went well beyond anything practised at home.

Demonstrators also copped it: police prepared a list of suspects who were banned unconditionally from the more sensitive areas for the duration. Others were allowed in under stringent conditions which included keeping a minimum distance of 300 metres from the action in case (and I am not kidding) they were carrying rocket launchers which had gone missing from an army store three years earlier. Police referred darkly to a protesters' manual advocating acts of violence; actually, it appeared to advocate civil disobedience and self-defence in the tradition of Gandhi. Vast areas of land, sea and sky were declared off-limits to all but the participants. And in spite of this massive exercise in overkill, when George W. Bush and his entourage arrived at the Intercontinental Hotel, they were met in the foyer by two bemused drinkers whom the crack security units had apparently overlooked. Oh well, at least we tried.

The madness rather overshadowed most serious discussion about what APEC was meant to achieve. Some, like Greens Senator Kerry Nettle, dismissed it as John Howard's $300-million campaign launch. Others, like the *Australian*'s Greg Sheridan, thought it was the biggest thing that had happened in generations, but it appeared he was creaming his jeans more over the all-star cast than in the hope of any real results. Some optimists had hoped that the tensions between the United States, China and Japan might also be on the agenda, but George W. Bush made it clear that for him at least, APEC was not all about China. Howard had spoken excitedly about a Sydney Declaration on climate change which would supersede Kyoto, but was already scaling back expectations. There would be a general commitment to free trade, but it seemed unlikely that the impasse which had stalled the Doha round would be broken in the course of a week.

Which left nothing much else except the chance to sign a few bilateral agreements and a hearty session of mutual back-slapping, or, in the case of Howard and Bush, mutual commiseration. This was no doubt a useful exercise; the more personal contact world leaders have with each other, the better. But it still seemed a lot of trouble for lunch, a cuddle with a koala and a silly photograph. Howard continued to describe the meeting as the most important and prestigious gathering ever to take place on Australian soil, so it was slightly surprising when he sent his deputy, the unobtrusive Mark Vaile, to welcome the most powerful man in the world to the event. (Our head of government had an appointment at a football awards night.) But the two got on well enough when they met next day, Bush praising his protégé as a man of steel, man of his word, a man not to be written off since, like Bush, he could come from behind. Alexander Downer smiled knowingly.

Apart from this shameless but possible counter-productive electioneering, the president confirmed a defence agreement which would allow more closely linked military operations (not exactly a vote-winner in the context of Iraq) and announced greater co-operation on nuclear matters, including a push for Australia to join the Global Nuclear Energy Partnership, which would mean, among other things, that Australia could be compelled to take back nuclear waste from countries to which it supplied uranium. Downer said it couldn't, and was wrong again. He was only slightly less embarrassing next day when he accepted the gift of a pair of pandas from Chinese President Hu; he was glad, he averred, not to have been born a panda because they didn't get enough sex. Alexander Downer, Australia's virility symbol.

Rudd stole the show at the welcoming lunch for Hu by addressing him, predictably enough, in Mandarin, but the Labor leader's 45-minute meeting with Bush was considered more newsworthy. Curiously Bush asked that the content be kept private, which suggested the two continued to agree to disagree about all the detail, while reaffirming the broad thrust of the alliance.

This was newsworthy? In the information drought of APEC it was. The enduring image of the event will be the footage of 21 heads of government in their colour-coded Drizabones, waving sheepishly with one hand while trying to conceal their unwanted Akubras with the other. It was fraught with embarrassment, and so it should have been. Not only did they look like a conga line of flashers caught emerging from a public toilet, but both separately and collectively they had achieved even less than their most severe critics had predicted. It is difficult to believe that anyone will ever take APEC seriously again.

Alexander Downer, of all people, got it right five months ago: when it comes to action on climate change, aspirational targets are not real targets at all; they are nothing more than political stunts. How then to describe the long-heralded Sydney Declaration, which failed even to set an aspirational target? It merely said that this should be one of the goals of the next United Nations climate-change meeting at Bali in December, a sort of aspiration to an aspiration. In the meantime, countries should aim to make equitable contributions with an emphasis on practical actions – sheer unadulterated waffle, which was precisely what the overwhelming majority of those present intended.

The Asian countries were never going to fall for the Australian–American idea of a separate forum, along the lines of the now all-but-forgotten AP6 group initiated by George W. Bush a few months earlier. For them, as for the Europeans, the serious negotiation would take place in Bali, where Australia and the United States, as non-ratifiers of Kyoto, would be admitted only as observers, not as full participants. For all Howard's posturing and grandstanding, the Sydney Declaration did not amount to a huff in a hurricane.

The bilateral deals Howard came up with were all sealed and delivered long ago: the defence and nuclear-power agreements with the US, and the sale of natural gas to China and uranium to Russia, had been settled at both a political and bureaucratic level, with only a signature required from the leaders. The only positive was the fact that they met face-to-face. Such first-hand contact was undoubtedly worthwhile, but was it worth $300 million? Given the outcomes, or the lack of them, even the profligate John Howard must have had his doubts.

The week was supposed to showcase Australia and Sydney, but the absurd security blanket ensured none of the VIP visitors saw very much of either. And the security didn't even work: the *Chaser* boys drove a horse and cart (well, a motorcade) through the $160-million ring of steel and were forced to give themselves up when no one could be found to stop them. Eventually the cops took out their frustrations on demonstrators after a peaceful and incident-free march had already finished in Hyde Park. Far from presenting Sydney as the friendly, open city overseas viewers might have remembered from the Olympic Games, APEC showed it to be an unwelcoming fortress reduced to a paranoid laughing stock.

The authorities, however, were not amused: the price of safety was iron-fisted repression. Back in July the government's resident Dementor, Attorney-General Phillip Ruddock, had berated a reporter who dared to query the need for his most recent restrictive measures. If they were not put into place and some terrible disaster took place as a result, the media would be asking him very different questions, he croaked. It was, as his authoritarian supporters in the media noted, a good argument. The trouble was that it was a little too good; it could be used to justify any form of repression under any circumstances. If we don't lock down the city, arrest all the usual suspects and a few more for good measure, arm the police with tactical nuclear weapons, impose an indefinite state of emergency, microchip every child at birth, require foreigners to wear electronic tracking devices at all times, and something terrible happens as a result, then you'll all be sorry, won't you? And of course if we adopt those restraints and nothing happens, it is proof positive that they are absolutely necessary. It's the old story about elephant repellent being 100 per cent effective. It must be: since wearing it, I have not been trampled by a single elephant.

The only APEC story to receive any significant overseas coverage was the crashing of security by *The Chaser*. Even the local media failed to respond to what Howard kept assuring them was the most significant gathering ever to take place on Australian soil. At the start the coverage of APEC was largely overwhelmed by concern about cancelled horse races, and by the end it had been overtaken by feverish leadership speculation. Oh, not again! Not still? Wasn't all that settled in 2006? Well, yes – up to a point.

> *The dancing pair, that simply sought renown*
> *By holding out, to tire the other down.*
> —OLIVER GOLDSMITH

★ 14.

THIS TIME IT WAS NOT YET ANOTHER feeble lurch by the Costello rump, or even a manifestation of the chronic twitching of the nervous nellies in marginal seats; the crisis was sparked by John Howard himself. The Newspoll had shaken him more than he was prepared to admit, and he was worried that it might be having the same effect on his loyal lieutenants. So he asked the most trusted (which was not saying very much), Alexander Downer, to sound out the rest of cabinet about how they felt about his leadership. Peter Costello, it was agreed, need not be included: everyone knew just how he felt. But it would be useful to know whether there were any other potential defectors in the ranks, if only so they could be brought back into line.

This was on the first Tuesday of September, during APEC. Then on Wednesday the *Australian*'s resident dominatrix, Janet Albrechtsen, contacted just a few of her close friends in the Liberal Party – Malcolm Turnbull, Nick Minchin and Tony Abbott – to tell them she was writing a column saying that she was about to join the other rats – Paul Sheehan, Andrew Bolt and David Barnett – in deserting her idol and benefactor and calling for Howard to step down. She might as well have hired a sky-writer; by Thursday the rumours of a new push for a change of leadership were thicker on the ground than APEC security. That night Downer held his meeting; those cabinet ministers who could not attend were kept in the loop by phone, always excepting Costello who claimed later that he did not even know it was taking place, ho ho ho. The consensus was clear: Howard had to go. If he was fair dinkum in his constant mantra that he would stay only as long as the party wanted him to and it was in the party's best interests for him to do so, then the time had come.

This presumably meant that he should toss the leadership in a hospital pass to Peter Costello, although how this was supposed to help the conservative cause was not really explained. Presumably the analogy to be drawn was with Labor in 1983, when Bill Hayden as leader made way for Bob Hawke, who subsequently swept to victory. However, seasoned political analysts might have detected just the hint of a couple of differences between the two situations. The first was that in 1983 the polls showed Labor already on track for a win; in 2007 they showed the Coalition headed for a crushing defeat. The second was that in 1983 Hawke was unquestionably the most popular politician in the country; in 2007 Costello was arguably the least popular.

Desperate times might call for desperate measures, but this was just ridiculous. Truly, those whom the gods seek to destroy they first make mad. Downer was given the job of conveying the bad news. He did so on Friday, the same day Albrechtsen's column appeared.

At this stage it is worth flashing back some sixteen years to 1991, when the heavies of the Labor Party had come to the same conclusion about their own leader. Kim Beazley, Gareth Evans and Michael Duffy, all long-time Hawke loyalists, were given the job Downer now assumed. Beazley explained to his political adviser, Gary O'Neill, how it would work: 'We're just going to go around to Bob and tell him that while he continues to enjoy our total support, we think it's time for him to go.' O'Neill was sceptical: 'And what are you going to do when he tells you to piss off?' he inquired delicately. Beazley scoffed at the idea: 'No, no, he'll never do that,' he replied. 'Bob will understand we're not plotting against him, it's just that there needs to be a way out of the situation ...' Beazley returned, morose, a couple of hours later. 'Well, what happened?' asked O'Neill. 'He told us to piss off,' said Beazley. Downer could not say he was not forewarned.

It says something about how out of touch Howard had been with his colleagues that he was astonished by Downer's report; he had expected, if not a standing ovation, at least a majority verdict that he was the party's last, best hope. Having told Downer to piss off, he realised he would need a new formula. When asked about the rumours that he might step down, he replied that as far as he was concerned the leadership question had been settled in 2006, which was fatuous: since then the political world had been turned upside down. He brooded through Saturday while continuing to go through the motions of the APEC round, and when it was over on Sunday he sought reassurance at what he called a family meeting. One suspects it went something like this:

> Tim, Melanie and Richard (in chorus): Dad, please don't consider our feelings at all. Whatever you do, please, *please* don't feel you have to give up politics to spend more time with your family. Please.
>
> Janette: Well, I'm not moving out of Kirribilli one instant before I absolutely have to, and that's final.
>
> John: Yes, dear.

His mind made up, Howard weathered the Nielsen poll in the Fairfax papers on Monday with something approaching equanimity, which is more than can be said for his troops: the raw figures weren't quite as bad as Newspoll, but once again they showed a drop in Coalition support. APEC, on first impressions at least, had not helped, and after APEC there was nothing on the horizon before the election. On Tuesday morning Sky News reported that Downer and Turnbull, thought of as Howard's rusted-on allies, had withdrawn their support. Stories about the ministers' Thursday meeting were now all over the place and backbenchers were desperate to find out what was really going on; as they reassembled in Canberra, there was an air of near panic.

The day was supposed to be ceremonial, an occasion for an address to parliament by Canadian Prime Minister Stephen Harper. (There was also to have been an address by Japanese Prime Minister Shinzo Abe, but he went home early and promptly resigned. APEC obviously didn't do him much good either.) Howard pre-empted a question at a joint press conference to announce that he had never run away from a fight in his life and he wasn't about to now: it was not entirely clear whether he was talking about the leadership or the election. Downer and Turnbull issued half-hearted statements denying the Sky report. But most significant was the reaction of Peter Costello: nothing, nought, zip. Like Howard, he was not about to break the habit of a lifetime; he wimped out again, even when he had the tacit support of his own cabinet colleagues.

So by Wednesday it was all over: with no alternative on offer, the party room stuck with Howard, who told them private polling said they could still win Eden-Monaro and hence the election. He then proceeded to question time, where not a single one of his once-loyal ministers would look him in the eye.

A week before, the story had been that he would call an election straight after APEC to break the cycle of bad news and take back control of the political agenda, but this was now out of the question: it was time for a makeover. This, he said bravely, would involve promoting his team more – a tacit admission that he could not beat Kevin Rudd one-on-one – and talking less about the past and present and more about his exciting plans for the future. When asked what these were, he couldn't yet say.

But he did make one significant flip-flop: he stated firmly that he would retire as prime minister sometime during his next term of office – assuming, of course, that there was one. Well, if then, why not now? Because he wanted to be around for his exciting plans for the future, whatever they might be. He looked old, tired and somewhat confused: perhaps, some viewers mused, he was now chasing the sympathy vote. At least there was no doubt that he was playing the underdog, if not the lame duck. He was, he explained rather plaintively, just being honest – not like those Labor premiers, Steve Bracks and now Peter Beattie, who had pulled the pin mid-term and with no warning. True, but it didn't sound like much of a campaign slogan: Re-elect Me So I Can Retire. And Peter Costello finally emerged to tell us what a courageous treasurer he'd been and what a worthy successor he would make. Opinion was, to put it mildly, divided.

However, Howard had at least made one thing clear: the election was to be fought seat by seat, which meant a strategy of pick-and-pork. Voters fortunate enough to be living in marginal seats, especially those held by the government, and swingers identified as a members of vulnerable groups, could expect to be all but buried by an avalanche of increasingly bizarre promises as the campaign progressed. These promises would, of course, be aspirational, meaning that no one in his right mind would take them seriously, but by golly they would sound good. The rest of us, the other 90-odd per cent of Australians, could go whistle. It was not an edifying prospect.

But at least the Rubicon had finally been crossed, the die had been cast and the bridges had been burned. The election campaign was to be run by a sort of dicephalous teratoid who would roam the countryside hurling goodies at the marginals with one pair of its arms, and mud at Kevin Rudd with the other. Costello would still be the lesser half of the partnership, the rear end of the pantomime donkey; Howard would make the big announcements, deliver the policy speech and conduct the debate with Rudd. In the age of television, electioneering is not a team sport, as Bill Hayden found in 1980 when the party strategists wedged him between the hugely popular NSW premier and party president, Neville Wran, and the even more popular ACTU leader, Bob Hawke, the latter about to enter parliament with the avowed intention of taking Hayden's job – and Hayden lost. Costello's role would be to sit dutifully behind Howard and applaud in the right places, much as he had been doing for the last eleven years, but he would have to share responsibility for the result. If, as still appeared likely, the Coalition was defeated, Costello would go down as the man who lost an election without even taking the reins.

★

Nevertheless, when parliament resumed for what was assumed to be the last time, a Coalition loss seemed slightly less inevitable. Newspoll retreated to where it had been for most of the year, showing the gap between the parties had narrowed to just 10 per cent. This would still have meant the loss of 33 seats, but it was a lot better than the avalanche predicted by the previous gap of 18 per cent. All it proved was that the previous poll had been a rogue, an aberration, and that the 55–45 result represented the status quo. But desperate backbenchers chose to interpret it as a big swing in their favour: they were, as the *Australian* breathlessly announced, back in the game. To celebrate, Costello announced solemnly that he would not challenge for the leadership. Given his flawless record of pusillanimity, no one doubted him for a second. This did not stop Kim Beazley, on the eve of a reluctant retirement, from noting that the press gallery was looking down on the prime minister like three rows of crows waiting for the sheep to die, yum yum. If only he had been as concise and colourful during his time as Opposition leader ...

There was an expectation that Howard would use the session to fulfil his promise to talk about the future, and for a moment he seemed about to oblige: there was to be a new nursing recruitment drive which would see them learning on the job at hospitals, rather than preserving their hard-won professional status gained through universities. But that was where the future began and ended: the rest of the fortnight was devoted to an increasingly hysterical 'get Rudd' exercise, which, in view of the failure of similar exercises in the past, suggested a Bourbon-like determination to learn nothing from history. Rudd's crimes ranged from a promise to sign the United Nations Declaration on Indigenous Rights, which meant he supported the abuse of Aboriginal children, to a propensity for setting up reviews and bureaucracies: he had promised 96 of the former and 67 of the latter. At the last count Howard was running 501 reviews alone, but it proved Howard was strong and Rudd was weak, not to mention phoney and manufactured. Then Rudd stumbled over a tax threshold; Howard had done the same in May. This, of course, demonstrated that not only was Howard strong where Rudd was weak, but that Rudd knew nothing about economics and was totally unfit for office.

Parliament was used to do what it does best, which is to generate an enormous amount of noise. Some government people got seriously carried away. Peter Lindsay, the member for Herbert, said that if families were suffering mortgage stress they should sell their furniture and sit on milk crates. Peter Phelps, chief of staff to Special Minister of State Gary Nairn, went to an election meeting of Nairn's opponent, Iraq veteran Mike Kelly, and accused him of acting like a guard at a Nazi concentration camp. Best of all, Alexander Downer was reported as yearning for the job of South Australian premier. Clearly he still had ideas above his station, but if he really wanted to stretch his talents, he might consider standing for Goolwa Council.

In the real world the news was not good for the government: a Sydney University study found that WorkChoices had resulted in women in the hospitality sector losing as much as 30 per cent in wages, and Spotlight, a company previously accused of misusing AWAs to dud its workers, announced it was abandoning them altogether for being too complicated and was going back to a collective award through the union. The OECD reported that Australia's spending on education, already parlous, had declined even further. And the Commonwealth had finally overtaken Coles to become the nation's largest advertiser, with an annual bill of $175 million: gold for Howard, gold, gold, gold.

But in what Peter Costello had sloppily assured us was parliament's last question time, it was all personal. Someone had leaked Rudd's medical records to Channel Nine, revealing that fifteen years earlier the Opposition leader had had routine heart surgery. Since then he had been a picture of robust health, walking the Kokoda Track as a holiday ramble, but after Mark Latham's pancreatitis any suggestion of infirmity has been a big political no-no. There was, of course, an upside: at least it confirmed that Rudd had a heart. John Howard was unlikely ever to need heart surgery, for the same reason that Alexander Downer would never suffer a brain tumour or Peter Costello succumb to testicular cancer.

But it was undoubtedly intended as a smear, and the last day of parliament turned into a screaming match of accusations and counter-accusations. For once, Rudd lost his cool and gave Costello a thorough going-over, which was a mistake. A large part of his appeal had been that he had remained aloof from the shit-fights which politicians and their aficionados enjoy, but which turn ordinary voters away in droves. His outburst undoubtedly did him far more harm than the original story about his heart surgery. Perhaps even more damaging was the glee it brought to the government: after months of unremitting effort, they had finally managed to get under Rudd's skin. It gave them great hopes for being able to do so again during the grind of the long, hot election campaign Howard was now clearly planning.

Howard himself made it perfectly plain where he stood: 'I can beat him without smears,' he yelled in a triumphant conclusion. Well, perhaps; but up till now he had not tried. He and other ministers indignantly denied the existence of a government dirt unit, and it is true that no office in parliament house bears a plate labelled 'Government Dirt Unit'. But there are plenty of government apparatchiks who see searching for mud to throw at the Opposition as part of their job. All the stuff about Rudd's recollections of his childhood, and the meetings with Brian Burke, and the visit to the New York strip club, did not emerge from an Opposition press release. To confirm that it was not simply a matter of Labor paranoia, Jason Koutsoukis wrote in the Melbourne *Age* of being invited to a minister's office to inspect a shit-sheet on Julia Gillard, which he declined to use.

The government argued that it happened on both sides of politics; the Poison Dwarf, Glenn Milne (who else?), revealed in the *Sunday Telegraph* that he had seen a document scurrilously alleging that a Liberal minister was a closet, but extremely active, homosexual. He admitted, however, that it had not come from the Labor Party. It was later reported that Milne's source was none other than Tony O'Leary, Howard's own press secretary. The rather more credible Laurie Oakes said he had also seen the document; it had been shown to him by a different Liberal minister. Not much honour among this pack of thieves. Tony Abbott, of all people, promised a clean campaign based on arguments about policy, not personality, but then added hurriedly that he thought his opponents' 'political character' was fair game – in other words, open slather.

On this cheerful note, parliament adjourned for what everyone fervently hoped would be the last time before the election. Howard was still prick-teasing: it was possible it could come back on 15 October, he mused. But there was no reason why: the year's legislative program had been well and truly wrapped up. The only outstanding item, the bills to open the way for nuclear power, had been quietly shelved; polling revealed that nukes were still irredeemably unpopular with the public.

★

Kevin Rudd, meanwhile, was fighting off accusations that he was getting cocky (he wasn't, but some of his sillier colleagues were) and doing a few back flips of his own. Previously Labor had accepted the electoral need to continue with the government's private-health-fund rebate, despite having correctly described it as one of the worst health policies of all time. Now it followed up by promising to continue the Medicare Safety Net, ignoring undeniable evidence that it was overwhelmingly for the benefit of the rich and hardly helped the needy at all. This piece of pragmatism undoubtedly avoided a wedge, but it also gave credence to the government's line about Rudd having no policies of his own and either adopting those of the government or those thrust upon him by the unions.

It was a damaging attack, and there were indications that it was starting to bite. Although the polls were still holding up overall, ominous signs were coming from the west, where the two vulnerable Labor seats of Cowan and Swan were said to be back in play. In South Australia Labor's glamour candidate for Boothby, Nicole Cornes, fumbled a question about industrial relations. Unfortunately the polls were showing she was already considered a blow-in and a bimbo, with the result that the slip made national headlines. There was a meeting with Al Gore, who endorsed Rudd – sort of. But apart from that, the best thing about the week was his fiftieth birthday; John Howard was 68 and a quarter. In Queensland the Nats unveiled an election slogan: 'Don't Risk Rudd'. It was not quite as absurdly negative as the 1972 reply to Labor's 'It's Time' – 'The Hell It Is' – but it was hardly visionary. Asked if and when the Nats were going to be positive, Mark Vaile said they had a story to tell but every campaign had two sides. It was clear which he believed was the more important.

But all this was taking place in a kind of electoral limbo. Howard continued to play the traditional prime-ministerial game of funny buggers, hinting at dates without ever naming them. The only thing that was clear was that he was going to follow the precedent of Billy McMahon in hanging on to power as long as possible, and for the same reason: sheer funk in the face of the opinion polls. And, of course, in the end Billy lost anyway. The superstitious noted that every leader who had held the election off until December had lost office – since World War II, anyway. The odds firmed for 24 November, with Costello dropping elephantine hints to that effect. Asked what qualities he could bring to the team that the current prime minister did not have, he replied modestly: 'Well, I think I bring a long-range vision for the future of the country. I think I bring a younger perspective. I think I bring a lot of energy and enthusiasm' – these, presumably, being the qualities John Howard lacked.

To prove that he was actually pretty hip, the prime minister announced a back flip on climate change. In the past he had dismissed the idea of targets for renewable energy as mere stunts, a waste of time and money. Now he announced that he would have one of his own – or rather that he would adopt the targets the states had already set: 15 per cent by 2010. Admittedly, this was for 'clean' power rather than renewable power, which enabled him to include the myth of clean coal and the threat of nuclear energy, but the emphasis was to be on solar, wind and water. One of his ministers, Fran Bailey, whose constituents find windmills unsightly, immediately retorted that wind power was all garbage and a cruel hoax, which didn't help Howard's sales pitch. There were also problems about costing and administration and everything else; yet again, it appeared to be an idea Howard had thought up in the bath.

The follow-up was an even more dramatic somersault from Alexander Downer, representing Australia at a United Nations conference in New York. The reason given for Australia's refusal to ratify Kyoto had always been that it imposed binding targets on industrialised nations, but not on developing ones. Now

Downer announced almost casually that this might have to be the reality, and that Australia could live with it. The switch caught everyone by surprise, not least his colleagues; when Environment Minister Malcolm Turnbull was asked to explain it, he gritted his expensive teeth and suggested that the question should be directed to the prime minister.

John Howard, however, was stuck in his electorate at Bennelong, frantically introducing himself to his constituents in a last-ditch effort to fend off Maxine McKew. In a shameless attempt to duchess the largely (and understandably) hostile Chinese-Australian community, his office sent out an invitation to a function celebrating the achievements and qualities of Chinese Australians, but through either pig ignorance or blind racism his office sent it not only to the Chinese but also to their traditional enemies, the Vietnamese and the Koreans – after all, they all look the same and they all have funny names, don't they? The threat of McKew cost Howard a week on the national trail.

He emerged only to undergo ritual booing at the Rugby League grand final. And the polls actually went slightly backwards for him. At least he knew to whom to address his prayers: he referred to Rupert Murdoch as God. He added that he was joking; but then, he would say that, wouldn't he? At least he knows that he has one of God's servants in his pocket. Seldom can a story have suffered such a massive beat-up as the *Australian*'s political editor, Dennis Shanahan, gave Kevin Rudd's switch over naming his ministers.

On Wednesday Rudd had said that if Labor won, all ministerial positions would be up for grabs, which was technically true; caucus would have to vote to endorse the personnel, after which Rudd would allocate the portfolios. Howard and Costello immediately launched into a prolonged frothing about how this was an admission that the dreaded Left was really in control and that the unions would force Rudd to install Julia Gillard (the horror! the horror!) as treasurer. To end the distraction, on Thursday Rudd said that yes, Wayne Swan (treasurer), Gillard (industrial relations) and Lindsay Tanner (finance) would keep their shadow positions, which no one had really doubted anyway. For most, a filler for the inside pages, but for Shanahan a hold-the-presses super-splash, an absolute jeans-creamer. It was a huge unforced error which allowed Howard and Costello to dictate political terms, he gibbered: Rudd's hand had been forced and he had lost the political week. To cooler observers it seemed more probable that Shanahan had lost his marbles.

Also, that he had missed the real story, which was that Rudd was now tearing up ALP rules and taking it upon himself to appoint his ministers without a caucus vote; and, more importantly still, that the faction leaders were prepared to let him get away with it. This gave Rudd more power than any Labor leader in the history of the party. Not Curtin, not Whitlam, not Hawke – no leader would have dreamed of pre-empting the system; they exerted what influence they could, but they accepted that the final choice lay with the party room. For the moment at least, Rudd assumed supremacy along the same absolutist lines as a leader of the Liberal Party.

Rudd decided to fill in the next week of waiting by undertaking a health crusade to sell his policy on hospitals and superclinics. Howard followed, and announced a plan for public hospitals to be taken away from the states and run by community boards – presumably an attempt to turn his Mersey Hospital stunt into a national policy. Hospitals were hugely expensive and rapidly becoming more so: as Rudd pointed out, it cost almost as much to run Sydney's Royal North Shore Hospital as it did to maintain Howard's taxpayer-funded advertising campaign, which was by now running at a staggering $1 million a day. The only way to rationalise the system was to keep a comprehensive base hospital in every major district, with smaller satellite hospitals for emergencies. This, of course, was exactly what the Tasmanian government was doing before Howard barged in with his Mersey rescue operation. To hand every hospital over to its own community would mean a huge amount of wasteful rivalry and duplication, more bureaucracy, less efficiency and far greater expense, and would also greatly advantage rich areas over poorer ones – all the hallmarks of wasteful and stupid Liberal policy on health funding. It reeked of populism, which was the whole point.

Julia Gillard said that another reason for it was to introduce AWAs in the hospitals, especially for nurses; Joe Hockey indignantly denied it, which was a little surprising. After all, he had spent thc previous week rubbishing a Sydney University report which once again showed that for those at the bottom of the heap, AWAs delivered $100 a week less than collective agreements. The researchers were biased, their figures were out of date and those who believed them were dupes, Hockey thundered: AWAs made everyone richer and happier, which was just what the government wanted. Then why not put nurses on them?

Strange ... or perhaps just reflecting the newly cautious mood. All over Australia, Coalition candidates were busily removing all reference to their party and its policies and especially its leader from their election material: they were no longer Howardites or even Liberals, but staunchly independent local members. Still more worryingly, the media was starting to treat Labor not as a ratbag Opposition, but as a government-in-waiting. On the same day the *Australian* had a piece by Paul

Kelly laying out approvingly the changes Rudd planned for the public service, and one by Alan Wood reluctantly admitting that a change of government would do no harm at all to economic policy. Only the Dominatrix, Janet Albrechtsen, stayed loyal – to the cause, if not to Howard. She sank her spurs into Kevin Rudd, whom she dismissed as 'a girly boy'. Hurtful, perhaps, but no more so than YouTube, where one contributor had christened Rudd 'Butch Firedong'. No one was game to ask Therese Rein what she thought of the nickname.

> *Dancing is a contact sport.*
> —Duffy Daugherty

★ 15.

As day followed dreary day, with politicians of all parties electioneering furiously in the hope that sooner or later Howard would either piss or get off the pot, the Dear Leader adopted a new strategy: it wasn't really happening. What he was doing, he unsmilingly maintained, was not to be confused with campaigning: he was *governing*. He was getting on with the serious business of running the country. And from this it followed that the bribes, pork-barrelling, sweeteners, backhanders, inducements and handouts he was announcing every day were not in any sense election promises: they were serious, deeply thought-out policy commitments which would be developed irrespective of any polling date which may or may not be announced sometime in the foreseeable future.

This was as bewildering to his colleagues as to the general public: Liberal ministers and backbenchers continued to insist that only by re-electing the government would their constituents get to taste the goodies dangled so enticingly before them. The *Sydney Morning Herald* published what it calculated to be the running total of promises from both sides:

Coalition $9.6 billion, Labor $8.8 billion. Finance Minister Nick Minchin's estimate for Labor was $17 billion, a figure he reached by claiming that Labor had promised to do everything the government would do in addition to its own promises. To most, the figures were as fanciful as the promises themselves. Howard's po-faced assertion that his should be taken seriously was treated with the contempt it deserved.

But in one area at least the government was governing: through gritted teeth Malcolm Turnbull announced that the chief scientist's review of the proposed Tamar Valley pulp mill had imposed new and stringent conditions, but had basically given it a tick, so he was doing the same. Perspiring vigorously, Peter Garrett muttered that Labor would also do the same, which prompted Bob Brown to say that Peter couldn't be his friend any more. Garrett bore the rejection with stoicism. You had to feel sorry for him. From being a trusted environmental warrior, Garrett had become a sell-out and a cipher, the shadow minister who didn't cast a shadow, as Geoffrey Cousins continually reminded us. As everyone had predicted, the Labor Party had chewed him up and spat him out. Once an idealist and a man of principle, Garrett was now just another politician.

Well yes, he was, and this was precisely the point. After spending his youth banging his impressive head against various brick walls in pursuit of noble causes, Garrett had grown up. In 2004 he became convinced that actually achieving change for the better, imperfect though it might be, was more useful than spending the rest of his life yearning for an unattainable green utopia. Whether consciously or not, he accepted the truth of Gough Whitlam's dictum: the impotent are always pure. He may even have turned it around: the pure are always impotent. From the start he knew politics would involve compromise, that he would no longer be the free spirit his fans had idolised at Midnight Oil concerts. He would have to balance the interests of the many against the dreams of a few. But he made the choice, and to his great credit he stuck with it.

Moreover, he saw how dire the consequences of uncompromising idealism could be. In 2004 Labor under Mark Latham went down the deep-green path in Tasmania. Seduced by Greens leader Bob Brown, Latham was persuaded that a policy of quarantining large areas of forests from loggers would be a vote-winner both in the island state and on the mainland. Garrett embraced the move and campaigned vigorously in the short time remaining before polling day. The result is now history: not only did Labor lose the seats of Bass and Braddon in Tasmania, but the party forfeited any chance of picking up mainland forestry seats like Eden-Monaro and Gippsland. The policy did not lose the election for Labor, although the contrast between Latham sneaking away from timber workers through an underground car park while Howard was cheered by them in a mass rally was one of the enduring images of the campaign, and one which would have swung many waverers to the government in the final week. But the net cost was at least two, probably three seats. In a tight election in 2007, those seats could make the difference.

There was no doubt that Garrett felt uncomfortable with the pulp-mill decision, or that he was hurt by the attacks from former friends and allies. But he could take more than marginal comfort from the fact that Labor's primary vote was running at 47 per cent, while the Greens were at just 7.6. As a result there was every possibility that in two months' time Peter Garrett, Australia's Minister for the Environment, would be signing the ratification documents for the Kyoto treaty and preparing to implement a radical and far-reaching program on sustainable energy, pollution control and climate change, while

Bob Brown, Greens leader in the Senate, would still be leading futile demonstrations against a pulp mill. Another of Gough Whitlam's favourite lines, quoting the Protestant French King Henri IV: Paris is worth a mass.

Other ministers were content to fill in the time by re-announcing previous commitments. Defence Minister Brendan Nelson unveiled plans to modernise the Mulwala munitions factory: as his Labor counterpart, Joel Fitzgibbon, pointed out, this was the tenth time since 2001 this promise had been made, and nothing had been done. Nelson's revelation of a contract for two new ships fared slightly better: this had only been announced six times since 2005. Howard followed suit by disclosing that the huge sums of money previously allocated to the Pacific Highway would now actually be spent, although not for a couple of years, and then only if the state government contributed huge sums of money which it did not have.

This act of generosity looked even trickier when it turned out that although the commonwealth blamed the states for everything, it had been short-changing them over the life of the Howard government; their share of revenue had fallen, in spite of the GST. In particular, the states had been paying a progressively greater share of the cost of running public hospitals, and the commonwealth a progressively smaller one. Given Howard's push to compel the states to install local hospital boards (and making specific grants to the Mersey and Grafton hospitals conditional on them doing so) the timing of this report was, at the very least, inconvenient.

Then the Wallabies lost, Howard conspicuously discarded his Wallaby tracksuit for his walk next morning, and Janette was reportedly seen shopping in Target, apparently preparing for straitened times ahead. Alexander Downer's wife, Nicola, was overheard telling her husband that the Coalition was gone for all money and could they please get on with their lives. Rudd was clearly getting on with his; it was revealed that he and his wife had been toying with the idea of acquiring a $5-million beach house at Noosa. Some suggested that this was hardly in the old Labor tradition, but the Libs, who had been inveighing against the politics of envy, could hardly complain – particularly when others asked why the Rudds didn't just pinch Kirribilli House, like the Howards had.

★

In this mood of almost unrelieved gloom, there was suddenly a glimmer of hope: Labor's foreign-affairs spokesman, Robert McClelland, made an unremarkable speech reiterating Labor's opposition to the death penalty, and foreshadowing a campaign to oppose its use in Asia. Opposition to the death penalty was supposedly bipartisan policy; Downer, for one, had spoken passionately for its universal abolition. But not this close to an election, and not close to the anniversary of the Bali bombing. In the circumstances a certain selectivity was also bipartisan. Rudd, sensing a wedge, said the Bali bombers should rot in gaol for life, and that he would never ask for clemency, except of course for Australians. Howard agreed, but added puzzlingly that Rudd was at fault for reprimanding McClelland for his timing; after all, McClelland was only restating Labor policy (which, he did not add, was also government policy). Downer said Rudd should take responsibility, in the way Downer had not during the AWB affair. Costello, suffering from media deprivation, hit the loud pedal and accused Labor of supporting the Bali bombers.

It was a fine exhibition of humbug from all sides and a useful distraction from a rather more serious piece of dog-whistling, coming, predictably, from the unwholesome immigration minister, Kevin Andrews. For much of the year a large proportion of Australia's quota of 12,000 refugees had been made up of Sudanese fleeing Darfur. But a few months earlier the United Nations High Commissioner on Refugees, who advises on such matters, apparently suggested that Australia might like to take more Iraqis and Burmese. This was seen as reasonable, so the Sudanese intake was reduced to make room for them. But with an election looming and no boat people who could be accused of throwing their children overboard to exploit, Andrews decided to play the race card.

There were, he warned, serious community concerns about the Sudanese. They were just not integrating. Hints of violent gangs, criminals. Bar your windows; lock up your daughters. Why, only last week a Sudanese youth had been bashed to death in a brawl in Melbourne. Well, yes, he had, but the two youths charged over the death were both white – although this was seldom mentioned. The police reported no evidence that the Sudanese were any more violent or criminal than any other group. But they were big, black and readily identifiable, which was what mattered. With cynical deliberation, Andrews turned what had been a normal administrative decision into a racist echo of Howard's notorious 'we will decide' mantra from 2001.

Australia has not been well served by Howard's immigration ministers. Philip Ruddock, cruel and calculating; Amanda Vanstone, blustering and incompetent; now Kevin Andrews, just plain nasty. And we were once considered good international citizens. In the circumstances, Labor's pledge of $45 million to combat preventable blindness in the Asia-Pacific region was very welcome. There were no votes in it; but that was exactly the point.

At this stage Howard decided to release his guidelines for the teaching of Australian history in years nine and ten of school. In summary at least they were not nearly as awful as had been anticipated; while there was a lot more of three cheers than of black armband, they were reasonably balanced and at least acknowledged the possibility of different viewpoints. They could have formed a sensible basis for negotiation with the teaching profession and the various state education authorities. But there was to be no negotiation: Howard ordered that they be accepted in toto, or the states would have their funding cut off, simple as that. Dissent was not an option. The children of Australia were to get the Howard version, and that was that. We'll teach the little bastards. And as for the Aborigines ...

Howard vigorously denied that he had undergone some sort of Damascene conversion over reconciliation between black and white Australia, and for once he was telling the truth. His unexpected announcement that he now accepted that symbolism had a role to play and that he had been partly to blame for the lack of progress in the past looked like a change in attitude only until you got down to what he was actually planning; then you realised that you'd heard it all before. His commitment to reconciliation had first been made in 1998; it was to have been the centrepiece of his second term. And the inclusion of a reference to Aborigines in the preamble to the constitution had been proposed in 1999, when Howard had torpedoed it by putting it together with the republic referendum and campaigning against both. This time he said he would campaign for it, but that was as far as he was prepared to go. The only symbol that mattered, an apology, remained out of the question.

'The challenge I have faced around indigenous identity politics is in part an artefact of who I am and when I grew up,' he explained pompously; but this was nonsense. The popular drive for a better deal for Aborigines came from Howard's contemporaries; I know, because I am one of them. We were at Sydney University together. It is hardly our fault if Howard never emerged from the grey confines of the law school while the rest of us were rearranging the universe. Not that he appeared to have learned much there: the point of his symbolic gesture, he claimed, was to 'recognise Aborigines in the constitution'. Aborigines have always been recognised in the constitution, and the final confirmation of their status as full citizens of Australia came with the 1967 referendum, which saw them counted in the census. Incidentally, it would be interesting to know how Howard voted on that historic occasion. If he was indeed a product of his times, he would have been part of the 90 per cent majority. Why, then, did one suspect he was one of the Neanderthal 10 per cent in opposition?

And why did one feel that the belated olive branch was intended more as a club to belt his opponents into submission than a peace offering – and that the fact it was being thrust on the Aborigines without consultation or the opportunity to negotiate was yet further proof that he didn't give a stuff about genuine reconciliation? John Howard, boasted John Howard, was the only one who could unite conservative and progressive Australia on the issue; it didn't seem to have occurred to him that it might be a good idea to bring Aborigines into the process as well. They were expected to be fawningly grateful for whatever they were offered. And what they were offered was a form of words to be determined within a hundred days and put to a referendum in eighteen months: take it or leave it. My way or the highway.

No, he had not undergone a Damascene conversion, or any other kind. However, the commentators bought it with enthusiasm, if some puzzlement: this was just not Howard's territory. Those Australians who really cared about reconciliation were hardly likely to swing to Howard, and most didn't care. Perhaps the old man was resigned to defeat and was simply trying for a slightly better entry in the history books. But next day he came out full-steam in defence of his mate Richard Pratt, the cardboard king who had admitted to the worst case of price-fixing in Australia's corporate history. Pratt, gushed the prime minister, was a fine and generous bloke: indeed he was especially generous to politicians generally and to the Liberal Party in particular, which was into him for about a million and a half. Arguably, Howard could be called a receiver of stolen goods; certainly the association made Rudd's lunch with Brian Burke look like tea with the vicar.

Meanwhile, Rudd's new mate Al Gore was picking up the Nobel Peace Prize and General Ricardo Sanchez said the war in Iraq had become a nightmare with no end – not a good note on which to start an election campaign. Fortunately Alexander Downer was there to set him right: actually, good progress was being made, our foreign minister assured us. As Robert McClelland pointed out, perhaps the wish was father to the thought: Downer had exhibited the same optimism once or twice before.

> 'Significant progress has already been made,' Downer had said in Parliament on 25 May 2004;
>
> 'Steady progress is being made in Iraq' in Parliament on 15 June 2004;
>
> 'I think that as a country it is making progress' in Parliament on 30 November 2004;
>
> 'I'm delighted with the progress that's been made' in an *AM* interview on 31 January 2005;
>
> 'Iraq as a country has made considerable progress' in Parliament on 20 June 2005;

> 'They have made good progress' in Parliament on 17 August 2005;
>
> 'Progress is being made' in a Washington DC doorstop on 19 September;
>
> 'They are making some real progress' in an ABC Radio interview on 23 June 2006;
>
> 'Progress is being made' in his *Meet The Press* interview on 2 July 2006;
>
> 'They've made good progress' on the *AM* program on 26 October 2006;
>
> 'I think progress has been made' in a New York doorstop on 18 January 2007;
>
> 'Progress is gradually being made' in a 2UE interview on 22 February 2007;
>
> 'I think at long last, after a big struggle, real progress is being made on the ground in Iraq and just as we are making progress there' in a 2UE interview on 13 September 2007.

He might not be very bright, but at least he was consistent. Perhaps that was why Howard continued to promote him as two short planks of stability in an uncertain world. Or perhaps it was because he didn't have anyone else.

★

On 14 October, having put out a manifesto replete with slogans cribbed in equal measure from Ronald Reagan ('strong, prosperous, secure') and, incredibly, Mark Latham ('float every boat'), John Winston Howard finally launched the official election campaign under the banner of 'The Right Leadership' – not Rudd's new leadership, certainly not old leadership, but the *right* leadership. Well, nobody thought it was Left leadership.

Next day's Newspoll showed the starting point was the same old gap: 56–44 on the two-party-preferred. It looked huge, but the Howard-huggers insisted it was not unbridgeable: much of the Labor vote was soft; the situation looked better in the marginals, particularly in Queensland, and Howard was still way in front on economic management. This was true, but as George Megalogenis mused in the *Australian*, perhaps the pollsters were asking the wrong question: what interested the voters was not just economic management, but how it affected their lives. Mussolini made the trains run on time, but Fascist Italy was not exactly a fun place to live. However, Howard was still popular; the punters were not sitting on the front porch with their baseball bats waiting for him to come past – although at the Billinudgel Hotel quite a few regulars were hoping he would catch fire in their vicinity, so they could refuse to piss on him and put him out. The problem was that Rudd was more popular – much more popular.

But on that first Monday no one was taking anything for granted. And to demonstrate the enormous advantage of incumbency, Howard and Costello immediately fired the biggest of their big guns: a five-year plan for $34 billion in tax cuts, the mother of all bribes. It might have been a bit early in the campaign, it might have been marred by the fact that a number of commentators saw it as inflationary and it certainly deflated when Howard blooped on interest rates on *A Current Affair*, putting the cash rate at 6.25 instead of the 6.5 it reached after the September rise. But it was sure going to be a hard act to follow.

Wisely, Kevin Rudd did not try to follow it – not immediately, anyway. He refused to be goaded by Howard and Costello and their supporters in the media, pointing out that when Howard was in Opposition in 1996 he did not release his tax policy until the third week of the campaign, and there was this proverb about the goose and the gander. And in the meantime Rudd could stick to his own agenda, which at that stage of the campaign was health and industrial relations, and what a re-elected Howard–Costello government would do with the latter.

In a bad-tempered interview with Kerry O'Brien, Howard complained that now it was Rudd who was running a scare campaign, and he shouldn't be because he was complaining about the government being negative. His frustration was understandable: Rudd was picking off Howard's L-plate and union-terror ads by stepping into them, switching them off and talking about another day, another scare. Howard now countered by stepping into Rudd's ad, turning him off and telling him to grow up; we now had Howard commenting on Rudd commenting on the Libs commenting on Labor, with the prospect of an endless regression which could only culminate in the revelation of a First Cause by one or the other.

But God's messengers were being determinedly neutral: the conservative Catholic Cardinal George Pell endorsed Labor's schools policy (why not – it involved keeping all the worst features of the government's for several years) and the even-more-conservative Anglican Archbishop Peter Jensen mused that it might be time for a change of government. Howard and Costello, used to being the anointed, now had to rely on the loonies. The Exclusive Brethren were once again campaigning for Howard, while Danny Nalliah of the Catch the Fire Ministry, after personal meetings with both men, announced he had been divinely ordered to endorse Howard and then prepare the way for the ascension of Costello. Since Nalliah also encouraged divine intervention to 'pull down' casinos, brothels, bottle shops, mosques and Buddhist and Hindu temples, it was a little surprising Howard and Costello accepted his support with effusive gratitude. Still, presumably they needed all the help they could get.

Some of their colleagues weren't exactly assisting. Tony Abbott dismissed the 650,000 Australians desperate for dental care as 'political stooges'. The Nationals' candidate for Leichhardt, Ian Crossland, snorted that the electorate was no place for a woman, an assertion disputed by the Liberal candidate with whom he was swapping preferences – she was in fact a woman. But Rudd was having his own problems: Gavan O'Connor, disendorsed from the seat of Corio by a union boss in a pre-selection battle, announced he was standing as an independent and claimed that Rudd had told him he was not strong enough to fight off the union push. Howard could scarcely believe his luck.

Apparently unhinged with joy, he announced that if he was re-elected, there was no reason why the economic boom could not go on forever. Cynics commented that it had better: including the tax cuts, his promises now topped $60 billion. Clearly warnings from the International Monetary Fund against excessive spending were not in the forefront of the Howard–Costello mind. Rudd, on the other hand, was trying to be responsible and conservative – so far. His finance spokesman, Lindsay Tanner, still insisted that all Labor's promises would be costed and paid for. But this did not solve the problem of how to reply to the Great Tax Bribe. The polls had consistently shown that not all wanted their tax simply returned to them; a lot, even a majority, would rather see the money spent on infrastructure, particularly schools, hospitals and transport.

The dilemma was whether to believe them or not. To do so was tempting: the opportunity was there for a massive rebuilding of an increasingly dilapidated system. But conventional wisdom said that it was always safer to back self-interest: the only adequate reply to a tax cut was another tax cut. Labor had spent the first week talking about hospitals, about housing affordability, about national broadband coverage and about work and family, but all the pundits wanted to know was whether Rudd would get his tax policy out in time for the leaders' debate. And at the end of the week the polls showed a slight movement back to the government. Only a slight movement and one that everybody had expected, but a movement nonetheless.

It was not an invitation for Rudd to be brave and visionary. Nonetheless he had to be a bit different, so he did the safe thing, which was to postpone the cuts for the very, very rich (boo! hiss!) and put the money into rebates for digitalising school children, as he rather ineptly put it, and reducing hospital waiting lists. Costello did a quick calculation to claim that 91.5 per cent of Labor's plan was identical to his but that there was a massive error because it ignored bracket creep, which meant that 45 per cent of taxpayers would be $600 a year worse off – in 2013. Wayne Swan retorted that he had simply followed Costello's figures and that Costello had made a bigger boo-boo by not nominating tax thresholds for 2012. No one had a clue what either was talking about, and since it was about something that wasn't going to happen for at least six years and quite likely not at all, no one cared.

For Coalition backbenchers the issue now was survival; they were still keeping any reference to John Howard and most references to their party off their campaign posters. However, Howard appeared prominently in Labor ads repeating his famously ill-advised comment that working families had never been better off. In retaliation, Howard took Costello's name off his own literature before attending the Eastwood Granny

Smith Festival in Bennelong, where he was still tied down by the indefatigable Maxine McKew.

★

The big event of the weekend was the Debate, which the media insisted on calling Great, but which Howard and his enforcers were determined to reduce to the most minimalist form they could get away with. So on a take-it-or-leave-it basis Rudd was offered a single debate right at the start of the campaign, hedged with enough terms and conditions to make it stultifying for the surprisingly large number of viewers prepared to desert *Kath & Kim* for a glimpse of the leaders. In the circumstances it is surprising that anyone watched it at all – except, of course, the worm. Howard had banned the worm, but Channel Nine refused to acquiesce. The National Press Club, acting as always in the interests of the establishment instead of the journalists who had founded and named it, therefore pulled Nine's direct feed of the debate, and then pulled a back-up feed from the ABC. Nine, undeterred, went to Sky News and the worm survived – rather better than the prime minister, in the general view.

Howard had always hated the worm and it was clear that the hatred was mutual: every time the camera moved to the prime minister the annelid burrowed its way to the depths of the screen, only to leap as if on steroids when Howard was replaced by Rudd. Tony Abbott concluded the worm was fixed. In the end the worm scored it 65–29, better than two-to-one Rudd's way, which most commentators agreed was about right. Howard looked old, tired and flat, while Rudd's initial nervousness was quickly transformed into a confidence verging on cockiness. But it should be stressed that the worm was no bleeding-heart, latte-sipping elitist; one of Howard's few good moments was when he defended his invasion of the Northern Territory. The worm didn't mind a bit of hardball. And for this reason its verdict probably mattered more than the Liberal spin-doctors were prepared to admit. On the night, Rudd won on the bedrock issues which were supposed to be Howard's ground. Unfortunately this would be at best a distant memory by the time people came to vote. Peter Costello's role in the event was to sit in the front row of the audience, make faces at Rudd and heckle until reprimanded by the excellent moderator, Sky TV's David Speers. Rudd said he'd like to take the pair of them on next time.

But for many true believers the best thing about the debate was that Rudd finally mounted a spirited defence of the trade-union movement, which had been so denigrated and demonised by Howard and Costello that it had become almost unmentionable in polite company. The crude caricature of the Faceless Union Bosses standing over benevolent employers and conning gullible workers through politically sponsored thuggery had been the staple of the Coalition campaign for some months, and if anything Rudd had encouraged it by his own policy of zero tolerance towards any officials who stepped out of line. This gave some validity to Howard's line about the awfulness of a frontbench with a 70 per cent membership of former union operatives: if their own leader was constantly demanding the expulsion of their colleagues from his party, they must have been a trifle suss.

The Coalition's line of attack had admittedly become a little confused: at least two of the Labor frontbenchers characterised as union officials, Wayne Swan and Craig Emerson, had never been anything of the sort. They were certainly rank-and-file union members, but even Howard admitted that was hardly a crime. Then Howard's own workplace relations minister, Joe

Hockey, claimed that the unions were essentially finished. Costello, on the other hand, insisted that they were poised to take over the government, destroy the mining industry, shatter small business and drive up inflation, unemployment and interest rates, bringing on a recession – 'this is fact!' screamed the man in charge of the national economy, who also wanted us to believe that the boom times could continue for ever and ever, but only if he became prime minister.

Rudd at last felt strong enough to point out that most union officials, like most members of parliament, were dedicated to serving their constituents and to the wider good; that they were by and large idealistic and hard-working, and that while some might get corrupted by the system – as indeed did some politicians – their calling was an honourable one, and by its very nature was good preparation for a wider political career. Far from being out of touch, they were in constant contact with ordinary workers and their problems, but had to view these in the context of economic and political reality. Union officials to have come to Canberra include John Curtin, Ben Chifley, Bob Hawke, Mick Young, Clyde Cameron and Ralph Willis, all universally acclaimed. As Howard retorted, none of them had ever run a business, unlike John Elliott, Alan Bond or Rodney Adler, but you can't have everything.

Howard's own cabinet consisted of one army officer, one bank economist, one doctor (who was also a former union boss), one stock and station agent, two farmers and twelve lawyers. Our choice, then, was between a government dominated by representatives of the workers or one dominated by the hired guns of the legal profession. Put that way, the unions didn't seem so bad.

Funnily enough, the Labor figure who excited most fear and loathing among the Libs was not a union boss, but a lawyer:

Julia Gillard, who, Costello revealed, was once a member of a university debating group called the Socialist Forum, along with (the horror! the horror!) some ex-communists. It followed that she had horns and a tail and was dedicated to the destruction of the Australian way of life. But others remembered Costello's own university days, when the long-haired left-wing firebrand was a dedicated zealot of the Social Democrats, even attending yearly training camps with his fellow revolutionaries. They had the pictures. For a moment at least, the personal attacks eased off.

Yet, as fellow conservatives, Howard and Rudd could agree on one thing. *The Chaser* ran a song which reminded us of the bad side of Don Bradman, Steve Irwin, Kerry Packer, Princess Di and others who were no longer with us. It was tasteless, outrageous and very funny: archetypal satire, in other words. A million and a half people watched it, and exactly six rang the ABC to comment – and three of those were in favour. Our fearless political leaders, however, were shocked and disgusted. Just five weeks to go: safety first.

> “*Dance till the stars come down with the rafters,*
> *Dance, dance, dance till you drop* —W.H. Auden

★ 16.

The consensus among the commentariat was that the first week had been a comfortable win for Howard – the leaders' debate had taken place after opinion polling closed, so was deemed to belong to the second week. The tax package had effectively set the policy agenda and the anti-union ads had dominated the negative side of the campaign. Rudd had been forced to play catch-up, and Howard had got at least some of his zing back: he was again looking like the Dear Leader we knew and loved/loathed, depending on our predilection.

The Newspoll on Tuesday, 23 October – undertaken before the debate – was thus all the more devastating: the government had actually gone backwards and was a horrendous sixteen points behind on the two-party-preferred. Rudd had increased his lead as preferred prime minister and, more ominously still, had closed the gap on economic management: he was just nine points behind Howard. If the poll was right, the government was gone for all money. All Howard could do was either slit his wrists on the spot or assume that the poll wasn't right and plough ahead as planned – which, being Howard, was what he did.

The week's big bribe was a $4-billion handout to pensioners and associated dependents, which was received with the now customary combination of greed and cynicism; the punters were perfectly happy to trouser any available cash, which they felt was long overdue, but they were buggered if they were going to show gratitude for it. Like Rudd's massive pre-debate child-care commitment, it grabbed the headlines for about 24 hours and was then buried in trivia such as Ian Crossland in the far north snarling that he wanted to go to Canberra so he could 'kick arse' – another reason that representing Leichhardt was no job for a woman, presumably; Kevin Rudd being mobbed by teenyboppers at a school, but being called a bastard and told he had ruined a party at an old-people's home; and Paul Keating mounting a stirring defence of the unions.

The latter was good news for the government, because it put two of their favourite targets together: anything Keating was in favour of was by definition bad, and vice versa. But among more thoughtful observers of the political scene, some doubts were developing about the ferocity of the government's approach. After all, while the public's knowledge of the unions was clearly limited, what they did know was not all bad. Two enduring images had been of Bill Shorten's sensitive handling of the Beaconsfield mine drama, and of Greg Combet's untiring efforts on behalf of the asbestos-affected workers from James Hardie. These were two of the fearsome 70 per cent who might be part of a Rudd government.

The really scary ones weren't going into parliament; indeed, Rudd was heaving them out of the party. Fortuitously, Joe McDonald, one of Howard's most used bogeymen, was cleared by the courts on one of many charges of trespass; he boasted, 'John's gone. You know that. I'll be back.' Rudd saw the innocuous line as a hanging offence, and demanded and obtained

McDonald's immediate expulsion. It made the claims that Rudd was the unions' patsy – he 'couldn't go three rounds with Winnie the Pooh', said Brian Courtice, a disaffected Labor man from Queensland – seem somewhat far-fetched, to say the least.

★

I took refuge at the Seabird Rescue Service at Ballina, in the interesting seat of Page, which was receiving a visit from Peter Garrett. Shy and self-effacing as always (at least when not on stage), Garrett seemed genuinely pleased to be among conservationists, even those who felt he had let them down over the pulp mill. He and the local candidate, Janelle Saffin, both liked the mood for change they were picking up on, and both were certain that WorkChoices was still the big issue: nothing the government said or did would convince workers that it was not a plot to lower wages and conditions – which, in a way, was hardly surprising, since that was exactly what WorkChoices was. What was surprising was how deeply the concern ran; the government had spent well over $120 million of taxpayers' money in trying to sell the bloody thing, and there was no evidence that it had won back a single vote.

Howard, perhaps for want of something better to do, promised to build two defence-force colleges, but like everyone else, he was marking time. The week, indeed the fortnight and very possibly the election, hinged on the inflation figures for the September quarter, which were released on the Wednesday. And they were not good news. The headline rate, the Consumer Price Index, which is supposed to measure the cost of a typical basket of household goods and services, was not too bad; but this was largely because a rising Australian dollar had held down the cost of imports. The underlying rate, which was what the Reserve Bank board members were paid to worry about, was either just under or just over 3 per cent, depending how you measured it, and that was too high.

The bank's governor, Glenn Stevens, had said that if the circumstances required a rise in interest rates, the bank would not hold off just because there was an election campaign on; to do so, he implied, would be a dereliction of duty. The all-but-unanimous view among professional economists was that the circumstances did require it. End of story, and quite possibly end of government. A November rise would be the sixth since Howard had won the 2004 election on the slogan 'Keeping Interest Rates Low'.

But incredibly, Howard still seemed to feel that he could wriggle out of the commitment; that by a suitable choice of weasel words he could convince the voters they had misunderstood what he had said; that he had actually kept his promise and those who believed otherwise were just stupid or perverse. First there was the old line that all he had ever said was that rates would always be lower under the Coalition than under Labor, and that was still true. Liberal Party advertising may have promised to keep rates at record lows, but that was the advertising, not him, and in any case it had only run for a couple of days so it didn't really count: it was just a two-day promise. But the words had never passed his lips, scout's honour, cross my heart and hope to die.

Actually, they had; Laurie Oakes unearthed the damning tape. Oh dear, said Howard. Well, how about that. But even then, he refused to own up; by an extraordinarily devious manipulation of the figures, comparing various obscure measures at particular times, you could still make the case that rates now were still, well, maybe not at *record* lows, but lower than they looked. Or something. All that legal training was paying off, but of course those with mortgages did not want to know that. Nor were they listening when Peter Costello helpfully added that rates now were still lower than they had been eleven years ago, when he was a boy. What they did know was that they were already stretched to the limit and another rise would push a lot of them past it, and they knew exactly what Howard had told them three years ago and they felt betrayed.

Many now accepted that Kevin Rudd was right; in the short term at least, there wasn't really much any government could do about inflation, and hence about interest rates. But Howard had told them he could, and would. And he hadn't. While they waited for the bank's fateful meeting on Melbourne Cup Day, they would talk of little else. And indeed, for the rest of the week they didn't.

Costello did his best to provide a distraction: apparently crazed by publicity deprivation (the most exciting thing he had done in the last week was attend a teddy bear's picnic), the treasurer crashed back onto the front pages to warn of an impending economic tsunami, a maelstrom of uncertainty which would engulf the region – at least, it would when China floated its currency, which obviously wasn't going to happen for quite a while yet and in any case would be done in stages, so perhaps there wouldn't be a tsunami after all, but golly it made a good headline. As George Megalogenis, among others, pointed out, the messages were really getting mixed. The boom could go on for years, or we could be hit by a tsunami overnight. We wanted the Reserve Bank to stop tightening the economy, but we were determined to keep throwing enormous amounts of money into it. Responsible, experienced economic management would keep everything on course, but we were utterly helpless in the face of China. Eh?

Howard, in an attempt to cut through, said it was really all about jobs and that full employment was a real possibility, but only under him. He promised $2 billion for 100 new technical colleges, a nice round figure. He remained, we were assured, very popular while doing his morning walk through the streets of Kirribilli. But we were also informed that the Howard family home (no, not Kirribilli House; the one at Wollstonecraft) was undergoing renovation, presumably in preparation for reoccupation. He then went campaigning with a candidate who was an electrician and also a trade unionist. Howard explained that he wasn't against trade unionists, good heavens no, he just didn't want them running the place. Joe Hockey, ever helpful, jumped in to reassure the voters that his party's advertising was not really negative at all: 'Our fear campaign is based on fact.' Try that again: 'Our fear campaign is based on fact.' The more you said it, the crazier it sounded.

To provide yet further light relief, some photos of a Family First candidate, Andrew Quah, appeared on the internet, including an unimpressive display of his privates. Quah's response was at best disarming: his first reaction was to say he must have been drunk at the time; his second to complain, 'That's not my penis.' Unmoved, the fuddy-duddies of Family First disendorsed him.

★

For Howard, though, things were a little more serious. The *Financial Review* reported that six weeks earlier Malcolm Turnbull had taken a submission to cabinet urging the government to finally ratify Kyoto. There was, Turnbull insisted, no good reason to hold back. Unlike many other countries, Australia would actually come close to reaching its very generous Kyoto target, and negotiations about a post-Kyoto protocol were about to begin. Only by ratifying the old agreement could Australia become a full participant in negotiating the new one.

Moreover, Australia's ratification, however belated, would put pressure on the United States to do the same.

It would also remove a major stumbling block to getting the developing countries, particularly India and China, involved in setting new targets for emission control; China had specifically referred to Australia's recalcitrance as a reason for refusing to sign up to any binding treaty. The argument was that developed countries like Australia were the ones responsible for the emissions already out there; it was a bit rich of them to ask developing countries to agree to controls on future development without at least token acknowledgement of the industrialised nations' past guilt in the area.

But forget, if you like, all this airy-fairy stuff about being a responsible international citizen: after all, it was hardly part of the great Liberal tradition. Concentrate on a more urgent matter: there might be votes in it. Turnbull told various colleagues that he reckoned ratifying Kyoto could be worth as much as 3 per cent nationally, which was probably wrong; certainly it didn't allow for cynical punters dismissing a deathbed repentance as nothing more than yet another act of monumental cynicism. However, it surely couldn't do any harm. But Howard wouldn't budge – or, as Turnbull rather more graphically put it, the little cunt was too fucking stubborn. (How good it was to hear that old nickname for our beloved prime minister back in use! What a reminder of his glorious younger days, when everything was so much clearer!)

Two days after the story broke, Glenn Milne, the Poison Dwarf, celebrated with a front-page screamer in the Sydney *Sunday Telegraph* headlined, 'Turnbull Betrays Cabinet'. According to Milne, members of the party believed that Turnbull himself had leaked the story in order to save his own seat. The conspiracy theory ran that Mr Turncoat, as he was now to be known, had already made up his mind that the election was lost and Howard was finished. But if he could just hang on in Wentworth, he could be a starter for the leadership against Peter Costello – who was, of course, Milne's own candidate for the job. So Turnbull was not a team player; he was putting his own interests ahead of the party. Well, how very Liberal of him. The Liberals are, after all, the party of the individual: not for them namby-pamby collectives and unions. And what a surprise: having devoted every waking moment to scrabbling as far up the greasy totem-pole as possible, Turnbull was determined to hold onto the bloody thing! Who would have thought it? Certainly not the pusillanimous Costello or his acolyte.

But perhaps Turnbull's little cunt might have recognised the symptoms, and even sympathised. For more than a decade Howard insisted that he would only be leader for as long as the party wanted him and it was in the party's best interests that he did so. Then when the party, through its senior parliamentary representatives, announced to him that the time had come, he told them all to get stuffed and said he would fight to the death to stay on, and bugger the party. It was Howard, of course, who had been Turnbull's mentor and benefactor – until now. If the phrase 'Liberal principles' was not an oxymoron, the master and his apprentice were applying them like never before. Nonetheless, the episode gave the impression of chaos and disunity, so it was an enormous relief when something similar happened to the other side.

Peter Garrett had always been a great supporter of Kyoto and its underlying premise that the developed nations had to take the lead in limiting their emissions. He now suggested that the same principle might apply to the post-Kyoto protocol: if the developing countries like China and India failed to sign up to binding targets, this need not be a deal-breaker; different conditions could be imposed on different countries. This was hardly revolutionary: Howard himself had reluctantly adopted the same position as part of the Sydney Declaration, and Downer had confirmed it at the United Nations conference which followed. But now Howard took it to mean that Labor would sign a new agreement which left China and India out altogether; there would be no conditions imposed on the developing countries whatsoever.

The *Australian*, sensing an opening, went completely ape: Dennis Shanahan and Paul Kelly were all over the paper in a frothing competition about which of them could misrepresent and denigrate Rudd most hysterically. Rudd and Garrett both issued clarifying statements; Howard screamed that this was total capitulation by Rudd, who now agreed with him about everything. Well, no; Howard was still not going to ratify Kyoto and Rudd was, just for starters. They did, however, agree that while different criteria might apply to the developed and the developing in a post-Kyoto agreement, all would have to make some form of commitment to reducing their emissions. This had always been the understanding from Kyoto and it had always been Labor's position; Howard had come to it in September. In fact, the confusion was on the government side. Turnbull still wanted to ratify Kyoto. Howard didn't. Alexander Downer thought we should wait and see what the American position was. Mark Vaile was still not convinced there was a problem at all. And Peter Costello told a group of schoolchildren that God made cactuses. But the *Australian* concluded that Labor was the party in dire trouble over climate change. The paper walked away with a Gold Mixmaster for the biggest beat up of the campaign to date.

While few if any readers would have been properly across the story (a survey in the *Daily Telegraph* revealed that 38 per cent of its readers thought Kyoto was the treaty that ended World War II, and 14 per cent thought it was a Japanese banquet), it did create the impression that Rudd and Garrett had committed a serious boo-boo. This rather spoiled Rudd's announcements of a 20 per cent renewable energy target by 2020 and $200 million to save the Great Barrier Reef. And it also gave Howard a boost at a time when things appeared to be moving his way. Once again the pundits had got it wrong: they scored the second week as an easy win to Rudd. Newspoll, however, lurched back to Howard: the two-party-preferred gap was now only eight points and Labor had lost 4 per cent of primaries in a week. It seemed unlikely. The commentators shook their huge heads and muttered that the voters were volatile, although all the other evidence was to the contrary.

★

The poll result gave a certain frisson to the debate between Peter Costello and Wayne Swan, an event which desperately needed one. Costello had talked about hammering Swan into the ground, which he should have done easily: he had been treasurer for eleven years and was acknowledged to be parliament's best and nastiest performer. To gain credibility, all Swan had to do was avoid a knockout. But he did better; most commentators gave him an honourable draw. The dreaded worm actually gave him a fairly easy win, which confirmed the Howard-huggers' worst suspicions about the filthy socialist crawler.

At least Costello had been there. For his scheduled debate with Nicola Roxon, Tony Abbott wasn't; he had been delayed in Melbourne. When he finally arrived at the National Press Club he was petulant and rude, which figured: he was not having a good time. The previous day Abbott had been confronted by

Bernie Banton, the leader of the James Hardie victims, with a petition requesting that a new drug be subsidised under the Pharmaceutical Benefits Scheme. Abbott sneered that it was just a stunt, and that just because someone was sick (Banton was in fact dying of mesothelioma) it did not mean they were pure of heart. Howard told him to apologise, which he did with some reluctance and manifest insincerity. It then turned out that the long-awaited takeover of the Mersey Hospital by the commonwealth would have to be postponed, because although the building was now saved, no one had made any employment arrangements for the doctors and nurses who were to staff it. The planned celebration was cancelled, and Abbott took tea with the domestic staff while workmen pulled down the unused marquee which had been erected to accommodate an assemblage of champagne-quaffing glitterati, including the Dear Leader himself.

In the circumstances, Howard's promise of $300 million for extra doctors and nurses across the nation seemed somewhat ill-timed. Rudd countered with a plan to cut back waiting lists for elective surgery as part of his own $2 billion package and then went to Grafton to offer its ailing hospital, in the marginal seat of Page, a no-strings bonanza of $24 million, upping Howard's conditional bid of $18 million. Rudd had said he would not match Howard's promises dollar for dollar, but he was hardly playing Scrooge.

At this stage Labor was clearly winning the week on points, thanks mainly to Tony Abbott's one big mistake – getting out of bed, which led to all the rest. But then Peter Garrett, who wasn't having the best of weeks either, made not one mistake but three. He assumed a shock-jock would have a sense of humour; he assumed a shock-jock would have a sense of proportion; and he assumed a shock-jock would have moral scruples. So when

Steve Price taunted him about copying Howard's policies, Garrett joked that Price shouldn't worry, in government Labor would change everything. Price rushed off to trumpet his scoop – Garrett's shock-horror admission of Rudd's secret agenda – and the Liberal bunker sprung into action. Costello shrieked that the greatest conspiracy in history was now unmasked, and that in office Rudd would shed his conservative disguise and embark on an orgy of rapine, pillage and slaughter, leading to the total destruction of civilisation. It was true, it was on the record, Garrett had confessed.

Rudd and Garrett wearily issued a press release saying that what Garrett had said had been a joke, that was J-O-K-E for the hard of hearing and the slow learners, and that while they did plan to change quite a bit, it was all there in their policies and they would stick to the policies, got it? The week ended in a draw, a result reflected in Monday's Nielsen poll, which showed that, yet again, nothing had changed: the gap remained at ten points.

What the week had proved was that not only were the public turned off – they had long since stopped listening and just wanted to vote and get it over with – but the media had gone stir-crazy and were now only interested in the bizarre. They had developed an obsession with the performance art provided by Howard's morning walk, which had now become a magnet for every show-off and exhibitionist in town, as well as for the traditional chorus of hecklers and supporters. There was an unhealthy interest in the fact that a woman who hugged Howard at a shopping centre boasted of not wearing undies, and that a Rudd supporter produced a squirrel glider from within her ample bust. An ancient video of Rudd eating his earwax became a movie sensation on the scale of *Star Wars*. The colour writers competed to find examples of slips, bloopers, blunders – anything that could be beaten up into a story to relieve the daily boredom.

There were some real issues around: the *Australian*'s Hedley Thomas had produced new evidence on the Haneef case which, if it could be proved, would see Kevin Andrews and others in his department and in the federal-police hierarchy perilously close to a charge of perverting the course of justice. But this was too complex for an election campaign based solidly on the eternal verities of fear, greed and opinion polls. Everything had to be portrayed in terms of gains and losses, of points for and against. Thus the gaffes by Garrett and the series of blunders by Abbott were given far more prominence than they deserved.

In Garrett's case, the solution was simple: he said he had learned a lesson, which was not to talk to Steve Price – or, he might have added, anyone else for the next fortnight. Labor was ahead, and didn't need to take risks. In Abbott's case, it was not so straightforward. To begin with, the man was clearly incorrigible: he had the record to prove it. And however thuggish and erratic he might be, he was also a key member of Howard's attack-dog team, which would have to be increasingly active in the time that was left. And there wasn't all that much of it. Over the weekend Rudd announced more plans for first-home owners and Howard re-announced massive road-building projects ('Super Sunday', he crowed rather optimistically), but for once the public gaze was firmly fixed on the future: Tuesday was the Melbourne Cup, a welcome break, but then would come Wednesday and the Reserve Bank's announcement on interest rates. New economic figures had made a rise a near certainty and both sides were digging in, preparing for the battles which would follow.

★

Howard's position was objectively untenable, since his entire 2004 campaign had been based on keeping rates low. All the economists had warned that his big-spending policies, and especially the promise of massive tax cuts, could only increase pressure on inflation and interest rates, but he remained determined to buy his way back into office; indeed, his campaign slogan, 'Go for Growth', could be seen as consciously thumbing his nose at the Reserve Bank and daring it to do its worst. Also, as Rudd had ceaselessly pointed out, Howard had for years failed to match growth with a supply of skilled labour and infrastructure sufficient to sustain productivity, and this had added considerably to the strain. He was a leader who had promised the impossible, contributed massively to the problem and continued to exacerbate it in order to fulfil his own ambition. There was only one way out: an even bigger lie than the one that had got him into the mess in the first place.

So yes, things had not turned out the way he had hoped. Of course it wasn't his fault; nothing ever was. This time we could blame the drought and petrol prices and the American subprime collapse, and yes, damn it, the unprecedented success of the Australian economy, and he was actually prepared to take his share of responsibility for the latter. It had to be admitted that there were, or at least there could be, troubled times ahead, again not his fault, and not nearly as troubled as Peter Costello had suggested with his silly talk of a tsunami; but, well, the odd squall, perhaps even a minor earth tremor or two. Nothing to panic about at present, because you had firm and experienced hands on the tiller, but the mere prospect of putting untried union-dominated sloganeers in charge should induce an instant feeling of mortal terror. Trust me – after all, you did before, didn't you, suckers.

This was not only outrageous but, as Rudd noted, supremely arrogant, the statement of a genuine megalomaniac. Yet, remembering what Goebbels said about the big lie, it was probably Howard's best bet – and he had, more than once, managed to turn adversity to advantage through mammoth leaps in logic. At least it fooled some on his own side: the Liberal member for Blair, Cameron Thompson, combining cynicism and optimism to an unprecedented degree, even opined that an interest-rate rise might be a good thing for the Coalition. So that was the fall-back position as the Reserve Bank moved into conclave and the rest of Australia wrestled with the Melbourne Cup form.

I awoke to the news that Rudd was about to visit the local State Emergency Service at Lismore. Nothing serious, I hoped, although I had heard rumours that he had injured his greeting hand. But it was worth going along for a look, and as it turned out he was as chipper as ever. Whatever else could be said about the man, he had stamina, and he had also developed a certain rapport; he seemed genuinely interested in inspecting the service's truck, and then its other truck. He listened attentively to the volunteers and chatted with them personably. He held a press conference and gave all the same answers to all the same questions over and over again. I could only feel that his pain and boredom thresholds must be extraordinarily high. Certainly, as the grand old strategist John Faulkner admitted appreciatively, he was remarkably disciplined. But Faulkner was not cheerful. His face now twisted into permanent frown from the many whips and scorns of time it has endured, he declined to be drawn on the progress of the campaign; the most he would say was that Labor remained competitive. Since that had also been his line throughout the Mark Latham campaign of 2004, I was not encouraged.

Rudd had been scheduled to perform one of those absurd meet-the-people exercises in the main shopping square, but this was switched to a busy street, where the few people strong and brave enough to thrust their way through the media pack were ceremonially greeted, photographed, interrogated by reporters nearly comatose with boredom, and sent on their way. The Labor leader proved his worker credentials with a brief session in a juice bar, and then entered a bookshop where he was sold the latest offering from best-selling local author Di Morissey. (The bookseller told him his wife might enjoy it.)

Lismore is a large chunk of Page, an electorate in which Labor needs a swing of 5.5 per cent. In other words, it could fall to Labor if a decent swing was on, but more likely wouldn't. Still, Rudd and the candidate, Janelle Saffin, were both very well received and appeared hopeful as they entered the Ballina RSL Club to watch the big event of the day. Rudd had originally tipped Maybe Better, which was a late scratching: not a good omen. Howard had tipped Mahler – only, Rudd and I agreed, to annoy Paul Keating, a devotee of the great composer. It ran a good third, but Rudd's new choice, Efficient, beat it in a withering run; the omens promptly reversed. The man was delighted, and his enthusiasm communicated itself to the rest of the room, which, with a few recalcitrant exceptions, seemed fairly solidly on his side; one enthusiastic patron even serenaded him in Italian. And on that happy note he departed to prepare for the interest-rate announcement.

For months Howard and Costello had been jawboning the media – and, through them, the Reserve Bank – that another rise would be unnecessary, even counterproductive. The international economy was slowing and unstable, the drought at home was an exceptional circumstance and the dollar was at an all-time high: surely the bank could at least hang off for a couple of months. Even when every economist in the land declared it inevitable, the government was still hoping desperately that the bank could be persuaded not to break the habit of a lifetime and put up rates in the middle of an election campaign. Costello had even told the ABC's Jon Faine (off the record, of course) that it definitely wouldn't. But of course, that's just what it did, with a scarcely veiled warning of more to come.

> *Will you, won't you, will you, won't you, will you join the dance?* —LEWIS CARROLL

★ 17.

AT LEAST THE RESERVE BANK'S DECISION came at a time when the government's fortunes could be said to be reviving, and fortunately Dennis Shanahan was still around to say it. In reality the Cup Day Newspoll showed very little movement; serious commentators saw what variation there was as little more than statistical noise. But by a judicious reallocation of preferences and rounding-off of decimals, the two-party-preferred was reduced to a mere six points, the smallest gap for months. Moreover, crowed Shanahan, support for one of Labor's key strengths had disintegrated: the previous week's gaffes by Garrett meant that Labor had lost control of the environment vote. Previous polling had given it a lead over the Coalition of 39–25; it was now only 29–24. True, but as the lost support had gone not to the Coalition but to the Greens, it would come straight back to Labor in the form of preferences. Not even Shanahan was serious about Howard winning over the conservationists.

But he and other Howard-huggers still believed that their man could sneak home on the economy; in spite of everything, the government was still regarded as the superior economic manager, and even the best bet when it came to interest rates. Thus, a great deal depended on how Wednesday's rise could be spun, especially by Howard. The answer was: not very well. Peter Hartcher, in the *Sydney Morning Herald*, put it best: 'Howard adds a new concept in evasiveness.'

Even at this critical moment in the campaign, with the evidence clear for all to see, the Dear Leader could not bring himself to admit that he had broken his undertaking of 2004: 'Keeping Interest Rates Low'. As always, John Howard insisted that he had never said what he was on record as saying, or if he did, it really meant something else: 'It's no one statement that totally, well very rarely is it one statement that sort of adumbrates the whole thing – it's the aggregate impression.' Apart from demonstrating that Howard had no idea of what the word 'adumbrates' actually meant, this was a world-class exhibition of weaselling, beaten only by his statement that he was sorry – but this was not to be taken as any kind of apology. As always, his behaviour had been faultless – and of course rates would always be lower under a Coalition government than under Labor ...

In desperation, the *Australian* weighed in with the headline, 'Business Backs PM Over Rates'. What the story in fact said was that Howard's stooge in the Associated Chambers of Commerce and Industry, Peter Hendy, remained loyal and that Stephen Knott, of the Australian Mining and Minerals Association, still liked AWAs. But funnily enough, business in general was not exactly delighted at the prospect of interest-rate rises continuing indefinitely. Heather Ridout of the Australian Industries Group, for one, made it clear she was not amused. And the tabloids treated Howard's pseudo-apology with something approaching contempt: the *Daily Telegraph* said, 'Not As Sorry As We Are', and the Hobart *Mercury*, 'Sorry, But It's Not My Fault'. The Brisbane *Courier-Mail* splashed simply, 'Endgame'.

In response Howard produced what would presumably be his last slogan: 'Aspirational Nationalism' having sunk without trace, we were now invited to embrace 'The Opportunity Society', a phrase which was quickly found to have been lifted without acknowledgement from a 2004 speech by Tony Blair. Kevin Rudd was still ploughing on with 'New Leadership'. If the polls were even half right, this had worked a treat with the under-40s, but the middle-aged and older were still likely to stick with Howard. Many of them had already paid off their mortgages; the key to the election now was probably whether those who had not done so believed Howard's current big lie about saving them from disaster. Or, as the *Sydney Morning Herald* economics writer Ross Gittins more delicately put it: 'Mr Howard has form when it comes to misleading the electorate about interest rates. Is it going to be so gullible as to be conned two elections in a row?'

The week concluded with a guest appearance by Mark Latham in the *Financial Review*, in which the former leader complained that it was all a farce, an episode of *Seinfeld* in which there was no real contest: two conservatives were competing for the same ground and whoever won, there would be no substantial change. While the Liberals were delighted to see Latham back in town, they were deeply depressed about his message: the whole point of their campaign was to paint Rudd as a dangerous radical, even a kind of heavily disguised reincarnation of Latham himself. If even his worst enemy regarded him as a pussycat, what hope was there? Paul Keating, while a more distant figure in the public mind, was a far more useful bogeyman.

And the other blast from the past, Bob Hawke, was definitely bad news for the government. Hawke had been working tirelessly and effectively in the marginals in a little-noticed campaign which must have left Rudd slightly ambivalent. While he welcomed the master populist's help, Hawke's larger-than-life persona provided an uncomfortable contrast to Rudd's own more self-effacing approach. Still, it appeared to be working: according to a Galaxy poll commissioned by the men's magazine *Zoo*, 34 per cent of respondents were keen to see Rudd naked, as opposed to 16 per cent who lusted after Howard. It would have been small consolation to the prime minister that he was slightly ahead among gay respondents.

By now it was clear that the young demographic belonged to Rudd, which could prove decisive: the various enrolment campaigns had produced a deluge of new voters, in spite of the government's sneaky attempts to lock them out. Howard's decision to run a long campaign might have been a mistake: his core supporters were dying off day by day. And it was hard to believe that the spectacle of the deputy prime minister, Mark Vaile, riding a skateboard through the streets of Tweed in a back-to-front baseball cap would recapture the devotion of the under-30s. Howard's promise of half a million dollars to preserve orangutans in Indonesia was more imaginative, and Kevin Rudd's promise of free visits to the dentist for teenagers more confronting. But none of them had any effect on the polls, and neither did anything else. Monday's Newspoll was back to its traditional 55–45. At least Howard had avoided taking a big hit from the interest-rate rise, which would have been terminal. He had not, however, made up one skerrick of ground in four solid weeks of formal campaigning, or, if you like, in nearly a year of hard electioneering. It was time to get serious; so, with just twelve days to go, he launched his campaign.

★

There was a time when campaign launches came, as their name suggests, at the start of the campaign; this continued until 1990. But then a convention emerged – actually a sweetheart deal between the major parties – that made the launch date the cut-off point for looting the public purse. Until the launch, taxpayers continued to fund the staff and travel costs of members, which were considerable; after the launch, the parties had to pay their own way. As a result, campaigns got longer and launches got later. By 2007 the launch marked not the start of the campaign, but the final desperate push.

For Howard, the push was more desperate than usual, and the circumstances more fraught. On the very day he was to make his last big bid for votes, the Reserve Bank issued another statement making it clear that further interest-rate rises were already in the pipeline and that the more money politicians hurled at the public, the higher rates would go. The message could not have been plainer: *Dear Mr Howard and Mr Rudd, Lay off the bribery.* The point could hardly have been lost on the Coalition: in 2004, as Peter Costello recounted, he had offered Howard a menu of spending promises from which he could choose. Slavering, the prime minister scoffed the lot: entrée, main course, dessert and the vegetarian option. In just twenty minutes of his campaign address he spent more than $6 billion. This could not be allowed to happen again.

And it wouldn't, insisted Liberal Party heavies. This year the promises would be responsible, restrained, even frugal. There would be no $6-billion splurge. And there wasn't: in 2007, the splurge was nearly $10 billion. A large chunk of it was tax rebates for schooling expenses, including school fees, a policy which brought paroxysms of delight from the non-government sector and accusations of a secret plan to privatise education from the public sector. Most of the rest was catching up with Rudd on housing affordability (where Howard incorporated a handy tax lurk for the rich) and child care – in other words, about trying to claw back Liberal voters who were defecting to Labor. This time the bribes were targeted, unlike the scattergun approach Howard had employed in 2004; but it didn't make them any cheaper. Even as the Dear Leader was making his triumphant exit from Brisbane's Lyric Theatre, commentators were warning that whoever was in office, a lot of the promises were going to have to be declared non-core.

I did not get a guernsey to the gala occasion: having only discovered that it was to take place on the preceding Thursday, I applied immediately for accreditation but was knocked back. The following email exchange is self-explanatory:

FROM: Jim Bonner
TO: Mungo
Mungo – unfortunately I have to decline your request for registration for the Coalition campaign launch – the close-off time for registration was extended to yesterday – I thought I would be able to get u in but I couldn't – sorry – Jim Bonner

FROM: Mungo
TO: Jim Bonner
Jim – this makes me very unhappy. I was not even aware of the timing of the launch until yesterday (Thursday) and immediately rang Howard's press office. I asked specifically for your number but they refused to give it to me and assured me someone would ring me back. There was no mention of any deadline or cut-off for registration. Of course no one rang me back, so this morning I rang the Libs' Canberra HQ who did give me your number, and you

know the rest. Neither of the two *Echo* newspapers (locals) for which I work had any notice of anything. I fail to see why it is so difficult to get me registered with four days to go – would a late application from someone working for News Ltd be treated similarly? Forgive me if I smell a rodent. Mungo

Unsurprisingly there was no reply, but my suspicions were confirmed later, when I learned that the ABC had arrived at the launch with an extra and unaccredited technician who was signed through by Bonner on the spot, no questions asked. But I was relieved to read that a member of the *Chaser* team had also been barred, and indeed incarcerated for the duration. It wasn't just me.

Reduced to watching on television, I was struck by how little had changed since 2004: the same Nuremberg-style setting, the same rousing muzak, the same overblown introduction from Brisbane Lord Mayor Campbell Newman, the same homespun drollery from the Nationals leader (Mark Vaile instead of John Anderson, but who noticed), the same brutal and envious sarcasm from Peter Costello, the same interminable speech from Howard and the climax of family hugs; the only real difference was that Hyacinth was in white rather than yellow and had snuck in a grandchild.

I suppose the timeless ritual was a source of comfort to the faithful in the audience (all the same people, but three years older), but there was something terribly dated about it. When Howard harked back to the great days of Sir Robert Menzies, he looked not so much yesterday's man as a relic from the last millennium – which, of course, he was.

The edited version on ABC television the following night was even worse: Howard's droning list of promises was interspersed with what were supposed to be reassuring cameos from his ministers, but they served only to remind us that most of them were either silly or horrible or, in the case of Alexander Downer, both. An appearance from the malevolent Philip Ruddock was a particularly bad idea.

However, the day held some comfort for Howard: Labor's candidate for the key seat of Eden-Monaro, Mike Kelly, cracked over the government's schools-funding policy and did a Garrett. Labor, he said, would come up with something more equitable and sensible. Howard screamed that Mark Latham's private school hit-list was back on the agenda and Rudd, who had promised to retain Howard's system for five years in order to avoid precisely this wedge, ordered an instant and grovelling retraction from Kelly. The importance of this became apparent when he delivered his own launch the next day.

★

For Rudd, as for the leader he replaced, education was the thing. They came at it from different directions: Kim Beazley's family was cultured and literate, and took the necessity of education for granted, while Rudd's was rural and underprivileged, and saw education as essential for advancement. But both men agreed on its centrality to Labor's ideals. Education, as Rudd said, was the engine room of equity, the engine room of opportunity and the engine room of the economy. He had begun his leadership – indeed, his parliamentary career – with a call for an Education Revolution, which coming from a neophyte back-bencher sounded a trifle pretentious; but since then the details had been slowly filled in, with a chapter here and a chapter there over the year's campaigning.

At his launch, Rudd finally pulled the pieces together and inserted what had been missing: the entire system to be rebuilt, from pre-school to postgraduate, with the unifying thread being modernisation. It knitted together with Rudd's promise of universal broadband to produce something like the revolution Rudd claimed. It was unquestionably a well-conceived and comprehensive plan, perhaps even a vision: by far the most far-sighted and important policy in an election sadly lacking in either.

I said to Beazley (he was present among the cheer-squad, along with Gough Whitlam, Bob Hawke and Paul Keating; Mark Latham wasn't) that there was a lot of Knowledge Nation in it, his own grand plan that was dismissed contemptuously as 'Noodle Nation' by Peter Costello because of an unwisely presented connectivity diagram; Costello's easy sneer had meant that it was nine years before anyone got serious about education reform again. The Bomber agreed without a trace of bitterness, and was enthusiastic about Rudd's prospects; he was always a big man – the best prime minister we never had.

For my money the Education Revolution was a winner in its own right, but wait, there was more. There was some urgent stuff on climate change, and a vote-winner that produced one of the biggest cheers of the speech, a promise to re-establish the Commonwealth Dental Health Program. And all this, as Rudd emphasised, for just a quarter of what Howard had spent in his great Monday splurge. To rapturous applause, Rudd declared that he would not match Howard's 'irresponsible spending spree', his 'spendathon'; there would be no 'feeding frenzy' like that witnessed at the Liberals' launch.

This was very good politics. Howard's near-$10-billion spree had raised the eyebrows of more than just the academic economists. In the face of the Reserve Bank warnings, it seemed provocative, even perverse. Howard and Costello insisted that it was not inflationary, but they were the only ones who thought so; real economists asked acidly which part of the phrase 'demand inflation' did the government not understand? Quite suddenly and unexpectedly the political reality had changed, and they had missed it.

In the great scheme of things Rudd's restraint did not add up to all that much; depending on who was doing the calculating, Rudd's promises now came to about $55 billion, compared to Howard's $64 billion; the difference was significant, but not enough to change the Reserve Bank's mind when the crunch next came, probably in February. But at least Rudd could say he was listening, however belatedly; Howard was just defiant and reckless. It gave extra points to the Labor line that he was not staying around to clean up the mess: Rudd was the one in it for the long haul and, it now appeared, the one with the safe pair of hands, the one you could trust.

Apart from that, as they say, all did not go well. The launch was held up for half an hour without explanation: rumours flew, the most imaginative being that Rudd had been assassinated and we had to wait for caucus to elect a new leader. I was comforted by the thought that the last leader to miss his own launch was Malcolm Fraser in 1975 (he postponed it due to flu), and he won in a landslide. The occasional attempts at razzamatazz failed; in particular the happy-clappies in 'New Leadership' T-shirts looked straight from the Hillsong Church. Both John Faulkner and Julia Gillard were unusually flat in their warm-ups and the sound system gave Rudd's voice a curious sibilance, as if he was recovering from a trip to the dentist.

But all of this was fixed for the television version that night, and the consensus both among the faithful and the travelling media was that Rudd had done enough to win. Most of the latter seemed to think it was all over; they reported incredulous surges of optimism in the Labor camp and what was described as a healthy sense of defeatism among the Libs and Nats. Even the most hopeful among the government's backers now acknowledged that they would lose a swag of seats; the only hope was that they might still scrape home with a couple of marginals to spare. But it looked a pretty unlikely hope as the Nielsen poll, taken after Howard's bonanza but mostly before Rudd's big push on fiscal responsibility, indicated that the gap still stood at eight points – a slight movement back to the government but not nearly enough. We were still in landslide territory. Howard insisted he could pull it back: 'There are still twelve days to go,' he said bravely. There weren't; there were ten. 'Knock-out blow,' he replied sarcastically when this was pointed out. And he was still pushing the economic-management line; after all, there was nothing else left. Rudd might claim to be an economic conservative, but look at his record: judge him not be what he says but what he does. Well, quite: Rudd wasn't the one hurling $10 billion at the electorate in a last mad attempt to buy votes.

★

To put the icing on Rudd's cake, the auditor-general released his report on the Regional Partnership Scheme, which he found had been horrendously rorted for years and transformed into something like a National Party slush fund. When bureaucrats had rejected grants to National electorates for failing the basic criteria, the (National) ministers had gone ahead regardless; amounts ranging from a few thousand to more than a million had been poured into what turned out to be bottomless cesspits. The *Sydney Morning Herald*'s headline said it all: 'The Bottom of the Pork Barrel'. The auditor-general himself was more measured, but no less damning: 'The operation of the scheme fell short of acceptable standards of public administration.'

This was not corruption on the grand scale, like the theft of hundreds of millions of taxpayers' dollars to pay for political advertising; it was more like tickling the till for a few bucks to pay for a gambling habit. But somehow its pettiness only made it worse – just another example of how tawdry and grubby the Howard gang had become after far too long in office. Mark Vaile, the Nationals' godfather, appeared nonplussed at all the fuss: well, sure, from time to time ministers overruled bureaucrats; that's what ministers were for. And if the decisions overwhelmingly favoured Coalition electorates, that was because there were more of them, particularly in the bush. He even suggested that there was something wrong and sinister about the auditor-general publishing his report during an election campaign, and proceeded to snaffle another $900,000 worth of handouts for his own electorate: this was not bypassing the system, he averred solemnly, it was a pre-election promise, which was something altogether different.

And just to show that you can't keep a mad minister down, Tony Abbott was sprung on video admitting that yes, WorkChoices had removed some protections – 'in inverted commas' – from the workers, and the Industrial Relations Commission had lost some of its powers. And if the workers were unhappy about their employers, they could always go out and get another job. Abbott, of course, said it was all out of context and not what he meant at all, and then, confronted with the full video, declared that its use by Labor proved that Rudd lacked honour and character and was unfit to be prime minister. On the other side of the country a schoolteacher was roughly handled by police when he attempted to present the real prime minister with a pooper-scooper. The *Sydney Morning Herald* ran an unflattering photo of Howard with the caption: 'This Man is One Week from Oblivion', which at least one reader saw as disrespectful.

It may have been, but on all the evidence it was also true. A Galaxy poll suggested that things might not be quite as grim as they appeared: the tide was turning in Queensland and Victoria, and the government might lose only eighteen seats, rather than the 34 predicted by Nielsen and Newspoll. But this was hardly calculated to get government backbenchers – or, for that matter, ministers – dancing in the streets. Nor were the weekend papers, which considered that it was all over. Not only did they treat Rudd as effectively the prime minister in waiting, but the Fairfax Sydney *Sun Herald* and the Murdoch Sydney *Sunday Telegraph* and Brisbane *Sunday Mail* all favoured voting for him – admittedly without a huge amount of enthusiasm, but hey, this is the filthy capitalist press we're talking about. It's a while since it endorsed the ALP. However the Murdoch Sundays in Victoria, Western Australia and South Australia stuck with Howard, proving that God was still moving in mysterious ways. The Fairfax Melbourne *Sunday Age* said snootily that there wasn't enough difference between the parties for it to recommend a vote for either. Well, if you don't vote, you shouldn't complain.

If the papers were divided about the candidates' merits, they were unanimous about the result. They hardly mentioned the campaign anymore; it was all about what Rudd would do when he won. His first action, it turned out, would be to ratify Kyoto. This fitted in well with the other weekend news, which was the release of the very scary fourth climate-change report from the Intergovernmental Panel on Climate Change, which in turn coincided with horrific flooding in Bangladesh. Rudd said it was a call to arms. Howard said it was a serious challenge but the world would not come to an end tomorrow. His government, in due course, would no doubt have acted promptly. His failed protégé in New South Wales, Peter Debnam, said he should have ratified Kyoto.

The prime minister attended a Korean church in his own electorate for the first time; he was allowed to give a little sermon in which he said God's teachings sat very comfortably with the values of his party; the deity must have been immensely gratified. Encouraged, Howard announced a new policy: drug offenders were henceforth to be treated like Aborigines, and have their earnings quarantined. It sounded bizarre and desperate, but then Rudd, in the far west, suggested that when the mining boom was finally over the Sandgropers could continue to flourish by acting as middlemen for wealthy Chinese seeking to purchase real estate in Latin America, or something like that. And the *Sunday Age* reckoned there was no difference between the parties.

Howard, now accompanied by Peter Costello, took up the subject: 'Labor's IR policy will end the mining boom.' This was too much for Howard-hugger Imre Salusinszky, who commented acidly: 'The idea that the abolition of Australian Workplace Agreements could threaten the demand for raw materials created by one billion Chinese took the Coalition's fear campaign against Kevin Rudd to a new level.' Howard and Costello continued their double act on commercial television, where Howard insisted that Costello would be elected as his successor unopposed (cop that, Malcolm Turnbull) and the two thought of nice things to say about each other. Howard said Costello was really smart and funny (implication: Howard wasn't) and Costello said Howard was a really hard worker (undisputed fact: Costello wasn't).

This sudden bonhomie between the old enemies failed to

cover the cracks appearing in what was left of the Coalition facade. The bitterness was now so open that the Sydney *Daily Telegraph* ran the headline 'Libs at War' over a list of accusations of stupidity, incompetence and outright treachery. The developing consensus appeared to be that the campaign had been complicated, contradictory and, above all, boring – in spite of his promises Howard had ignored his team and hogged the limelight, to the detriment of the party – and that the behaviour of some ministers, notably Abbott and Turnbull, had been nothing short of appalling. They might be becoming resigned to the idea of defeat, but they were going to go down fighting, if only among themselves.

Rudd was still trying not to appear cocky, but with an increasing lack of success. He cancelled a scheduled appearance on the ABC's *Insiders* program, sending Julia Gillard instead; as always she was smart and competent, but it smacked a little of arrogance, especially when he turned up instead on Rove McManus's variety show. Certainly it had a bigger audience and the viewers were more likely to be swinging voters, but it confirmed the view of some serious commentators that Rudd was a bit too keen on the soft option; he wanted to keep informed questioning about his policies to a minimum.

Howard, in contrast, complained that not enough senior journalists got out on the campaign trail; they stayed at home writing comment pieces. This was true, but it was partly his own fault. The campaign trail was now so tightly controlled that it never produced anything of substance and very seldom anything of even passing interest. From being a kind of political magical mystery tour, it had become a trek of quite unimaginable tedium. The old hands dropped in on it from time to time, but generally it was left to the young and healthy as a political boot camp where they could prove their dedication.

By the last week, even the toughest had begun to wilt. Howard and Rudd, powered by an inexhaustible supply of ambition and adrenaline, continued to rush frantically from one side of the country to the other, but the media pack could no longer see the point. The pundits believed that it was probably over anyway, but if there was movement left anywhere, it would be in New South Wales, Queensland and Western Australia. Labor would make a clean sweep of Tasmania, and win three seats in South Australia and one in the Northern Territory; that could now be taken as a given. But the west looked dicey; it was not impossible that the Coalition could pick up one or even both of Swan and Cowan. If that happened, Labor would need as many as a dozen from the eastern seaboard. There were no real marginals left in Victoria; anything there would be a bonus. New South Wales continued to look pretty good, but it would need to: Queensland was puzzling.

Labor strategists had always assumed that having a Queenslander as potential prime minister, backed up by another in Wayne Swan as potential treasurer, would be a major vote-winner in the parochial Sunshine State. Yet it wasn't turning out that way; indeed, there were some signs that Kevin07 was a positive turn-off in what should have been his natural habitat. The overall polling was still fine: with just four days to go, Newspoll was maintaining the unshakeable eight-point gap. But those atavistic fears about whether the vote would translate into seats had started to resurface among Labor's army of pessimists.

> *For yesterday and for all tomorrows we dance the best we know.* —KATE SEREDY

★ 18.

T.S. ELIOT RECKONED THAT APRIL was the cruellest month. Well, he didn't have to survive November 2007. The last days of the interminable campaign were harrowing for everyone, but perhaps particularly for Labor: after all, it had more to gain. The Australian Left had been crushed by John Howard so thoroughly and for so long that not only was it out of the habit of winning; in its collective subconscious, it almost felt that it did not deserve to. To have Labor in power in Canberra would be a violation of the natural order of things. This did not mean that Labor supporters accepted that the other side was born to rule – far from it. But deep down, eleven years on the wrong side of the speaker had nourished the suspicion that they were born losers. Thus the prospect of power, suddenly so close, seemed surreal. For months the opinion polls had seemed too good to be true; now, with just four sleeps to go, they were still predicting a comfortable win for Kevin Rudd. He was so close to the Lodge you could almost detect a waft of those vile cigars Bob Hawke used to smoke. The suspense was unbearable.

From the government side it was equally hard to believe, but there was little choice, so shoulders were squared and teeth were gritted. The general feeling was that, as Howard bravely maintained, it was still possible to win – just – but in those last hours absolutely everything had to go right. Thus when the week began with the Administrative Review Tribunal agreeing to the suppression of documents outlining possible adaptations of WorkChoices, and the government being accused of covering up draconian plans for future grinding of the workers, whatever slim hopes were left began to dissipate. The documents dated back to 2005, and the government claimed they canvassed options which had been long since rejected; why, then, the obsession with keeping them secret?

Because they were cabinet documents, apparently. But a lot of them weren't, and the reason for suppression given by the tribunal's deputy president, Stephanie Forgie, was that to release them might 'lead to speculation about further workplace-relations reforms which were not government policy'. It was nice of her to try and help; but the speculation was going on anyway and had been since both Peter Costello and Nick Minchin had been sprung promising their supporters that there was another round to come. Howard strenuously denied it, which brought an unusually terse reply from Rudd: 'Pigs might fly.' In any case, Howard was retiring; what he promised had a very limited shelf life. It was known that the secret documents had included 'options to rationalise federal/state workplace relations and possible initiatives in relation to the setting of federal minimum and trainees' wages'. It sounded pretty scary. This was not a good start. There was a moment of hope when, at last, a boatload of asylum-seekers appeared on the horizon, but it passed. You only get one *Tampa*, and the government had used its up.

Howard went to Tasmania for the first time in the campaign, but it was not to be a re-run of his triumphal tour of 2004. He drove past the still-deserted Mersey Hospital at high speed, and when at a safe distance re-announced some old road promises for the island state. He then returned to the mainland for a final interview with his traditional adversary, Kerry O'Brien. As O'Brien acknowledged, it was to Howard's credit that he had not ducked the *7.30 Report* while in office, and he held up fairly well this time; but he could not help sounding as if he was running out of puff. He lapsed into the third person ('Some people might think that Howard hasn't done so badly') and fell back on an old Paul Keating line, which was that if you change the government, you change the country; only, revealingly, he put it in the negative: 'Don't think that you can change the government without changing the country.'

Rudd, in his wind-up at the National Press Club next day, made it clear that this was exactly what he intended; in the speech of a prime-minister-in-waiting, he talked about reforming the whole process of government as well as the big policy picture. Alexander Downer said that Rudd was smug and shallow. Yes, Alexander Downer said that. Oh dear. Dauntless to the last, Janet Albrechtsen wrote a long and somewhat incoherent column in the *Australian* about why Rudd still wouldn't win. Given that she had written off Howard's chances the month before, just who the Dominatrix thought would be in charge on Monday was something of a mystery. Rupert Murdoch, perhaps?

★

Labor was continuing with policy launches even in the final week: the indefatigable Anthony Albanese put out a big water-saving plan, but no one really noticed. Of more interest was the belated intervention of the minister for vocational and further education, Andrew Robb, nicknamed 'The Tradesman' by John Howard. The name was disconcertingly appropriate; as a former apparatchik, Robb's approach was similar to that of the Watergate plumbers. He demonstrated this skill with a shock allegation that no less than thirteen Labor candidates could be ineligible for election. This turned out to be based on a Google search, which revealed that said candidates had all been public employees; had they resigned before nominating, as required? The charge had been proved to have some merit (maybe) in the case of George Newhouse, the candidate for Wentworth, but for the other dozen it was just fanciful. In media terms, though, it was a badly needed point for the government.

Then Julia Gillard turned up fifteen minutes late for a scheduled radio debate with Peter Costello, prompting harsh exchanges between the pair. Costello joked that he had been forced to debate himself, and had had a win on points. His supporters grumbled that he was due for one; and Howard's prediction that Costello would succeed him unopposed as leader was apparently confirmed when Downer stated, to no one's surprise, that he would not be a contender; more importantly, Malcolm Turnbull did likewise. This was assuming that the government was returned and Howard kept his seat – hardly safe bets. But it prompted the *Australian* to declare, 'Libs Lock In Behind Costello.' It was unclear whether this was supposed to be good news. In the *Sydney Morning Herald* Paul Keating continued his long-awaited revenge on Howard with an article explaining that a change of government was essential to 'restoring a moral basis to our public life' after the erosion of values during the Howard years.

And then, as if to prove him right, the Libs were caught red-handed pushing the racist line in the marginal electorate of Lindsay, and any hope of a rousing finish by the Dear Leader disappeared. The offending item purported to be a message from the non-existent Islamic Australia Federation urging Muslims to vote Labor because Labor supported the release of the Bali bombers and the building of mosques in Sydney's west. It was clearly a fake: if nothing else the concluding exhortation, 'Ala Akba' (presumably intended to be 'Allah Akbar'), was a dead give-away. But its crudeness did not make it any less dirty.

Acting on a tip-off from a disaffected Liberal member, a group of unionists ambushed a team that was letterboxing the non-Muslim voters of Lindsay with the leaflet. The team included Greg Chijoff, the husband of Liberal candidate Karen Chijoff; Jeff Egan, a member of the Liberal Party state executive; and Gary Clark, the husband of retiring member Jackie Kelly. Reportedly on the advice of Tony Abbott (who else?), Kelly heroically tried to dismiss it as a prank, a bit of jape – the sort of thing *The Chaser* did every week. The *Chaser* team responded by offering her a job and Peter Beattie offered her life membership of the Labor Party as a reward for services rendered. The Libs' state director, Graham Jaeschke, insisted that those involved had been identified and expelled from the party. Howard, sensing disaster, disowned everybody and deplored the incident, but refused to include Chijoff herself in his condemnation. These were modern times, he declared: a woman should not be held responsible for her husband's mistakes. True, but surely she should not be allowed to benefit from them either. And the Kelly gang, it turned out, had form: Ken Higgs surfaced in Tasmania to say that during the 2001 election they and he had run a fake how-to-vote ticket purporting to be from a residents' action group urging a Liberal vote, when in fact the group was preferencing Labor.

What was left of the Liberals in Lindsay stopped returning calls.

It was not the first example of the Coalition adapting the theme 'If you want a nigger for a neighbour, vote Labour,' as the British Tories put it more directly in the 1960s. In my own electorate of Richmond in 2001 the sitting National, Larry Anthony, had been worried about the residents of caravan parks, who were spitting chips about the application of the GST to their site payments. Two days before the election, a pamphlet appeared on every van's doorstep warning that Labor had a secret plan to close the detention centres and relocate the boat people to, you guessed it, north-coast caravan parks. Anthony claimed total mystification, admittedly his usual state of mind; but after the election National campaigners were bragging about the tactic in every pub. Note the common factors: the dirty trick came from the conservative side of politics and relied on a covert appeal to racism. And, of course, Howard himself spent most of the 2001 campaign talking about how Labor was soft on border protection and would let the queue-jumpers with all their exotic diseases and suspected terrorists and child-murderers into the country while, if re-elected, We Will Decide, etc. Really, he was hardly in a position to take the high moral ground. It was satisfying that the dog of racism, so assiduously whistled up by the Dear Leader over the years, had at last come back to bite him on the bum.

From his point of view, the worst thing was not the evilness of the trick, but the distraction it provided. His address to the National Press Club was supposed to be the climax of his campaign, the final appeal to the nation that brought it all together. Instead, most of question time was devoted to the Lindsay pamphlet: Howard was forced to make an increasingly agitated and petulant defence of his position. By the end of it he was shaking. Kevin Rudd, now almost insufferably prime ministerial, simply noted that it was the ultimate example of the government's desperation and negativity, and indisputable proof that it had nothing left to offer the country; and that was the position as the campaign hit its final 24 hours. Surely it was all over.

★

Not quite. Friday morning brought two new polls: Nielsen, which was talking super-tsunami, with the gap at fourteen points; and Galaxy, which was hinting at a cliff-hanger, with the gap at just four. As the ABC's Anthony Green noted sagely, they couldn't both be right. Galaxy had a pretty good reputation, but no one else had detected any sign of a late swing back to the Coalition, although Morgan, which had a gap of ten, said that Howard was looking good in the west. He certainly didn't sound good in a sort of postscript interview on the ABC's *AM*: in fact, he sounded a bit like Bryan Dawe's senile Blimp, Sir Murray Rivers. His final message appeared to be: 'Please vote for me, because if you don't things just might get even worse.' Kevin Rudd sounded almost as tired, but rather more positive and coherent; if the swingers really were waiting till the last minute to make up their minds, he was clearly the best bet in a not-very-inspiring field.

This was also the view of the *Sydney Morning Herald*, the Sydney *Daily Telegraph*, the Brisbane *Courier-Mail*, the Hobart *Mercury*, the *Northern Territory News*, the *Canberra Times* and the *Australian*, which came out for Labor. The *Financial Review*, the Melbourne *Herald Sun*, the Adelaide *Advertiser* and the *West Australian* stuck with Howard. The Melbourne *Age* remained too precious to vote. These days it is doubtful if the editorials sway a lot of votes, especially when they no longer carry the imprimatur of the legendary proprietorial moguls: Murdoch, the only one left, had honoured his promise to leave the decisions to his individual editors, who were showing a commendable diversity of opinion. But the editors were obviously looking to their readers, and if the high Whigs of Granny *Herald* and the Tory battlers of the *Tele* were both looking Rudd-ward, then the swing was well and truly on – in New South Wales, at least.

But not according to Newspoll, which was released prematurely that evening. It agreed with Galaxy; the gap had shrunk to four points, and with two of the four major polls in lockstep, the possibility had to be taken seriously. It was hard to explain: by any normal standards the Coalition had had a diabolical last week, and the one before hadn't been much better. However, as the first two weeks had shown, these things don't always work logically – there are hidden forces at work. Some suspected sympathetic magic: Howard had plagiarised yet another slogan, 'Heading in the Right Direction.' This had last been used by Labor's Morris Iemma at the start of the year, and had led to the re-election of his universally loathed New South Wales state government; could it provide the same miracle federally? It seemed unlikely, but so did the polls. Another possibility was that the voters had suddenly gone sentimental: *Look, we've stuck with the old boy for all these years; we can't really cast him aside like a worn-out sock just because he's past it.*

But whatever the reason, Newspoll threw an almighty scare into Labor's supporters. Their hopes had been building for the whole year: surely the fates could not be so cruel and unjust as to dash them now? Well, why not? After all, that's what fates were for. In the circumstances I was hardly surprised to wake on election day to grey and miserable weather: always start the day the way you intend to continue. But the skies cleared, and on analysis the news was not as bad as it had seemed. Even on the most pessimistic reading, Newspoll suggested that Labor would still get there, albeit not as comfortably as had been predicted earlier. And the late mail from Queensland – the key state, where both leaders had spent the last day of the campaign – was particularly good. Old hands said the mood was reminiscent not only of the Labor win of 1983, but of the glorious year of 1972 and the It's Time election. Perhaps most encouraging of all, the betting market, in recent elections a far more reliable forecaster than any of the polls, still had Labor as a very short odds-on favourite. The general view was a Labor majority of around six seats – no landslide, but perfectly acceptable, thank you very much. And the mood in the front bar of the Billinudgel was optimistic to the point of serious obscenity.

★

And so, at long last, to the traditional boozy evening in front of the television, when the nation's future is decided. It did not start well; the Tasmanian seats that should have fallen in minutes were disconcertingly stubborn, and the early figures from New South Wales and Victoria, while at times promising, were all over the place. But then South Australia firmed things up, and when Queensland came in, the Coalition collapsed like a house of cards. Western Australia, as expected, was the government's best result, but it was too little and too late. The battle was over, and it was time for the survivors to start preparing for the war ahead. Malcolm Turnbull held Wentworth comfortably and made a triumphal speech which left no doubt that he would be a leadership contender. Peter Costello was equally smug and seemingly unstoppable, but didn't quite get around to giving us the real news, which – we later discovered – was that he had decided that being Opposition leader would be just too much like hard work. Too old at 50, too lazy at any time. His waffle was mercifully curtailed to make way for John Howard.

Obviously, it was a terrible moment for the Dear Leader. His electorate of Bennelong had been up and down all night; as he entered the ballroom of the Wentworth Hotel to surrender his government, he was not certain whether it was all over or whether he would still have to resign his seat in order to put the voters of Bennelong through a by-election so they could finally elect Maxine McKew. But he remained defiant about his record, and broke the habit of a lifetime by accepting responsibility – both for the campaign and for the defeat – before descending into senile ramblings, during which he compared his wife Hyacinth to cement. And on that note, he slid smoothly around the S-bend of history.

Kevin Rudd made a gung-ho victory speech more suited to the start of a campaign than to its finish, and demonstrated that one of his first jobs should be to hire a new speechwriter. After ten minutes it was still not entirely clear where we were going. But we knew all too well where we had been. For more than eleven years, John Howard led us on a voyage driven by greed and fear, into parochialism and paranoia, selfishness and racism, bigotry and corruption, and other dark places in the Australian psyche where we never should have gone. It was a mean and ugly trip, and it will take us all a long time to recover. As he left the Wentworth Hotel surrounded by his weeping and cheering entourage of orcs, my main feeling was not of exultation or even euphoria, but of relief – the same sort of reaction as I had to Cathy Freeman's win at the Sydney Olympics, or at the moment, seventeen years ago, when I stubbed out my last cigarette. The result was long anticipated and a fine achievement, but how dreadful I and many others would have felt if it had not happened.

And on that note, spare a thought for Labor's patriarch, Gough Whitlam, who against most expectations has survived to see another Labor government in Canberra. The final word should be his: a great quotation which he used in another context altogether, but which is utterly appropriate for 24 November 2007: *E quindi uscimmo a riveder le stelle.* It is the last line of Dante's *Inferno*, describing the poet's return from hell, and it means: And thence we emerged, to see the stars again.